T0037689

The publisher and the University of California Press Foundation gratefully acknowledge the generous support of the Atkinson Family Foundation Imprint in Higher Education.

IS GRAD SCHOOL FOR ME?

IS GRAD SCHOOL FOR ME?

Demystifying the Application Process
for First-Gen BIPOC Students

||||||||||||||||||||||||||||||||||||||||||||||||||||||||||||||||||||||||||||||||||||||||||||||||||||

YVETTE MARTÍNEZ-VU AND MIROSLAVA CHÁVEZ-GARCÍA

UNIVERSITY OF CALIFORNIA PRESS

University of California Press
Oakland, California

© 2024 by Yvette Martínez-Vu and Miroslava Chávez-García

Library of Congress Cataloging-in-Publication Data

Names: Martínez-Vu, Yvette, author. | Chávez-García, Miroslava, author.
Title: Is grad school for me? : demystifying the application process for first-gen
    BIPOC students / Yvette Martínez-Vu and Miroslava Chávez-García.
Description: [Oakland, California] : University of California Press, [2024] |
    Includes bibliographical references and index.
Identifiers: LCCN 2023026379 (print) | LCCN 2023026380 (ebook) |
    ISBN 9780520393967 (hardback) | ISBN 9780520393981 (paperback) |
    ISBN 9780520393998 (ebook)
Subjects: LCSH: Minorities—Education (Graduate—United States. |
    Universities and colleges—United States—Admission.
Classification: LCC LC3727 .M37 2024 (print) | LCC LC3727 (ebook) |
    DDC 378.1/610973—dc23/eng/20230719
LC record available at https://lccn.loc.gov/2023026379
LC ebook record available at https://lccn.loc.gov/2023026380

Manufactured in the United States of America

32   31   30   29   28   27   26   25   24
10   9   8   7   6   5   4   3   2   1

To Emiliano and Ely
And to all of our femtors and femtees
—YMV

To all those who have lacked the opportunities of our society
—MCG

Contents

INTRODUCTION

The Journey to *Is Grad School for Me?*

And so, lifting as we climb, onward and upward we go, struggling and striving, and hoping that the buds and blossoms of our desires will burst into glorious fruition 'ere long.

MARY CHURCH TERRELL[1]

THE JOURNEY TO *IS GRAD SCHOOL FOR ME?* and our commitment to provide a candid and practical approach to applying to graduate school is intimately connected to our professional and personal lives as well as our identities, culture, and history. As first-generation, low-income Students of Color, we (Yvette and Miroslava) faced many of the stresses of navigating predominantly middle- and upper-class, white-dominated spaces where our experiences and those of our communities were absent in the curriculum and infrequently reflected in our instructors and professors. While we did not face the specific challenges of nontraditional students, who return to higher education after a prolonged absence, we did encounter similar challenges, dealing with the loss of a parent (in Yvette's case) and both parents (in Miroslava's case) at the age of twelve. These losses meant having our childhoods cut short, having the rug pulled out from under us, and having to take on more responsibilities than any pre-teen would have wanted. It also meant living with increased financial precarity, given that Yvette had to rely on her now-single mother and Miroslava had to rely on the state to provide support. Fortunately, Miroslava also had the backing of her aunt and uncle who took her and her brother into their household and raised them along with their two younger daughters. Nevertheless, we persisted (and continue to persist) in our personal lives and developed a social-support network not simply to survive but to thrive in academic and non-academic spaces.

In thinking about graduate school and wondering if it's the right decision for you, we want you to know that no single path exists to a graduate degree. Rather, you map out that route or trajectory based on your needs and those of your family and community as well as the resources that are available to you. Accessing those sources of support is not always simple or transparent, as we know from first-hand experience and has been confirmed in the literature on the "hidden curriculum," that is, the unspoken cultural beliefs and practices that help socially and/or economically privileged students navigate academia. To assist you along your journey, we developed *Is Grad School for Me?* Its tools and tips will help you become familiar with the expectations and demands of graduate programs before, during, and after you apply. To demystify the graduate school experience, we begin with our own stories of how we landed in graduate school.

WHY WE ATTENDED GRADUATE SCHOOL
Yvette

For me, the decision to attend graduate school was easy, as I felt, at that time, as if I had no other option. I was going to graduate with a bachelor's degree in English literature with few job prospects and could not afford to move back home with my single mother of six without some income. I had also always been told I was "good" at school and was unafraid to take on more schooling. The thought of getting paid to attend graduate school was appealing because it meant I could pay my bills to study something I loved, even if money was tight. What made it more feasible was the support, femtorship, and mentorship I received from the UCLA Mellon Mays Undergraduate Fellowship, a two-year program funded by the Mellon Foundation for underrepresented students in the humanities, arts, and social sciences who intend to pursue a PhD and a career in academia. That program helped me apply to graduate school in my senior year of college. As part of UCLA's inaugural cohort, the fellows, myself included, had some added pressure to apply and get into graduate school. I did not really understand at the time that I had more career options than going to graduate school right after my bachelor's. Little did I realize that I had the capacity to apply and get a job with my existing research and writing skills. I also did not understand that the option to attend graduate school does not diminish or go away if you take a year—or many years—to return to school. I only learned about this possibility when I walked into a graduate program with cohort-mates who had much more life and job experience than I. And I also did not realize what a big decision it was to commit six years of my life to a doctoral program. Despite the Mellon Mays support, many aspects of graduate school remained hidden to me, including the expectations and my job prospects after the PhD.

Throughout my time in graduate school, I faced many instances of culture and academic shock, which was further compounded by my deep belief that I was not good enough and did not belong. As a twenty-one-year-old recent graduate with little job experience, I immediately felt "less-than" my cohort-mates who were older and had master's degrees and/or professional careers in my area of study, theater and performance (for example, costume design, lighting design, dramaturgy, directing, acting, and dancing). In contrast, I was a young Chicana from a disenfranchised, heavily Latinx region of the San Fernando Valley, California. Until then, I had only performed in school plays and college student organization performances. I had not even majored in theater as an undergraduate in college, as had many of my graduate school peers, and I felt I had a lot of catching up to do.

My first day of graduate school seminars felt so foggy. I could hardly understand my professors, who spoke using theoretical jargon. Similar to my experience as an undergraduate, I found myself taking excessive notes in class, then going home to look up terms and names of scholars I did not recognize. I struggled to participate in class due to my fear of being caught as an impostor. I believed they would discover that I was the person who was admitted by mistake or that I was ill-prepared to facilitate graduate-level discussions or write doctoral-level seminar papers. At the same time, I attended graduate school in a hostile and tense environment that neither acknowledged my assets nor validated my identity. As I got to know my cohort-mates, I realized we were all just as afraid to participate, we all struggled with our writing, we all were intimidated by our professors, and we all shared similar experiences. To my surprise, they were also intimidated by me, the young scholar who, according to them, seemed so prepared and on top of things. It took time for me to realize that my feelings of inadequacy and lack of belonging was actually a product of deep structural problems and inequities in higher education. Reminding other scholars with similar experiences to my own that they are not alone is one of my motivations for writing this book. Our stories deserve to be told. Our knowledge deserves to be validated. And we—people like you and I—deserve to attend graduate school without the added barriers that come from a lack of institutional and individual support along the path to the degree.

Miroslava

Yvette and I share similar experiences, even though I started my graduate program years before she did. I, too, decided to apply to graduate school because I did not think or know I had other options after graduating from UCLA with an undergraduate degree in history. I knew, however, that I had a passion for history and research, which was cultivated in my Chicana/o history classes and through a summer research program for underrepresented students where I had the opportunity to work with a professor exploring the experiences of Spanish-Mexican women in nineteenth-century California. Slowly but surely over the course of eight weeks, I found my calling for research, though I had yet to learn anything about a career in academia. Looking back, I now realize I had no idea what I was getting myself into. I briefly considered law school but, after perusing the course catalog and seeing the corporate-style language and the lack of representation of people of color, it was obvious that the curriculum was not for me.

Like many of my peers, I did not contemplate returning home to my family because I wanted to carve my own future. My aunt and uncle had raised me and my older brother after our parents died in a car accident in 1981 and I felt that I could no longer continue to occupy space in their household. Certainly, my aunt and uncle welcomed me with open arms but we had a small house—a one-bath, 800-square-foot home with four to five other people already living in that space—and I had to abide by the general rules of the house. Plus, like most young people, I wanted to explore the world (in my case, Los Angeles) and establish my identity. My thought was to stay in school until I could figure out what I would do next.

As such, when I ended up in graduate school, which was made possible by a mentor who fought for my admission to UCLA's History Department as a first-generation, low-income, immigrant, and self-identified Chicana, I aimlessly followed the path established by the institution. I took courses, worked with peers, and received feedback from professors, which resulted in the message that I was ill-prepared for graduate school. Essentially, as I came to learn, I lacked the reading, writing, and analytical skills necessary to communicate my ideas effectively. Coming from a tiny, under-resourced, all-girls Catholic high school, I had struggled with acclimating myself to the space and pace I encountered as an undergraduate (also at UCLA), especially its predominantly upper- and middle-class white culture. By my second year, I navigated the campus and my courses fairly well, even though the sting of not belonging and feeling invisible remained. With a massive undergraduate population at UCLA, and infrequent interaction with professors and graduate students, I received little academic attention, particularly regarding the tools I would later need to advance in graduate school. Today, looking back at my early graduate school career, I realize that few of the faculty, except for a small handful of mentors, believed I was "grad school material," that is, that I had the skills and intellect needed to make it in academia. I will never forget, years later, at my PhD hooding, the surprised look on the face of a former history professor-turned-associate dean, who was handing out diplomas on stage at Royce Hall at UCLA. "Miroslava!" he said with surprise, when he handed me my degree. That experience did not tear me down. Rather, it emboldened me to work harder to make sure students like myself receive equal access and support in higher education.

My lack of preparation and understanding of the rigors of graduate school resulted in a constant battle with self-doubt and desire to drop out—not just at the beginning or end of the quarter, but on a weekly basis, particularly in my first year. I recall that I would come home with a throbbing headache. In productive moments, I argued with myself, debating the merits of staying in school. I had limited funding for the first year but I found ways to make it work and, fortunately, the same mentor who assisted me earlier made it possible for me to receive a multi-year package going into my second year. Ultimately, however, the only thing that kept me in graduate school were my subjects of historical research: Spanish-speaking women in nineteenth-century California. I asked myself, if I didn't complete the project I had set out to do, which was to recover and rewrite history through their lived experiences, who would? I owed it to them, I reasoned, and to all the women of Spanish-Mexican origin who had sacrificed so much for their families and communities to survive and thrive in the nineteenth and into the twentieth centuries.

My commitment to my subjects is what kept me, and still keeps me, focused on reaching for my goals, but at the time it did not provide me with the knowledge and skills to access and navigate graduate school successfully. Fortunately, generous, tireless, and invaluable mentors, my twenty-year-plus journey in academia, and my deep passion for creating a more diverse, equitable, and inclusive environment in higher education, have all helped me learn what it takes to navigate successful paths to graduate school for first-generation, low-income, and/or nontraditional Students of Color. Certainly, no one mold fits everyone's needs and desires, but in this guide we share the key tenets to make it possible for you to achieve your professional and personal goals.

WHY *IS GRAD SCHOOL FOR ME?*

Is Grad School for Me? is a useful tool for first-generation, low-income, and/or nontraditional Students of Color who are exploring or seriously considering graduate school as a viable path to professional and personal success. *Is Grad School for Me?* helps you not only make the right decision but also successfully apply to graduate school, even if you are not familiar or have little understanding of what goes on behind closed doors. Both of us have spent many years as students and workers at graduate institutions and are still figuring out what goes on behind the academic veil or curtain. In *Is Grad School for Me?* we share those insights and walk you through the process, step-by-step, for thinking about what you need to do to achieve your goals.

Part 1 focuses on what you need to consider before applying. Chapter 1 pays attention to demystifying graduate school by teaching you the key differences in graduate programs and giving you an insider's perspective on the graduate school admissions process. We discuss what committees have historically looked for in an applicant's profile as well as the ways that implicit forms of bias have influenced decisions. We also provide you with insights on what you can do to take control of your education to ensure you get what you need from the programs you're applying to. In chapter 2, we turn our attention to helping you decide if graduate school is the right step for you by addressing the wrong reasons to attend and discussing how graduate school may impact you depending on your life and career stage as well as your intersectional identity—that is, the combination of your race, ethnicity, class, gender, sexuality, disability, and so on. Chapter 3 focuses on debunking common misconceptions about graduate school and sharing the expectations of admissions committees once they review your application. This chapter also covers the common obstacles that first-generation, low-income, and/or nontraditional Students of Color face—including impostor phenomenon, family achievement guilt, and feelings of doubt—and how to manage them.

Part 2 focuses on the application process and the components of a successful application with real-world examples of essays. Chapter 4 focuses on how to get started by learning organizational, time-management, and productivity strategies to help you get your application done without burning yourself out. This chapter also discusses how to create a graduate school list and questions to ask yourself and others during this process. Chapter 5 focuses on the statement of purpose and walks you through the components of that statement. It includes sample statements, showing you a variety of approaches from different disciplines across the humanities, social sciences, and STEM fields. Chapter 6 pays attention to the personal and diversity statements, and like chapter 5, contains sample statements. Chapter 7 teaches you everything you need to know about letters of recommendation: what they mean, who to ask for them, and how to obtain them. It also looks at other components of the application process as well, including hidden costs.

Part 3 turns our attention to what you need to do once you have submitted your application. Chapter 8 goes over the application review process, what a typical admissions timeline looks like, and when and how to consider a "Plan B." In chapter 9, we discuss how to prepare for a graduate school interview and the preview day or open house, how to establish solid relationships with the key people in your career, what graduate school funding packages may look like for you, and how to negotiate for better terms. Chapter 10 rounds out part 3, and the book, with an in-depth review of what to do after you've accepted a graduate school offer—this includes how to prepare for a big move, how to practice self-care and stress-management, the grim realities of the academic job market, and how to carry out career planning.

WHO BENEFITS FROM *IS GRAD SCHOOL FOR ME?*

We have written this book with first-generation, low-income, and/or nontraditional Students of Color in mind, though we welcome anyone with interest in learning the challenges and rewards of graduate study. When using the term *first-generation student,* we refer to a person "whose parents did not complete a baccalaureate degree or . . . any individual who regularly resided with and received support from only one parent, an individual whose only such parent did not complete a baccalaureate degree."[2] First-generation students are often the first in their families to attend college and navigate the higher education context without access to the same set of educational resources and cultural knowledge that second-generation or later students have benefited from as a result of personal experiences, social networks, and generational wealth. While some first-generation students might have siblings who attend or have attended college, the term refers to those who are in the first generation of their families—not the first in family—to experience undergraduate and graduate education.

In this guide, we define *low-income* students using California guide-lines on poverty, although for us this term is also inclusive of any populations who come from disenfranchised or under-resourced com-munities. In 2021 in California, an individual living in a family of four earning less than $97,200 qualifies as low income, which is a generous measure compared to that of the federal government, which sets the same threshold at $26,500. In some parts of the United States, including California and other states with high costs of living, an income of $26,500 for a family of four is extreme poverty, while in others with lower costs, the rate is more reasonable. Wealth, or poverty in this case, is relative. As such, we understand the potential for variation in financial opportunities from state to state and across different commu-nities within these states. We advise our readers to pay attention to the costs of any college or university, no matter its location, and consider what it means to you and your family's budget.

An equally important marker of experience shaping the lives of the students foregrounded in this book is the nontraditional pathway. According to the National Center for Education Statistics, *nontradi-tional students* are twenty-five or over. These adult students often have family and work responsibilities that can interfere with successful com-pletion of educational goals. Nontraditional students are no longer fac-ing barriers to education alone. Indeed, the Center for Postsecondary and Economic Success finds that the "typical college student is no longer an 18-year-old recent high-school graduate who enrolls full-time and has limited work and family obligations. Students today are older, more diverse, and have more work and family obligations to balance."[3] Nontraditional students are also more likely to be women and people of color, to be employed (frequently full-time), and to be enrolled in non-degree occupational programs. As compared to traditional stu-dents, nontraditional students face additional obstacles applying to col-lege, often as a result of taking a break between high school and their continued education, having to work full-time or enroll in school part-time in a community college to meet family responsibilities, and living off-campus and commuting. Other characteristics can include being a parent or caregiver, returning to college after previously attending and not finishing ("stop-out students"), and/or attending college as a formerly incarcerated student. Unfortunately, colleges and universities often do not provide the support or resources these students need to successfully navigate their educational experiences and achieve their goals, as institutions of higher education continue to cater almost exclusively to the needs of traditional students, that is, those eighteen to twenty-four years of age who matriculate from undergraduate to graduate school with no or only a short break. In contrast, this book prioritizes the experiences of nontraditional students to highlight the many ways that the disconnect between the university and their life circumstances can get in the way of pursuing an education beyond the bachelor's degree.

In this book, we also focus on the experiences of *Students of Color* and use that term throughout the book, as well as the term *Black, Indigenous, and People of Color (BIPOC)*, specifically to refer to Black and Brown students as well as any other non-white students who have been historically excluded from institutions of higher education and who continue to face institutional racism and discrimination in predominantly white and colonizing academic spaces. This includes, and is not limited to, Arab/Arab Americans, South/Asian/Asian Americans, Black/African/African Americans, Indigenous peoples, Latin Americans, Pacific Islanders, and other students hailing from the Global South, as well as those who are sometimes referred to as members of the global majority. We aim to decenter whiteness in the graduate admissions discourse and acknowledge the ways that colorism, anti-Blackness, and settler colonialism intersect with other forms of oppression such as sexism, classism, ableism, homophobia, among many others, which marginalize and push out many students, especially those who are also first-generation, low-income, and/or nontraditional.

We also want to acknowledge that terms like "BIPOC," "Students of Color," "first-generation," "low-income," and "nontraditional" are also contested terms and we use them in this book to call attention to populations often excluded in dominant academic spaces. By calling attention to the added barriers, we aim to empower you, the students who are especially the audience of this book, with the knowledge to make informed decisions about how to navigate hurdles in your education, careers, and ultimately, your lives.

WHY THIS AUDIENCE?

As we, in the United States, become increasingly diverse, so does higher education, though at a much slower pace than society in general. It is not surprising, then, that the population of first-generation, low-income, and/or nontraditional Students of Color has increased in recent years, requiring colleges and universities to pay attention to their needs, though not yet adequately or effectively.[4] According to the Center for First-Generation Student Success, 42 percent of students who graduated with a bachelor's degree in 2016 were first-generation students, a significant increase from the figure of 26 percent found a decade earlier.[5] Certainly, it is a great benefit to have more students from families without college or university degrees attending four-year institutions, as an educated population means the preparation of a workforce for the twenty-first century, increased incomes and reduced disparities in wealth, and an informed electorate, among other benefits. Yet as mentioned, first-generation students require assistance with navigating the uncharted waters of higher education, as most have not had access to the knowledge, behavior, and skills of institutions that come with previous generations' teachings and insights about that experience. Second and continuing-generation students, for instance, will likely have help from their parents or grandparents about how to navigate admissions or approach professors. First-generation students, in contrast, must figure out how to apply, take appropriate coursework, meet the benchmarks in their majors, and learn the social and cultural etiquette on their own or with other students who are in similar situations.

The numbers of low-income and nontraditional students, like those of first-generation students, are on the rise. According to the American Council on Education, the share of low-income students—calculated at 150 percent of the federal poverty level—increased from 26.7 percent to 43.1 percent from 2000 to 2016. Given economic stratification in the United States, Students of Color are more likely to be low-income than their white peers. The majority of low-income students, slightly more than half, however, attend two-year institutions, or community colleges, while one quarter, or 25 percent, attend four-year public institutions.[6] While community colleges are known as entry points for nontraditional students to access bachelor's degrees, they also often do not have the same level of resources and opportunities found in four-year colleges and universities. Low-income students can find it particularly difficult to transfer from community colleges to four-year institutions and to graduate, largely as a result of financial needs, family responsibilities, and lack of mentorship. Despite those hurdles, today, nontraditional students are more commonly found in institutions of higher education than in the past. Studies suggest that "40% of the current undergraduate population at American colleges and universities are non-traditional."[7] The changing demographic of colleges and universities means that what is meant by "typical" and "traditional" needs to be revised, as first-generation, low-income, and/or nontraditional Students of Color are more likely to fill the profile of what it means to a college student.

First-generation, low-income, and/or nontraditional Students of Color are also a diverse set of individuals who have faced (and continue to face) a variety of roadblocks along their path to higher education, both undergraduate and graduate school. As a group, however, they share challenges within institutions of higher education that will affect how they apply to and navigate graduate school. Most recently, as we finished up the edits to this book, we all witnessed the implementation of yet another barrier at the federal level when, in June 2023, the US Supreme Court struck down affirmative action. Generally known as a set of policies and practices aimed at providing historically underrepresented, ethnic and racial minoritized peoples a path for inclusion in exclusive, white-dominated, and discriminatory institutions, such as colleges and universities, affirmative action made it possible for us—Yvette and Miroslava—and thousands of others to achieve our collective educational goals and to provide uplift for our families and communities. Affirmative action forced the opening of many doors that had been sealed shut for decades, if not centuries, for BIPOC folks. While we are not able to dive fully into this topic, what we can say is that we have learned much from similar bans at the state level in places like California, our home state. We know that the conservative court's decision will have a direct impact on the admissions of BIPOC students in colleges and graduate school across the country. And yet, we also know that first-generation, low-income, and/or nontraditional BIPOC individuals and allies will continue to find new and creative ways to diversify higher education. Thus, the advice that we provide in this book about strengthening our relationships and sense of community not only continues to hold true but also is now more pressing and relevant than ever.

Much of the literature on higher education, however, fails to recognize the barriers faced by first-generation, low-income, and/or nontraditional Students of Color, which are often hidden, unspoken, and institutionalized. As such, these studies neglect the specific experiences of these students along their journey of applying to graduate school. Instead, studies tend to focus on a generic audience, often presumed to be white, male, straight, cisgender, middle-class, neurotypical, and able-bodied, among other overrepresented identities. Mainstream published work fails to take into account that, for many individuals, particularly nontraditional students, having a less-than-stellar competitive grade point average, struggles with standardized testing, and a gap between college and graduate school, are real impediments to applying, let alone being admitted and receiving financial support.

Fortunately, scholars generally, and Scholars of Color particularly, have recently begun to address the inequities in the research on educational attainment, paying attention to the experiences of first-generation, low-income, and/or nontraditional Students of Color. Specialists in the fields of education, critical race studies, and ethnic studies, for instance, have brought attention to the structural and individual challenges students face in pursuing a graduate degree. The literature is especially rich in identifying the cultural and environmental challenges that Students of Color face when they access higher education as first-year or transfer students. They demonstrate that unequal educational outcomes are not a result of individual failures and community deficits but, rather, deeply rooted systemic institutional neglect.[8]

Building on this rich literature, we review common and uncommon scenarios preventing students from successfully applying to graduate school and provide specific, measurable, action-oriented, results-driven, and timely (SMART) tips, templates, sample materials, as well as investigating myths vs. facts, to engage a variety of learners. With a strong focus on demystifying higher education and teaching the hidden curriculum, this guide aims to empower traditionally marginalized populations with the resources they need to enroll in a graduate program that is the best fit for their needs and purposes. The long-term goal of the book is to diversify a wide range of professions, including the professoriate, nonprofits, government, industry, and entrepreneurship, among others.

FEMTORING WITHIN *IS GRAD SCHOOL FOR ME?*

We developed and use the term *femtoring* as a foundational framework for this book, to call attention to the importance of using an intersectional feminist lens in mentoring first-generation, low-income, and/or nontraditional Students of Color as they pursue graduate school. For us, an intersectional feminist lens calls for an understanding of how race, ethnicity, class, gender, sexuality, disability, age, and legal status work in tandem to condition our lived experiences in our communities and the larger society. It is an appreciation of how our identities, cultures, and histories influence our access (or not) to resources, including higher education. As such, we take a holistic approach to understanding the systemic challenges—that is, poverty, poor educational and health outcomes, high rates of unemployment, underemployment, underearning, as well as incarceration and detention, among others—facing first-generation, low-income, and/or nontraditional Students of Color and their families. We seek to empower aspiring and current students by using specific language and examples that serve as mirrors and inspirational role models to move us closer to achieving our professional and personal goals.

Mentoring, in contrast to femtoring, is broadly defined as a process of guiding, teaching, and learning that happens between the mentor—the guide or teacher—and the mentee—the student or learner—in a variety of contexts and with a wide range of goals. According to leading graduate schools, mentors also commit to attending to the well-being and professional development of a mentee. Mentoring is a professional relationship that *both* the mentor and mentee actively create, a relationship that evolves over time. Moreover, because no single mentor can provide all of the information and support that a graduate student may need, "[e]ffective mentoring is a community effort."[9] Yet mentoring, as we have seen it operate, doesn't always include attention to identity, culture, and history. As such, it may lack the qualities of femtoring. Even further removed from our vision of holistic, culturally relevant support is *advising,* which is provided through an advisor usually assigned within the first few weeks of enrolling in a program. Though useful for guiding students along the academic track—that is, on course requirements, exams, and exam preparation, and writing and defending the thesis and/or dissertation—advisors do not usually focus on much more, including personal aspirations. Advisors, mentors, and femtors are sometimes the same person and sometimes not (more is said about the differences in chapter 1) and we encourage you to seek out a variety of these individuals not only in graduate school but also beyond your formal education. For our purposes, *femtoring* is mentorship that prioritizes individual and community empowerment as well as social justice and calls attention to how this type of service work is gendered. Moreover, as feminist scholars have shown, tenured and untenured female Faculty of Color in particular face an expectation and burden of service-oriented emotional labor that goes unrecognized and unrewarded.[10] Femtoring allows us to call out the visible and invisible inherent hierarchies in the policies and practices of institutions, allowing us to build more diverse, equitable, and inclusive spaces. Femtoring, we argue, is crucial in diversifying academia and the professional world.

We would be remiss if we did not disclose that the genesis for this guide comes from The Grad School Femtoring Podcast, which Yvette launched in 2019. The ideas, *platicas* (talks), and *testimonios* (testimonials) found scattered throughout these pages originate with her decision to femtor an online community of first-generation Students of Color interested in successfully applying to and navigating graduate school. For her listeners, the podcast has cultivated a welcoming and nurturing space. As Jeffrey Merino, a listener-turned-guest, noted:

> I've been following [the podcast] since the very early days. I think I might have been either in my graduate program, and I just wanted to be in a space or surrounded by . . . all the support. I think when I found your podcast it was . . . a way to decompress and know that there's someone out there that's looking out for first-generation, BIPOC individuals that are trying to navigate higher education. I definitely looked forward, always . . . to when you dropped a new episode. It was kind of like a therapy session, just hearing the stories, your advice, and then the stories of others,

and just knowing that . . . whatever I'm going through right now . . . there is an end in sight. [And, that] there are also other people that are just as ambitious and have goals like me.[11]

IS GRAD SCHOOL FOR ME? MATTERS IN THE HISTORY OF GRADUATE EDUCATION

Jeffrey Merino's narrative reminds us of the significance of making an intervention in the status quo or "business as usual" of graduate education. For centuries, it has remained beyond the reach of what we now call first-generation, low-income, and/or nontraditional Students of Color precisely because, as many of us have heard, these spaces were not created for people like us. History tells us that, for much of the nineteenth and early twentieth centuries, *higher education,* that is, formal study and training beyond primary and secondary grades—also known as the bachelor's, master's, and doctoral degrees—remained the purview of upper-class white men and was modeled on Eurocentric traditions. For decades, until the 1860s, the bachelor's was the primary higher degree obtainable in the United States. Growing demands for expanded access to research-based training programs in the sciences and humanities, however, as had been developed in Germany in the early 1800s, and the pressure to establish graduate programs in the United States, resulted in the opening of doctoral-degree-granting colleges. Though unregulated and haphazard in their course of training, US institutions generally included a prescribed course of study and successful defense of a thesis or dissertation. Master's degrees, developed much earlier than doctorates but later maligned as inconsequential and honorific, were retooled and gained prestige alongside the doctoral degree.[12] By the early 1900s, six of the leading universities in the United States enrolled some six thousand graduate students and had granted over two hundred PhDs, with the great majority going to white upper-class men. Increasingly, however, white men from the growing middle class as well as their female counterparts began to attend master's and doctoral programs as the result of the growth of new fields, such as social work, psychology, and education, as well as the professionalization of many previously established trades that had earlier relied largely on apprenticeship, including teaching, nursing, and medicine. The result was the awarding of growing numbers of doctoral degrees to white men and a small number of white women.[13]

Excluded from the vast majority of these predominantly white institutions were Black people. Institutional slavery, which was legally abolished in 1865 but reinstated through the Black Codes, as well as physical and sexual violence and grinding poverty, made access to formal education nearly impossible for most Black men and women, particularly in the US south. The convict lease system—the "leasing" of prisoners to the highest bidders—and legal segregation, allowed through the 1896 US Supreme Court decision in *Plessy v. Ferguson* and implemented through the "separate but equal" Jim Crow law, further worked to bar Blacks from most forms of formal schooling, including higher education. Despite the repression and potentially deadly consequences for teaching or learning how to read throughout this period, Black people pursued literacy. As education scholar Derrick P. Alridge writes, during slavery:

> African American conducted clandestine schools that taught reading and writing despite slaveholders' prohibitions. After emancipation, African Americans maintained their faith in education and by 1870, one-fourth of black school-aged children in the southern states attended school. By 1910 only 45.4 percent of the African American school-age population was enrolled. In the area of literacy, in 1890, less than half of black southerners, aged 10 years or older, were literate. By 1930, however, four-fifths—80 percent—of the southern black population was literate.[14]

Despite the seemingly insurmountable barriers to education and higher education, Black students not only attended colleges and universities but also secured master's and doctoral degrees in the late nineteenth and early twentieth centuries. Largely in response to entrenched racism and exclusion from predominantly white institutions, the mid-to-late nineteenth century witnessed a steady growth and expansion of Black colleges and universities in the north and, eventually, in the south. From the 1850s to the 1870s, some twenty-two programs were established with nearly forty graduates. By 1890, the nation's first historically black college for women had been founded, along with some sixty-three other colleges. Ten years later, in 1900, that figure had jumped to seventy-seven, contributing to the awarding of some 2,000 degrees in higher education to Black graduates, with approximately 390 of these granted by predominantly white colleges and universities.[15]

Access to doctoral programs was much more limited in this same period, however. Among the most well-known were earned by Edward Alexander Bouchet (in physics, from Yale College, now Yale University), in 1876, and by W. E. B. Du Bois (in history, from Harvard University) in 1895. Though Bouchet earned his degrees in a predominantly white institution and sought employment in similar places, he was turned down. Instead, Bouchet taught chemistry and physics for twenty-six years at the Institute for Colored Youth, an all-Black high school in Philadelphia, and later held a variety of teaching-related posts.[16] Du Bois, in contrast, willingly and by preference taught history, sociology, and economics at all-Black colleges, including Atlanta University, for he had witnessed the extremes of racist policies and practices in the predominantly white schools and sought to protect young Black males and females from those experiences. As Alridge writes, Du Bois believed that "African Americans must provide education for their children and the 'college-bred Negro' must take up his or her responsibility."[17] Preaching "voluntary separation," Du Bois nevertheless supported and fought for economic integration as a path to full citizenship.[18]

Despite the expansion of educational and professional opportunities in the early twentieth century, as experienced by middle-class white men and women, the numbers of Black men and women who obtained PhDs remained relatively low, though they expanded somewhat over time. From 1907 to 1930, for instance, nearly ten Black men and the first three women—all in 1921—secured their degrees. Despite the onset of the Great Depression in the early 1930s and its dire impact on Black folks and communities across the United States, especially in previously economically depressed regions, some 117 historically Black institutions of higher education, including 36 public and 81 private, had been established, with 5 exclusively devoted to graduate level education. By the 1940s and the 1950s, Black men and women increasingly filled the roles of professors not only at Black colleges and universities but also at predominantly white institutions, largely as a result of the boom in demand for higher education following World War II.

Latinas and Latinos, who we refer to in this book as Latinx people (although we also acknowledge the use of other inclusive terms like Latine), including Mexican Americans and Puerto Ricans, also lacked access to predominantly white institutions of higher education for most of the nineteenth and the first half of the twentieth centuries. Their inability to gain educational opportunities stemmed from racial discrimination, segregation, poverty, and, for many, a rural existence with a dual wage labor system—one for whites and the other for non-whites—in agricultural work. The most they could hope for was an eighth-grade education. Latinx peoples' preference for culturally relevant curriculum and Spanish language instruction also meant that those who had the ability to attend school studied primarily at Catholic colleges, teacher training schools, and junior colleges. Despite few opportunities to gain a high school and college education, a handful of Mexican Americans did obtain doctorates and made significant contributions to the study of Mexican-origin people. They include George I. Sánchez, who received his doctorate in educational administration from Berkeley in 1935 and became one of the foremost advocates of bilingual education. Three decades later in 1962, Martha Bernal, a

Tejana or Mexican American woman from Texas, became the first Latina to receive a PhD in psychology, from the University of Indiana at Bloomington. Later, Dr. Bernal would make it her mission to fight for Students of Color to have access to graduate training, specifically in her field of study, clinical psychology, which remained predominantly white. During her time with the American Psychological Association, she joined committees fighting for diversity, equity, and inclusion for racial and ethnic minorities as well as gays and lesbians.[19]

Native Americans, too, faced barriers to formal education in the United States prior to the 1940s and 1950s, but their experiences were brutal in a unique way. For hundreds of years, Native peoples not only faced racial discrimination, segregation, and disenfranchisement, but also outright war, violence, and murder. After decades of removal and campaigns of genocide against them, Native Americans faced another harrowing experience at the hands of US government officials attempting to subdue them: the forced removal of their children to be placed in "boarding schools" where they would be forcibly inculcated with American values and beliefs and, ideally, have their native cultures excised. Relying on a US military regimen, Native children were forced into gender-specific labor and training to prepare them for employment with non-Native families in agricultural and other industries. The result was few, if any, opportunities for other formal education. After they left or managed to escape, most Native people remained as distant as possible from US government-associated institutions and programs. Instead, they established their own schools and tribal colleges.[20]

The doors to higher education swung wide open in the post-World War II period. Not everyone, however, was welcomed or allowed to pass through. White middle- and working-class men and their families passed easily as beneficiaries of government programs generally made unavailable to women and racial and ethnic minorities as well as disabled people. Those benefits for middle- and working-class white men became available shortly before the end of the war. Anticipating the conclusion of the war and the need to prepare an educated workforce, government officials drafted the GI Bill providing enhanced unemployment benefits, job training, and college access to veterans regardless of race or ethnicity. The goal was not only to prepare veterans for the rise of the science and technology sector of the post-war era but also to advance democratic ideals in the Cold War era battle against communism and fascism across the globe. Administrators did not anticipate that many would take advantage of the GI Bill, as rates of college attendance remained low in the 1940s. By some estimates only 5 percent of Americans had a bachelor's degree and less than half had finished high school. Among non-white people, women, and disabled individuals, those rates were even lower.

Contrary to expectations, however, white male veterans in droves took advantage of the subsidies of the GI Bill, including the free tuition and stipend for books and living expenses. Many used it to attend private and prestigious as well as state and public institutions, leading to the rapid expansion of college enrollment and demand for access to higher education in the 1950s and the 1960s. That desire, in turn, created intense pressure for the expansion of existing colleges and universities and the development of new institutions across the country, leading to the establishment of many community colleges and four-year institutions. The rising availability of classes and programs along with the GI Bill allowed white working-class men and their families to have access to the middle class and, in turn, enabled the white middle class to expand and secure generational wealth for their families.

Largely excluded or overlooked from the program were Black and Latinx war veterans, as well as women across racial and ethnic groups, for the majority had not gone to war and had been expected (or were forced) to stay home. Though entitled to benefits, Black veterans in the US south were turned away by local level administrators who steered them towards other forms of support provided by the bill. Like Black veterans, Mexican American veterans had trouble accessing benefits, leaving many families of Mexican origin unable to pay the costs of higher education as well as the expenses of supporting their families while they studied. As the overwhelming beneficiaries of the GI Bill, white middle- and working-class men had the ability to enter the increasingly technologically oriented, managerial, and professional class, while non-whites continued to lag in educational attainment and career aspirations as well as access to generational wealth.[21]

Black, Latinx, and Native American people were not only limited in their access to undergraduate education but also graduate study, which experienced significant growth in the 1960s and 1970s. That came about following the Soviet Union's launch of the Sputnik satellite in 1957 and the Cold War. In response to the USSR's technological advancement in space and nuclear power, and in what would become known as the space race or the arms race, the US government poured support into the growth and expansion of research institutions, particularly those awarding doctorates in related fields. As the National Science Foundation reports,

> The number of doctorate-granting institutions grew by 73 in the 1960s and by another 87 in the 1970s. By the mid-1960s, institutions with doctoral programs were in all 50 U.S. states, the District of Columbia, and Puerto Rico. The rate of growth in the number of new doctorate-granting institutions slowed in the 1980s and 1990s, although the number of doctorates awarded continued to rise.[22]

The news was not so bright for aspiring students across predominantly impoverished communities of color. National data on doctoral attainment across race and ethnicity from the 1970 through the end of the 1990s demonstrates the vast inequities in educational opportunities and attainment. (Unfortunately, government officials failed to keep data on racial and ethnic differences prior to the 1970s.) During the last quarter of the twentieth century, the overwhelming majority of doctorates went to three groups: white US citizens (68 percent), Asian foreign nationals (14 percent), and white foreign nationals (8 percent). At the same time, Hispanics, those of Spanish ancestry, obtained a tiny proportion, between 2 and nearly 4 percent of PhDs in all disciplines. Most of those minute gains, however, were not representative of the majority of people of Hispanic descent, Mexican Americans and Puerto Ricans. Instead, "Other Hispanics"—Cuban Americans, who enjoyed many government benefits available to them as political refugees fleeing communist Cuba, as well as Central and South Americans, Dominicans, and Spanish peoples—gained nearly half of all these doctorates. While Mexican Americans with PhDs increased their numbers from 900 (of 2,000 awarded to "Hispanics" in 1979) to 1600 (of 5,100 in 1999), their proportion fell from 45 percent to 31 percent of the "Hispanic" group, demonstrating increased need for resources in higher education, both at the undergraduate and graduate levels. Black people witnessed slightly larger gains, from about 4.1 percent to 5.2 percent of the overall pool, an increase from 5,200 earned PhDs in 1975 to about 7,000 by 1997. Asian/Pacific Islanders hovered between 2 and 4.1 percent, while American Indians remained at less than 1 percent through the twenty-five year period.[23] PhD attainment in STEM fields specifically was even more dire for Hispanics as a group. Maricel Quintana-Baker found that from 1983 to 1997, "Hispanics earned 2.2% of all the STEM doctorates[.]"[24] Ten years later, in the new millennium, Latinx and Black people had seen limited gains. "In 2008," according to Elvia Ramírez, "Latinos earned just 5.7% of all doctorates, whereas Whites, Asian Americans, and Blacks received 75.4%, 8.3%, and 6.6%, respectively."[25]

Today, doctoral completion rates have improved among first-generation, low-income, and/or nontraditional Students of Color, but not as rapidly as we would hope, prompting our urgency to carry out this project. With this history in mind, it is no wonder that so many of us feel excluded, like we don't belong, and unworthy of occupying academic spaces. How many times have we been in colleges and universities where we see portraits hanging on walls or names plastered on buildings that look and sound familiar? How many times have we seen statues of people who look like our parents, grandparents, *abuelitos* and *abuelitas*? How many times have we been in classrooms taught by people with similar backgrounds as us? Institutions of higher education were not built for people who look like us or have shared experiences with us, and yet here we are. We invite you to consider graduate school as one way, of many, that you can participate in the larger struggle for community empowerment and liberation from the daily constraints we experience in the larger society. We don't expect graduate school to be right for everyone, nor do we expect you to achieve your personal and professional goals overnight. But know that no matter if graduate school is (or is not) the right next step for you, with the support of femtors and mentors, as well as diverse, equitable, and inclusive institutional policies and practices, we can achieve our dreams and desires for stronger families and happier and healthier lives for us and future generations. *Sí se puede.*

PART ONE

BEFORE APPLYING

1

DEMYSTIFYING GRADUATE SCHOOL AND THE HIDDEN CURRICULUM

||

WE DEDICATE THIS CHAPTER to demystifying what many scholars have called the *hidden curriculum of academia*. Most simply, the hidden curriculum is the set of cultural beliefs and practices of the institution that you are expected to know but are not explicitly taught.[1] Since the late 1960s, with the democratization of higher education and its slowly but steadily access to white women and people of color, scholars have worked to unpack the hidden curriculum and the ways it has excluded first-generation, low-income, and/or nontraditional Students of Color.[2] Given their lesser familiarity with higher education generally as compared to their second- and continuing-generation, middle- and upper-class white peers, navigating the hidden curriculum is a challenging prospect and is beset with real (that is, material or economic) barriers. Unlike formal curriculum, which is taught in classrooms, the hidden curriculum remains hidden, as Jennifer McCrory Calarco argues, because it's taken for granted, as it involves ways of performing essential functions that are not usually written down or recorded. These include how to carry out, write, and talk about your research; how to navigate the university bureaucracy; and how to approach and communicate with faculty and staff.

The hidden curriculum also remains invisible because its teaching is not rewarded. Professors at research-intensive universities are primarily advanced for their research, publications, projects, and creative activities, and less so for teaching and service, which is where advising and mentoring fall. Increasingly, universities are recognizing and rewarding diversity work, including mentoring underrepresented students and developing diverse curriculum, as valuable to the campus community. Yet, the bulk of the prestige—merits and promotions—remains with research and publishing. Professors at teaching-intensive institutions, including state college and liberal arts colleges, do take more time than their peers at research institutions to prepare their students for potential graduate education. But heavy teaching loads, limited means (especially for state colleges), and emphasis on master's programs leaves much of the hidden curriculum, particularly in doctoral programs that students might encounter after their master's degrees, still veiled.

The consequences of the hidden curriculum, along with systemic inequalities, have led to stark imbalances in the awarding of doctoral degrees to underrepresented students. According to Julie Posselt, a leading researcher on graduate admissions:

> Women and U.S. residents of color remain less likely than men and whites to attend research universities, and they continue to receive fewer doctorates than we would expect given their share of both the overall population and the population of baccalaureates awarded. African American and Latinos comprised 13 percent and 16 percent, respectively, of the U.S. population in the 2010 Census, but received just 6 and 7 percent of the doctorates awarded that year—numbers that reflect little change from the previous decade. Meanwhile, Native American doctoral attainment has fallen to its lowest point in twenty years.[3]

These disparities are a consequence not only of the hidden curriculum but also of the gatekeeping that takes place in academia. *Gatekeeping,* or keeping out members from certain populations, as Posselt has found, happens at many levels in higher education. In departments, it happens when faculty are confronted with applicants who look different from them or have divergent interests. Admissions committees are more likely than not to pause when they see applications from candidates who are first-generation or nontraditional Students of Color and likely will need mentorship or who have a declared passion for working beyond academic spaces. Gatekeeping, also a form of institutional racism, occurs when programs are focused on raising their status by increasing admissions criteria and competition, making it more difficult to obtain admission. Posselt reports that fiscal concerns over being able to support the students as well as uncertain employment prospects have led departments to reduce the numbers of students they admit, allowing them to justify their selectivity. The increased demand for graduate education as a result of *degree inflation,* that is, the need to have higher degrees for positions that in the past required bachelor's degrees or no degrees, and the shrinking supply of spaces for graduate students, has rendered admissions highly competitive and often beyond reach, especially for first-generation, low-income, and/or nontraditional Students of Color.[4]

Contrary to popular belief, graduate admissions, Posselt argues, are not based on choosing the applicants who are "most likely to succeed." Rather, it reflects and is driven by "institutional interest such as prestige, diversity, collegiality, efficiency, and fiscal responsibility," which gives the process "legitimacy in the eyes of the stakeholders."[5] Admissions, she continues, are used to pursue a variety of interests and reflect "multiple hierarchies of priorities [that] simultaneously and interactively shape an applicant's odds of being admitted."[6] Despite calls for diversity, equity, and inclusion, faculty may knowingly or unknowingly use admissions criteria that undermine those same goals. *Implicit bias,* what Posselt calls "informal discrimination and unconscious . . . biases," as well as a *colorblind approach,* what psychologist Derald W. Sue names the avowed commitment not to see or pay attention to racial or ethnic differences, mask racism, sexism, homophobia, and ableism, among other "isms," and are used to justify "fit" and admissibility, ultimately leading to rejection.[7] Colorblindness, Sue argues, increases disparities, rather than preventing or decreasing them, for it lessens "the ability to monitor inequities and encourage[s] greater discrimination." Colorblindness, he continues, "blind[s] people to real, meaningful differences that exist between groups in educational opportunities, civil rights protections, race-specific medical conditions, and so forth."[8]

Given the continuing disparities and structural challenges in higher education, we write as femtors with first-generation, low income, and/ or nontraditional Students of Color in mind, focusing on the most significant yet unspoken aspects of graduate admissions and graduate school more generally. We see this work as contributing to the building of *cultural capital,* that is, the knowledge and skills necessary to successfully navigate cultural institutions, like graduate school, for the inclusion of historically marginalized populations. Exclusion from schooling, at whatever level, as education scholars David Hemphill and Erin Blakely remind us, "often serves as the gatekeeper for attaining cultural capital," which schools preserve and distribute.[9]

We understand that limited exposure to and contact with individuals—either family members or friends—who hold graduate degrees like a master's or doctorate may also make pursuing such a degree seem like a far-off dream or an idea disconnected to your past, present, or future. Indeed, without knowledge or access to the language, beliefs, and practices of the institution, let alone the admissions process, successfully applying to graduate school appears a lofty goal. As such, we also allocate space in this chapter to exploring key elements of graduate school and the nature and variety of degree programs that are available, focusing on the differences between interdisciplinary and disciplinary programs or fields, and whether taking a gap year is right for you. Finally, we consider the mindset shift that is necessary for folks who are uncomfortable or unfamiliar with taking time from their everyday roles and responsibilities to improve themselves and their careers. For nontraditional applicants who have been away from school for five, ten, or more years, the idea of returning to school among younger and seemingly "brighter" people is a tall order. Returning to school is not, we argue, insurmountable. We hope that this overview familiarizes you with the particularities of graduate school, how it evolved, how and where you fit in, and why it makes sense (or not) for you to apply.

We are inspired by the words of Sirenia Sánchez on the power of "ethical *chisme*" (gossip) in helping to dismantle the hidden curriculum. In a Grad School Femtoring Podcast special guest appearance, Sirenia talked about the need to engage in ethical *chisme*—the sharing of insider knowledge in navigating higher education and academia—to expose the hidden curriculum and empower oneself. "Sadly," she laments, "ethical *chisme* is not as commonly found as you might think. While we might share accomplishments and achievements, we often say much less about our struggles and uncomfortable experiences in academia. Really trying to normalize a culture in which we're transparent . . . [is] the ultimate goal . . . because there's just hidden norms and curriculums in grad school. We don't know what's normal. We don't know what it's like to maneuver this space. Because of that, it is hard to identify someone who will be open and receptive." To combat this culture, Sirenia invites us to reach out to student organizations to get involved and to reach out to newer, fresher faces in the crowd. "I think that's a way of also developing communities . . . [by] initiating and creating that safe space for students."[10]

WHAT IS GRADUATE SCHOOL?

We use *graduate school* to mean any advanced academic degree that goes beyond the undergraduate degree. This can include post-baccalaureate (or postbacc), combined bachelor's and master's (i.e., BA/ MA or BS/MS), master's, and doctoral programs. We also include research-based and professional programs. This book focuses on assisting first-generation, low-income, and/or nontraditional Students of Color to prepare and apply for graduate programs, primarily master's and doctor of philosophy programs, in a wide range of humanities, social science, and science, technology, engineering, and math (STEM) fields. We do not cover applications for admission into professional programs such as medical school, law school, or business school. Those call for a specific set of tools outside our purview.

Moving from the undergraduate to the graduate school experience may seem like a daunting prospect, especially when the opportunity to study and learn in both environments is uncommon in our families and communities and we have little understanding of what's involved or what it takes to apply, enroll, and succeed. Undergraduate and graduate degrees reflect varying levels of duration, specialization, and commitment, among other differences. Undergraduate degree programs usually consist of two-year (associate's degree) and four-year (bachelor's degrees) programs, whereas graduate study can range from two to three years for the master's and from four to five years and, especially in the arts and humanities, up to six, seven, eight, or more years for a doctorate. Undergraduate programs cover general education courses required by the college or university as well as curriculum specific to a major, such as economics or biology, though they also include opportunities for lower-level, short-term research. Graduate programs are specialized in nature and offer an in-depth approach either to a discipline or an interdisciplinary field, which consists of multiple approaches and methodologies from a variety of fields that have been woven into a new and innovative field. Graduate programs are also generally research- and writing-intensive and involve highly specialized coursework. Although the number of courses you will take every semester is smaller than at the undergraduate level, the courses are demanding, requiring many more hours to complete than those for bachelor's programs. Graduate courses are also smaller than undergraduate classes, allowing students to develop one-on-one relationships with professors in seminars and labs. Undergraduate programs or majors are relatively easy to switch, but not so with graduate studies; switching programs will require navigating institutional bureaucracy as well as delicate personal and political relations within your home department. Landing on a field of study that ticks off the most important boxes for you is, therefore, important when considering your options.

What may be surprising to many is that, unlike in undergraduate classes, graduate programs generally pay less attention to grades during the academic year, diminishing, though not eliminating, competition among students. In highly desirable environments, the faculty pay attention to students and their needs and focus on the quality and innovative nature of the research. In contrast to undergraduates who must follow a pre-set curriculum, graduate students have less structure and more independence and freedom to shape their own learning. This is especially true when they are working on their thesis or *dissertation,* the long piece of writing based on original research that is often required to obtain a doctoral degree. This period of research and writing is when the built-in, day-to-day support or structure found in the classroom is largely absent. Graduate students in STEM fields, for instance, who have passed their exams, may spend the next twelve to sixteen months in a lab or at a research site conducting investigations without immediate guidance from an advisor. Similarly, graduate students in arts, humanities, and social sciences spend months, sometimes years, reading, producing creative works, and/or collecting field data, with potentially infrequent meetings with advisors. This autonomy might mean less direction and guidance, depending on your advisor and department, and implies the need for you to figure out in what environment you learn best and to make those needs known to your advisor and others on your master's or dissertation committee.

A *dissertation committee* refers to the members of faculty (typically three to five) who supervise a graduate student's work and may serve as mentors, provide constructive feedback, and evaluate the work before a final exam or defense. Presumably, your advisor will already know your working style; if they do not, you will again need to communicate how you work best and what you need to complete your work. Other major differences between graduate and undergraduate studies include the admissions process, responsibilities outside of school, residential patterns, and costs.

Researching and writing a master's thesis or doctoral dissertation and doing so relatively independently is part and parcel of academic training for the professor track, even though fewer and fewer graduate students today have plans or can afford to plan a career as a tenure track professor, given the declining job market. Certainly, experiences and relationships may vary with advisors, but independent thinking and development as a scholar is an essential goal of doctoral education. From our own experience and generally speaking, graduate programs are more intensive and stress-inducing than those at the undergraduate level. Depending on the size of the institution and availability of faculty and resources, undergraduate students have the opportunity to remain in contact with faculty and/or graduate students for the duration of their careers. Or, if preferred, they can fly below the radar, hiding out until coursework and studies are completed. This is not usually, if at all, possible in graduate school.

If your advisor is doing their job responsibly, they will track your progress, as will the department level faculty graduate advisor, the staff graduate advisor, and frequently other faculty working in your area of expertise. Essentially, graduate students must thrive and survive living under a microscope—while at the same time effectively managing their own time during long periods out of the classroom, as noted above. Certainly, not all programs run this way. Communicate with potential advisors and home departments about general expectations or, if possible, contact the graduate advisor, who can provide you with the information of a current graduate student who has a similar racial, ethnic, and/or gender identity to yours and who is willing to talk frankly with you. The more you learn about the norms and expectations—the hidden curriculum—of your program of interest, the more prepared you will be in applying for and transitioning from the undergraduate to graduate experience.

WHAT ARE POST-BACCALAUREATE PROGRAMS?

Post-baccalaureate (postbacc) programs are completed after graduating with a bachelor's degree and almost always before a master's or doctoral degree. Students enroll in postbacc programs for many different reasons. Some choose to do it to acquire additional training or skills to fill a gap in their academic and research profile or to gain mastery in a new area or training or research. A postbacc program can provide foundational coursework to help prepare for a major transition or to build a bridge onto a new area of expertise. They can specialize in assisting first-generation, low-income, and/or nontraditional Students of Color. Many students attend postbacc programs to gain a certificate or specialization, enabling them to become competitive applicants for doctoral programs. Postbaccalaureate programs are also an excellent option for students who need to boost their GPA or exam scores. Most also provide additional support with graduate school applications, as they know most students are interested in pursuing their studies further. In such instances, they will provide tutorials on the doctoral program application process, provide exam preparation courses, and often have high placement rates in competitive programs.

Postbacc programs typically range from one to two years and, while they are similar to master's programs, they do not usually grant that degree. Some may do so, while others will provide you with a certificate of completion. What makes postbacc programs stand out from master's programs is that they are designed to support you in transitioning to other professional and research graduate programs. Many postbacc programs are highly competitive and come with full or partial funding, but it is not guaranteed. Postbacc programs are plentiful in STEM fields and less common in the humanities and social sciences. Do not discount the opportunity of pursuing a postbacc if you are in a non-STEM field, however. They are available, though it may take longer to find them.

WHAT ARE BA/MA AND BS/MS PROGRAMS?

A combined or concurrent bachelor's and master's degree program allows you to complete an undergraduate and graduate degree in about four to five years, much less time than it would take to finish them separately. These accelerated programs are often touted as cost-effective and efficient means to prepare for professional fields, such as teaching, counseling, or management, and for advanced doctoral work. They are advertised, too, as opportunities to transition seamlessly from undergraduate to graduate study. Students gravitate to these programs because they are frequently almost assured of employment opportunities once they are done, as many are linked to programs that will hire them. In most cases, you are required to apply directly to the BA/MA or BS/MS program as a first-year student, as this will allow you to prepare and organize your course of study to ensure you complete it within the allowable time frame. In some institutions, you are allowed to move from a BA/BS to BA/MA or BS/MS course of study in your junior year, before you have moved too far along. These programs are popular as they include internships, training, and/or some other practical skills and knowledge that can open doors to many career opportunities.

While dual programs provide many advantages, they also present significant disadvantages, including a highly competitive admissions process (such as requiring high grade point average, academic achievements), a heavy course load, and a commitment of around five years, along with tuition and related costs. Like with any program, the key to success is determining if the course of study is right for you. We advise you to speak to advisors, current students with similar backgrounds, and alumni to get a feel for what the programs are like on a day-to-day basis as well as their long-term impact.

WHAT ARE MASTER'S PROGRAMS?

A *master's degree* is another credential that you can earn after completing your bachelor's. This includes the *terminal master's degree*, which refers to master's degrees in fields where no PhD is available, such as a Master of Fine Arts, or MFA. In some doctoral programs, graduate students may opt to leave with a master's degree if they are unable to or unwilling to commit to a five-to-eight-year PhD program and the financial and personal costs that come with it. Master's degrees are also key to increasing opportunities for increased salary and career opportunities. They are a great option, too, for individuals who would like more research experience before pursuing a doctoral degree or for professionals who are considering a pivot in their careers that requires or strongly encourages enhanced educational experience.

A master's degree includes research-based as well as applied or professional terminal programs. The research-based training in a nonterminal program generally works under the assumption that you will continue onto a doctoral degree, whereas the terminal master's programs may provide capstone projects and internships to support you in securing a full-time job or career. What is true of most master's programs is that they offer little to no funding. While it is possible to secure a fully or partially funded master's program, especially if your advisor has a significant research grant, it is less common than in doctoral programs. If financial support is a concern or deal breaker, make sure to contact the department, bursar's office, graduate school, and/or current graduate students to find out what sources of support are available. (We say more about funding in chapter 9.)

Master's programs, in contrast to doctoral programs, generally consist of one or two years of coursework followed by a set of exams or the research and writing of a thesis. In some institutions, written exams—carried out over a set period of time or over the course of a day or two—are provided in lieu of research or the writing of a master's thesis. The exams reflect the nature of the coursework and the specialization of the field. A thesis, in turn, is based on fieldwork and is informed by the relevant body of literature, methodologies, and interpretive frameworks or theoretical concepts that best suits the research. A thesis, like a doctoral dissertation, is intended to make what is called "an intervention in the literature," that is, a contribution or correction to what is already known about a particular topic, subject, or issue. The candidate's task is to make a significant addition to knowledge and to make that transparent. Though the writing of a thesis can take longer than anticipated and the final product can range from fifty to one hundred pages or more, depending on the field, it is considered completed when the main advisor signs off along with the other committee members, usually two to three faculty from the relevant department or unit. Their role is to read, comment on, and approve the work.

WHAT ARE DOCTORAL PROGRAMS?

A *doctoral degree* is the highest degree that you can earn in a field. Doctor of Philosophy programs in particular are for individuals who are interested in pursuing a career in research or in higher education. Many individuals with PhDs are trained to become professors or to take on research-based positions. Professional doctoral programs train Doctors of Education (EdD), Doctors of Psychology (PsyD), Juris Doctors (JD), and Doctors of Medicine (MD), and are intended for individuals who are pursuing a specific career track. In such cases, individuals know that they want to be a lawyer or medical doctor and this degree is required for their profession of interest. PhD programs have a higher chance than master's programs of providing full funding, especially for students who identify as low-income, first-generation, or diverse, or nontraditional in some way. Professional programs, in contrast, rarely if ever promise full funding because of the expectation that graduates will get a high-salary job and be able to repay loans, if they did not pay for their education out of pocket.

Professional doctoral programs usually have a set time limit of three to four years. PhD programs, however, are less structured and can range in length from three years to as many as eight or more years. Generally, the *time to degree,* or total time from enrollment to graduation, for those in STEM (science, technology, engineering, and math) ranges from about five to six years. Those in social sciences take about eight, and those in humanities—the longest—average about nine years. Differences in program length usually have to do with the program's structure, requirements, and funding. In exceptional cases, individuals can take longer than nine years to complete a doctoral program as a result of personal and professional decisions to take time off, prolonged conflicts with an advisor, uncontrollable circumstances, or a lack of financial support that forces them to work to make ends meet.

An unspoken truth is the relatively high rate of people who do not complete their doctoral programs. Indeed, studies demonstrate that 50 percent of *ABDs* or *all but dissertation* students—students who have completed all doctoral requirements except for their dissertation—do not finish, "equaling a loss of approximately 40,000 doctoral students annually across all disciplines."[11] Not all fields fare this badly. Biomedical and general sciences, where students enter faculty-supervised labs, have lower rates of attrition, at about 25 percent, while arts and humanities, where students tend to have less structure, see the highest losses, at around 67 percent. Moreover, *attrition*—dropping out or getting pushed out—is not concentrated at a specific moment but happens across the program and results in substantial debt. Research shows that those who leave accumulate more financial losses than those who stay and graduate.

The research also shows that most graduate students struggle to complete their work as a result of personal and familial reasons, not because—as faculty, administrators, and institutions contend—they are unprepared or incompetent. Those who leave without their degrees are just as ready and able to complete the work as those who stay. Women, Students of Color, those with less funding, and those less integrated with their peers and faculty members also are more likely to leave their programs without finishing.[12] Dropping out and getting pushed out is real, especially for first-generation, low-income, and/or nontraditional Students of Color who often lack the support to succeed. Leaving their programs before they graduate is also not welcomed by the administration. "No one likes it," writes Leonard Cassuto. "Not graduate schools, which prize their completion numbers; not departments, which prize placement of Ph.D.'s, and presumably not students, who invest time and money and then don't complete their programs." "Attrition," Cassuto reminds us, "carries the taint of loss, failure, and despair."[13] That is not to say that anyone who chooses to leave their program should internalize any shame or carry the weight of failure as a negative outcome; this choice can redirect the individual to more positive long-term outcomes as well. While quitting graduate school is not desired or the intended outcome when you apply, we do want to acknowledge that it is sometimes the right thing to do.

Doctoral programs usually consist of two to three years of coursework as well as written and oral exams, followed by the research and writing of the dissertation or completion of some comparably major project. The coursework is normally carried out in the main department with some opportunities for cross-fertilization and taking courses in other fields, depending on the policies and practices of the home unit. Exams are normally carried out at the end of the second or third or even fourth years. Written portions may reflect coursework as well as an extensive further reading list; they may also have an oral component. In some programs the oral segment is focused on the *prospectus,* which is essentially an academic proposal for the dissertation. In some departments, the prospectus defense is the focal point and functions like a rite of passage, while in others the prospectus is treated as an ongoing, developing project. As a proposal, it lays out the main objectives of the dissertation, including the project overview; central questions or hypotheses; contribution to the literature; sources, methodology, and theoretical frameworks; chapter summaries; and, if possible, a timeline to completion. Dissertation lengths can vary from one to several hundred pages, depending on fields and expectations.

Remember, every program and department has its own policies and practices as well as culture. Learn it and make it work for you. If you need accommodations, ask for them. Graduate committees are known to make changes to degree requirements, especially when faced with internal and external pressure from graduate students and their allies. I, Miroslava, have witnessed a significant shift in my department in the structure of the qualifying exams over the years, giving the graduate students more time to reflect and write their responses. The preliminary results have been successful, as the students are allowed to demonstrate the strengths of their analysis and writing and faculty have the opportunity to review ideas that have been fully formed and explained. We know that not all departments will have a streamlined process for preparing and taking exams and for developing a prospectus with a viable project, making the experience especially challenging for first-generation, low-income, and/or nontraditional Students of Color. But we agree that it is better to prepare and be aware of what you might face.[14]

Like master's theses, dissertations are considered complete when the advisor as well as the committee members sign off. Unlike most master's theses, many departments require a *dissertation defense* where the candidate is asked to "defend" or entertain any lingering questions or concerns about the study before it is officially submitted and considered completed. Though defenses can seem nerve-wracking and grueling, especially for those unfamiliar with such processes, most defenses are opportunities to engage committee members in conversation with your ideas, arguments, and evidence. In graduate and academic careers generally, you will have few opportunities to have a community of scholars read and comment on your work and offer critical insights and new vantage points. Defenses are usually great opportunities to grow your work, too, and discuss how to take it to the next level of intellectual thought and academic rigor. Talk with your femtor, mentor, advisor, and/or trusted colleagues who have come before you so you know what to expect, and try to attend one or two defenses in your department so you know what they are usually like. No one should allow you to step into that room if you are not yet ready, a decision your advisor and the committee will usually make.

AN INTERDISCIPLINARY OR A DISCIPLINE-SPECIFIC FIELD?

When considering graduate programs, odds are that you will come across both discipline-specific fields as well as interdisciplinary approaches. While disciplinary fields have been around for more than a hundred years, interdisciplinary programs have been around for no more than fifty years. Beginning with their reinvention in the nineteenth century, universities operated in three well-defined clusters of academic disciplines, namely the sciences (the study of nature), the social sciences (the study of human behavior and society), and the arts (the study of human creativity originating in the mind). Over time, these areas of study subdivided and further subdivided into a wide range of specialty fields, including math, anthropology, literature, and ecology. These areas or classifications are reflected in the kinds of programs that are provided at universities and are generally believed to provide a rich foundation for knowledge production. More recently, scholars have found that combining theories, approaches, and methods, among other aspects of scholarly disciplines, across a variety of disciplines "leads to invaluable insights," which may not have been possible without an interdisciplinary approach.[15] Interdisciplinarity, scholars increasingly argue, generates new knowledge and new ways of understanding and solving complex issues such as mass incarceration, environmental degradation, and global warming. Interdisciplinary approaches in academia are not only for building bridges across fields but also for building entirely new ways of—and new fields for—producing knowledge.

As Steven G. Brint writes, "the growth of interdisciplinary research and teaching is now widely recognized as a notable feature of academic change over the last 30 years."[16] It is not only this research that has increased sharply but also investment by private and public government agencies supporting such work. Advocates in academia and respected national organizations have started to produce, in turn, what academics and writers call "best practices" for interdisciplinarity, leading to supportive environments. These, in turn, Brint argues, have "influenced the value faculty members place on different forms of knowledge." Today, scholars are more likely to support interdisciplinarity than in years past.

Many scholars have argued that the growth of interdisciplinary activities, particularly in the arts, humanities, and social sciences, is also a result of the growing presence of underrepresented scholars in academia. Indeed, in past three decades, underrepresented academics dedicated to studying the lives of Blacks, Latinx, Native American, LGBTQ+, disabled, and other marginalized peoples in the United States have developed interdisciplinary fields, such as Black, Chicana/o, Latina/o, Native American, Disability, and Gender Studies, among others, where they can combine the most culturally relevant and specific theories, approaches, methods, and sources to understand the totality of their subjects' lived experiences. This approach, in turn, allows them to develop and use innovative fields of study that are more effective than traditional fields for understanding the particularities of a group within a specific context. Ethnic studies, for instance, is an interdisciplinary field that often applies comparative approaches to the study of two or more ethnic and racial groups. Depending on the strengths of the program's faculty and the students' interests and needs, projects are developed with the subject in mind rather than the discipline. Feminist studies, in turn, reflects the combination or amalgamation of traditional fields, such as sociology, literature, history, and film, as well as the innovation of interdisciplinary fields, to create alternative theoretical frameworks and methodologies for the study of gender and sexuality.

In contrast, discipline-specific programs such as political science, history, and English utilize theoretical concepts, approaches, and sources or data specific to the conceptualization of the field. While disciplinary fields tend to be more rigid in terms of academic boundaries (that is, what is and what is not acceptable as knowledge production), they have more clearly defined criteria than those in interdisciplinary fields. Though approaches to interdisciplinarity vary across institutional contexts, which in turn leads to variability and inconsistency of the fields, they often allow for creativity, originality, and, potentially, increased productivity.

Whatever appeals to you, interdisciplinarity or disciplinarity, take the steps you need to make sure you understand what is involved in the field of your choice. To do that, we suggest you go to the departments' websites and study the faculty's research projects—their publications and creative projects—as well as those of the graduate students. Be sure to contact faculty and staff too, since websites are not updated often. While it is highly likely that the majority of faculty will not have interdisciplinary degrees, given the recent development and slow acceptance of these fields in academia, which is invested in and legitimized by the status quo, the majority will likely be involved in interdisciplinary and multidisciplinary activities and projects. Look up the books, essays, and creative works produced by members of the department as well as the courses and seminars offered in that program. Do they appeal to you? If so, why? And do they make you want to carry out similar work? Approach discipline-specific units with the same curiosity and questions.

If you are interested in interdisciplinary scholarship and pursuing an academic position, namely a tenure-track or full-time teaching position, know that it can be challenging for interdisciplinary scholars to find employment in disciplinary fields unless they have specific degrees and training in those fields. Deep-rooted biases against interdisciplinarity persist, as leading voices in the academy generally assume that interdisciplinary scholars lack the expertise, training, or rigor necessary for academic legitimacy. This lack of understanding often leads to dim prospects on the academic job market. With the right support and understanding of interdisciplinarity, scholars trained in interdisciplinary studies as well as those pursuing interdisciplinary interests within disciplinary programs, we believe, are able to land jobs in traditional fields. A student of Miroslava's who obtained her doctorate in Chicana and Chicano Studies ended up as a tenure-track assistant professor in a history department at a research-intensive university. Fortunately, that department had faculty who knew the training, rigor, and value of interdisciplinarity and the multilevel and diverse perspectives it brings to scholarship in history. But not all programs or departments function in this way.

At the same time, discipline-specific scholars often face fewer barriers than do their interdisciplinary peers in landing positions in interdisciplinary programs. As sociologist Jessica McCrory Calarco has found, "interdisciplinary schools and programs (e.g., education, public health, public policy/administration) [often] hire a bigger mix of scholars, including some trained in disciplinary departments and others with interdisciplinary degrees."[17] In thinking about what kind of program you will pursue, you will need to consider your long-term professional and personal goals and how they square with your training in graduate school. Do you want a highly structured and potentially rigid discipline-specific program? Or do you prefer a loosely structured, creative, and self-directed interdisciplinary program? Or do you want something in between, such as a traditional program open to interdisciplinary collaboration or a more structured and rigid interdisciplinary program? Remember, you have options. Know how you work best and what is best for your research interests and future career plans.

TAKING A PAUSE BEFORE APPLYING: THE GAP YEAR OR YEARS

Beginning a disciplinary or interdisciplinary program in a doctoral, master's, or postbacc program months after finishing an undergraduate degree is not the right decision for everyone. Instead, more and more these days we hear advice cautioning students against going straight from undergraduate to graduate studies and encouraging them to take a gap year or two.[18] A *gap year* is when a student decides to take a break from their educational careers, typically for twelve months, or sometimes longer, and usually between undergraduate and graduate school or between undergraduate and a professional degree program, to help build their experience and resume. Until the 1980s, the white elite or upper class was the social group most commonly associated with gap years, as they were treated as moments of rest or interludes to regain the strength needed to continue with the rigor of higher education. More recently, as colleges and universities have democratized or expanded their student bodies, increased demand and pressure to access higher education has become intense, especially among many sectors of the middle and working classes, which see education as the key to social mobility. According to admissions officers, the rigorous planning and preparation—often from early childhood—for accessing "top" schools has led to burnout for many of these students.[19] Today, the advice is to take the time that is needed to gain "experiential learning . . . to deepen one's practical, professional, and personal awareness."[20] According to Nina Hoe Gallagher, "gap years can take place either domestically or internationally, but must involve, 'increasing self-awareness, learning about different cultural perspectives, and experimenting with future possible careers.'"[21] For the majority of the working class, including whites and People of Color, gap years have been and remain elusive. Rather than resting and reflecting on their future possibilities, low-income students and recent graduates have the real need to secure employment to make ends meet for themselves or family members, who are equally poor, and may depend on their contribution to the household economy.

A gap year, however, is not beyond your reach, even if you do not have the luxury of spending time engaging in "experiential" tours or programs, which come with their own costs. Depending on how you plan the year or years between your undergraduate and graduate career, it might allow you to gain perspective on your goals, to earn and save money, and to develop your confidence from your time in the workforce. Gap years also allow you the time you might need to take additional courses at a community college or specific language classes to meet the requirements of a graduate program. Some students we know decided to work in a related area to gain practical skills and insider knowledge of what goes on in the field before committing to it for a significant period of their lives. And for others, a gap year is the only viable decision when a loved one or family member is in need of care and attention and the costs for a nurse or nursing facility is out of the question.

For many students with whom we've worked, gap years have been the right solutions for their needs. But, again, take the time to research and determine if a gap year is right for *you* and your circumstances. Lay out the benefits as well as the challenges and assess what seems feasible. In doing so, be sure to set out your support systems (such as family and friends), who can assist you when you need it most, and your sources of independence, savings and work, which will allow you the freedom to pursue your goals. Plan out the gap year, considering when and how you will apply to graduate school, how you will maintain relationships with faculty for letters of recommendation, and what you will do to prepare for potential interviews and/or campus visits. Find or develop an online or in-person support group to keep you on track with meeting deadlines and other commitments. Once you are back in school as a graduate student, you will need to think about the ways that you might need to catch up to speed with the work or productivity or hours demanded in a lab or seminar. Might you consider hiring a continuing graduate student as a tutor? Are you willing to visit faculty in office hours regularly for assistance? Will you be comfortable, in some instances, in working with much younger and likely white, middle-class, privileged peers? While you can't predict future outcomes, you can make an informed decision based on what is best for you and those who matter most to you.[22]

LEANING INTO YOUR NEW IDENTITY

If you're a nontraditional student and you're thinking about returning to school to possibly enter a new field as well as to grow professionally and personally, you will likely struggle with finding comfort with your new identity. You may have a lot of negative self-talk or limiting beliefs, telling yourself that you are not capable of succeeding ("I'm not smart enough"), do not have the resources ("how will I pay my bills?"), or lack the self-worth ("who am I to want to lead a life of the mind?"), to continue your education in pursuit of your love for art, history, or science. Your family and friends may also find your interest in developing yourself and your new identity difficult to understand or accept, especially if you are a first-generation, low-income, and/or nontraditional Student of Color. We know from first-hand experience, particularly when it comes to Latinx cultures, that we don't know how to talk about issues of personal growth or development in our families or communities for fear of rejection or ridicule or, simply, misunderstanding. Many times our religious beliefs hold us back, too, especially when we're taught that we should appreciate what we've been given and we should resist making too many demands, for fear of retribution or punishment.

Certainly, our loved ones mean well and often support us in the best ways they can. But, unfortunately, they are not always able to understand our needs and desires and they may also fear the unknown, which includes predominantly white, middle- and upper-class spaces of privilege and power such as higher education. To reach your goals, you need to find ways to manage your internal and external critics or the voices telling you that it's too risky, too scary, and too challenging to do something. How do you do that? How do you turn off negative talk and limiting beliefs and cope with the feelings of uncertainty, anxiety, and tension? Certainly, mindfully reflecting about your future is helpful and productive for a lot of people, but it may not get the job done alone. A helpful approach is to shift your mindset about who you are and what you can and will become and take the steps necessary to do so. As business coach Wendy Amara explains, shifting your mindset is about "taking consistent radical action in your life, doing the thing, feeling the uncomfortable feeling, and doing it anyways . . . that's what builds the muscle, that's what creates the change."[23] We agree that consistency, or taking consistent action, is what is going to convince you—show you, not tell you—that graduate school is the right decision for you. Even though you may think you don't have what it takes, apply to graduate school and if it doesn't work out as you intended, take the necessary steps to improve your application and apply again. Don't give up easily. Prove to yourself that you have the will and the capacity to achieve your aims and aspirations. Afterwards, upon receiving a graduate school acceptance—all it takes is one—you will be on your way to continually improving and proving to yourself your capabilities. As Amara reminds us, venturing outside of our comfort zones is a fear-inducing prospect. Yet, as we know, fear will always be present in our lives, whether we stay in our regular lives or decide to go to graduate school. Don't let fear of failure hold you back.

Personally, we both have learned just as much, if not more, from our failures than from our successes, as we both reflect and contemplate on our steps and processes along the way. We have both faced fears of being the first in our families to attend college and graduate school in the pursuit of obtaining fulfilling careers but we have also dealt with different dilemmas, as we represent two distinct pathways to higher education. One of us pursued the tenure-track, earned tenure, then moved up the ranks to become a full professor at a research institution, while the other shifted disciplines between undergrad and graduate school, got her PhD, left the tenure-track job market, pursued an academic staff career, and then left higher education altogether to start an academic coaching business. As such, we offer you differing points of view on the traumas as well as the payoffs of the graduate school admissions process, one looking inside-out and the other peering outside-in.

No matter your career outcome, if graduate school is necessary for you, we believe that our points of view will offer you the comfort you need to rid yourself of your fears and will provide the insight and motivation to pursue your goals. Before concluding this chapter, we ask you to complete the following exercise by answering these key life-planning and lifestyle design questions:

- Where or who do you plan to be in five years? In ten years?
- What excites you? What inspires you? What nourishes you?
- What are your personal values? Your mission? Your vision?
- And, if you had no limits, what would be possible for you? What does your ideal life look like?

Once you've landed on a few answers, think about how you are going to realize that future person and map it out by working backwards, or rather, reverse engineering, from the end to the beginning, considering the steps it will take to get there. Rest assured that you're not alone. With our guidance and this book in hand, we believe you can and you will develop your own graduate school admissions map.

We hope this introductory overview of graduate school has not alienated or frightened you away from the prospect of a graduate education. Rather, we provide this frank and open conversation for you to understand the potential challenges and successes that lie ahead for you on your journey to enrich your learning and enhance your wellbeing and that of your family and community. We also believe that the more information you have at your disposal, the more empowered you will be to make informed decisions. Remember, you are not alone. We are with you on this path of self-discovery and affirmation. We invite you to join us for the next chapter where you will learn all about whether graduate school is the best next step for you.

KEY TAKEAWAYS

- In this chapter, we defined and reviewed the many graduate programs available, including postbaccalaureate, the combined bachelor's and master's, the master's, and the doctoral program. We reviewed the difference between "professional" programs and research degrees.

- We discussed the differences between discipline-specific and interdisciplinary programs, and the challenges and opportunities in both.

- In thinking about your options, we asked that you consider or think about a gap year and what role it plays in preparing prospective applicants for graduate school.

- We also encouraged you to take the necessary steps to work towards embracing your new identity and your life goals by building a plan or roadmap that begins at the end and works backwards to help you figure out the steps you will need to take to achieve your stated objectives.

2

IS GRADUATE SCHOOL
RIGHT FOR ME?

||||||||||||||||||||||||||||||||||||||||||||||||||||||||||||||||||||||||||||||||||||||||||||||||||||||||||||||||||||||||||||||||||||||||||||||||||||||||||||||||||||||||||||||||||||||||

WHEN CONSIDERING APPLYING to graduate school, one of
the first things you should think about is whether graduate
school is the right step for you in your career and life. To do
that, you need to take time to reflect on your goals. Ask
yourself: What is my current career objective? Is graduate
school a requirement for this career? Do I need an advanced
degree to have access to and ascend the ranks of my intended
profession? Besides academic training, what else do I hope to
gain from a graduate program? What graduate programs
have other individuals in my similar career trajectory completed? Is it possible to gain the necessary skills and resources
without enrolling in a graduate program? What are the benefits and challenges of graduate school in my area of interest
and/or discipline? Who are the people, that is, the femtors
and mentors, who can guide me in my decision to pursue (or
not) a graduate program? Before you go further, spend two
minutes reflecting and recording your thoughts and ideas.

For some individuals, choosing to go to graduate school is a relatively easy decision because it is a requirement to advance in or enter a field of interest or discipline. Social workers as well as professors, for instance, require advanced degrees to launch their careers. For other individuals who are not expected to have a master's or doctoral degree, but may be transitioning careers, a graduate program might provide the much-needed structure, knowledge, and networking necessary to advance in new areas. Some individuals who already have careers choose to attend graduate programs to gain the additional expertise, skills, and certification necessary to make a significant impact in or contribution to their specialty. That is the rationale Amanda Peña cites for pursuing a master's degree. Amanda started her career in e-commerce marketing and learned how to research consumer behavior, which then led to her starting her own business and taking on a role in a design firm that focused on user experiences of the future, specifically for autonomous vehicles. As part of her work, she researched and learned about topics that fascinated her, including the user-end experience, facial recognition, and the role of artificial intelligence. Soon after, however, Amanda realized that she needed formal validation of her expertise and the nearly 10,000 hours she had invested in her line of work. In the business world, she said bluntly, "I'm not an expert, because I don't have the degree. And, . .. to be quite frank, . . . no one was . . . giving me that chance." No one took her under their wing, she said, and told her, "we know how smart you are. You don't need any other stuff. We're gonna just kind of vouch for you. Unfortunately, I didn't have that," she said. When she interviewed for positions, she recalled, prospective employers said to her, "but you know . . . there's other MBA candidates and if you had a master's degree. . . ." That moment, she recalled, stayed with her. "I see," she thought. "if I had a master's degree, you would pay me this amount or you would take me a little bit more seriously."[1]

It was at that crucial moment that she made her decision to pursue an interdisciplinary master's degree that encompassed her interests.

Amanda's experience tells us that, whatever your circumstances, the decision to attend graduate school involves acknowledging your professional and personal goals and considering the expectations as well as the hurdles and rewards you will encounter throughout the process. For many others, deciding to go to graduate school is not an easy decision, and not everyone needs to attend. We have seen many people pursue programs for all the wrong reasons. Here are a few common reasons *not* to pursue a graduate degree:

I'm struggling to secure a job.
Going to graduate school will not guarantee that you will gain employment or a career. In some cases, attending graduate school only delays the process or derails you from finding the work that best suits your interests and talents. Rather than sink your resources into graduate school, determine the gaps in your employment record and preparedness for the work you want to pursue and seek out training and opportunities that will help you secure your dream job. These might be short-term internships, three- to six-month certification programs, or longer one- to two-year technical degree programs. Explore your options. Consider shadowing someone who is on track to achieve the career goals you want to pursue. Or think about talking to a career coach or to others who have reconsidered their professional and personal goals.

My best friend, who recently completed a master's program, recommended I go too.
Graduate school is a significant commitment and no one else will complete the program for you. We do not encourage you to pursue graduate school for the sake of pleasing others, including friends or parents who might want you to apply to professional and applied master's programs that may offer promises of landing high-paying industry jobs after graduation. Acknowledge their best intentions but, at the same

time, determine what you want from your career and life and pursue those dreams and desires. Ultimately, you will be the one living with the decision to make the sacrifices needed to invest in your future in this particular way. Make the commitment because you have a passion for the field and for furthering your knowledge of it. Ultimately, your purpose in graduate school is to make a contribution—to add something new to what we already know—to your area of study. What you do with those skills after your program is up to you.

I'm bored and don't know what to do.
Some individuals go to graduate school because they are bored, they have no other idea of what to do with their lives at the moment, or they believe they have no other options. While graduate school may keep you busy and stop you from ruminating about your choices in life, it will not ensure that you will pursue a career path that is right for you or will fulfill you and meet your needs. Delaying introspection and an honest assessment of the self is not a viable reason to pursue graduate school.

I want to lead the life of an intellectual—it looks so glamorous!
Romanticized interpretations of the life of a professor, whether in films or novels, often portray them as driven, mysterious, and well-off. No wonder people have the wrong idea about professors and the lives they lead. The reality is that professors and lecturers (who from the point of undergraduates may look identical, but who lack employment security), face long hours, often alone, with disgruntled co-workers, demanding students, and, increasingly, unstable and low paying jobs. Like most professions, the life of an academic carries its own set of challenges and benefits but, ultimately, you must find your reasons for doing this work and for upholding your commitment to the field. To demystify the day-to-day experience, ask a trusted source about the different stages of their career. What does a typical day look like for a

professor and/or lecturer in your field? Does this change according to the stages and ranks within your career? If so, how? And what are the immediate and long-term expectations?

I want to continue deferring my student loans.
Some students decide to continue with their schooling as a means to continue delaying the inevitable—student loan debt. They figure if they go to graduate school, they can continue deferring their loans for a few more years and that will give them some time to "figure things out" financially. If you don't make it a point to learn about financial literacy now, it is less likely that you'll do so in graduate school because you'll have more commitments and in some cases less time than as an undergraduate. Why take on more debt only to defer your undergraduate loans? If you fear that you will have a high monthly loan payment after your deferment period ends, please know you have different payment options depending on your income. You can also find free online debt payment resources that can help you make a plan so that you can work towards paying off your student debt over time rather than avoiding it altogether.

THE IMPACT OF LIFE AND CAREER STAGE

Once you decide to apply, you should keep in mind that graduate school is not a singular experience. As we mentioned in chapter 1, graduate programs come in all shapes and sizes. While some are applied, lasting one to two years, others are research and theory oriented, continuing five to six or more years. Regardless of the kind of program you pursue, your life experiences as well as your educational career will impact your graduate school experience. Issues to consider: Are you a first-generation student, that is, are you among the first in your generation to attend a four-year college?[2] Are you a nontraditional and/or a re-entry student? Are you an enhancer, looking to advance your career?

Are you low-income, according to state and federal guidelines, or working-class? Is your identity—for example, Latinx, BIPOC, LGBTQ+, and/or disabled—underrepresented in your field? Are you a late bloomer or someone with substantial gaps in your academic record who is seeking to return to an educational setting under different circumstances? In this chapter we'll cover how each of those as well as other circumstances may impact your graduate school application process and educational career.

Today, colleges and universities seem to be making a lot of fuss about being first-generation, whether it's at the undergraduate or graduate level. What's that about? Institutions of higher learning are finally acknowledging what civil rights and social justice activists have argued for decades: the need to demystify academia and dismantle the hidden curriculum for first-time college students. The hidden curriculum also refers to cultural capital—the knowledge and intellectual skills necessary for social mobility, which is often needed to successfully navigate higher education. First-generation students normally have little exposure to what academic life looks like on a daily basis or even what a campus looks like, for that matter. First-generation students must find ways to figure out negotiating university bureaucracy, communicating with professors, choosing the right classes, and networking in and outside of the classroom, all unspoken and unwritten pathways to advancement.

Fortunately, most four-year institutions now have a series of different graduate school preparation programs, courses, and workshops available to students, including those for first-generation, low-income, and/or nontraditional Students of Color. If you are currently enrolled in a college campus, be on the lookout for such resources. Does your institution have a Ronald E. McNair Scholars Program, a Mellon Mays Undergraduate Fellowship, University of California Leadership Excellence through Advanced Degrees (UC LEADS) Program, or other similar one- to two-year graduate school preparation program? Does your institution offer opportunities for you to take part in a departmental honors or senior capstone project where you could work closely with a faculty mentor who could guide you in research and in your graduate school application process? Are there any summer opportunities, within and outside of your institution, that you are eligible to apply for, such as the Summer Undergraduate Research Fellowship (SURF), the Research Experience for Undergraduates (REU) Program, the Big Ten Academic Alliance Summer Research Program, the Leadership Alliance Program, and more? Have you also considered checking out if your institution has a Career Center or Career Services office where you could meet with a career counselor, attend career-prep workshops, and network with other professionals in your discipline, industry, or area of interest? Outside of the college campus, there are also free and low-cost resources and events available to alumni that you can look into at your alma mater. You could certainly borrow books, e-books, and audiobooks related to graduate school and career preparation from your local library. You can also consider working closely with an academic or career coach to support you in this application process. You have many resources available to you and likely ones that you didn't even realize existed, which is why we emphasize being on the lookout for them now before you start your application process.

From personal experience, we know that, as first-generation students, we often don't know what we don't know or we may struggle to ask for help. While some of us may think we have the answers to the most pressing questions needed to navigate institutional spaces, we do not realize the opportunities, contacts, and networks that are available to assist along our educational journey. As such, we do not seek them out or take advantage of them, not realizing that many, if not most, of our second and continuing-generation peers have been taught—either explicitly or by example—how to advocate for themselves in the classroom and beyond. As the children and grandchildren of parents and grandparents who attended colleges and universities, second- and continuing-generation students often have familiarity with campus social and cultural environments as well as strategies for approaching faculty and staff who can help them navigate the system. Without such knowledge, first-generation students face barriers to gaining access to and advancing in their programs.

Dr. Jasmine Escalera, a PhD in pharmacology from Yale University, career coach, and self-described Latina who grew up in the projects in Brooklyn, New York, had a similar experience as a first-generation student when she arrived in New Haven, Connecticut. "When I stepped out into the college world," she told Yvette in an interview, "especially grad[uate] school at Yale, and then later into my career, I felt like I saw less and less of people who look like me . . . and was around less and less of people who had the same background as me. And that truly affected the way that I saw myself, what I believed I could accomplish and do, and the confidence that I used to have as that young girl who was in her own community. I don't think I was adequately prepared for what it was truly going to be like out there in the real world, not because no one wanted to prepare me for it, but because they truly have not had those experiences."[3] She rebuilt her confidence, she explains, "through mindset work, through using empowering tactics, and through connecting back to my Latina heritage, to who I truly was and what my community had given me, which was strength and resilience, and true competence." "I really had to do that," she continued, "to build myself internally in order to really be able to step out into this space as the only Latina in STEM, and truly be the woman who was going to build her career her way."[4]

Fortunately, first-generation students like Dr. Escalera are not alone. Many first-generation staff and faculty, second- and continuing-generation allies at institutions of higher education across the United States, and committed femtors like ourselves are working diligently to break down and unlock the little-known aspects of the undergraduate and graduate school curriculum, including the application process.

From low- to no-cost online seminars and workshops, to free websites, podcasts, and publications, prospective graduate students have many resources at their fingertips.[5] Navigating those sources of information, however, and figuring out which ones are trustworthy, legitimate, and current can be overwhelming. Our goal is to assist you in figuring out what it takes to successfully access graduate school, which has been out of reach for far too long.

The application process, though seemingly straightforward, will vary depending on where and when in your educational career you decide to apply. (We will cover everything you need to know about the application in part 2 of this book.) For first-time graduate school applicants, the process of applying usually begins in the fall or early winter term with the expectation that you will be notified of admissions decisions in the late winter or spring terms. As you prepare your documents, keep in mind that doctoral programs tend to have earlier deadlines and make decisions sooner than in master's programs. The same goes for students who are re-applying to graduate programs after leaving their current program to transfer into a new program. However, when students take a leave of absence and return to the same program, they will likely follow a trajectory they have negotiated with their specific advisor and graduate staff program advisor.

Your and your family's financial circumstances, as well as your student status, will impact your application process. There are many potential hidden costs of applying, including processing fees, requesting transcripts, studying and taking standardized exams (particularly for those in the sciences), submitting exam scores, and in some cases, processing recommendation letters via electronic dossier services. Low-income students may therefore struggle to fund the beginning of their educational journey. In many cases, those who meet state and/or federal low-income thresholds are able to secure fee waivers for application costs but those require separate applications and deadlines, which adds time and labor to the process. To determine the ins and outs, review the details at the campus website or contact an administrator via email. Other costs can involve identifying the right programs, which calls for visiting the college or university as well as meeting with people who can give you insights about the department and campus community. While you might be able to do this in one day, getting to know a campus often includes travel and meal expenses that can add up quickly. Another cost-effective option, though not ideal, is to schedule a virtual visit with the admissions division in the graduate school of choice. They will have many chances for you to get to know the surroundings or meet with current faculty or students without necessarily investing all your resources to do so.

To make graduate school a reality, low-income students and those without financial safety nets will need to find ways to finance their education. For many that includes obtaining fellowships and grants as well as teaching or research assistantships, while for others it consists of finding on- or off-campus employment. It may also include taking out loans, both private and public. Ideally, you want to finance your graduate school career with funds you do not have to repay, namely *fellowships,* which provide you with stipends sufficient to cover anywhere from three to twelve months of expenses, allowing you the opportunity to advance in your program without having to hustle to find employment. *Grants,* in contrast, provide money for specific research- or project-related activities, including maintaining labs in STEM fields, fostering interdisciplinary collaboration across the humanities and social sciences, and/or carrying out a number of archival, recovery, or digital projects. Teaching assistantships, or TAships, or Research assistantships, or RAships, require you to work from ten to twenty hours a week. TAs assist a professor who is teaching a large lecture course. RAs may assist a professor with their research in various ways, but may also manage their research lab or team, usually consisting of other graduate and undergraduate assistants, respectively. TAships are a great opportunity to gain teaching experience in seminar-style classrooms but they require constant involvement with and monitoring of academic coursework, including managing discussion sections of eighteen to twenty students, grading dozens of student papers, and holding weekly office hours. If you are a Student of Color, an LGBTQ+ student, and/or a disabled student, you may have undergraduates with similar profiles reaching out to you for support and mentorship. Both of us had similar experiences throughout our time as graduate students at UCLA, albeit years apart. Working as an RA might not put you in the direct path of undergraduates but it will expose you to new areas of research, though it might not always directly relate to your own work. Both RAships and TAships can, for all these reasons, derail your progress. Remember, on top of any RAship or TAship, you will need to take courses and complete related assignments. Despite those challenges, TAships and RAships are practical training opportunities, and sometime provide the only chance to gain an income without having to repay any loans.

Other forms of employment, such as working as a mentor, coordinator, or advocate on campus or in the local community, can assist you in the development of many valuable skills that you can later tap in your career. Mentoring Students of Color in graduate prep and research programs, coordinating a women's or student-parent center, or advocating for disabled students in a disability or accessibility services office, for instance, can help you sharpen your listening and communication skills as well as help build life-long professional and personal networks. Loans also have their advantages, as they allow you to pursue your dreams without having to worry about how you are going to pay your tuition, rent, and grocery bills, especially if you have dependents. Pay attention to the differences between federal loans (both subsidized and unsubsidized) and private loans, however. With exorbitant interest rates and less flexible repayment schedules, private loans may set you back for years to come, and as such we do not encourage students to take out these loans unless you have no other alternative.

NAVIGATING AN INTERSECTIONAL IDENTITY
IN GRADUATE SCHOOL

Many first-generation, low-income, and/or nontraditional Students of Color apply to graduate school working under the assumption that the application reviewers know who they are and the communities they come from. They do not. Researchers have shown that graduate school administrators are overwhelmingly white—85 percent of them—and, while the number of non-white administrators is on the rise, it has fallen behind the increasing rate of diverse student populations on college and university campuses.[6] Every applicant must decide, then, how much or how little of their identity they wish to disclose in a graduate school application. More and more these days, it is advantageous to reveal the diverse perspective and experience you bring to the academic table, as it will allow you to articulate your assets and, in turn, enable the college or university to match you with the best resources at its disposal. And, even though you might choose to withhold aspects of your identity because you don't want to stand out or for fear of shame, stigmatization, or discrimination, once you are in graduate school, your identity (that is, the intersection of your racial, ethnic, class, gender, sexual, and dis/ability profile, as well as your age) will shape how people perceive, respond, and relate to you. Your identity, too, will influence how you encounter and deal with the challenges of racism, classism, sexism, homophobia, and ableism at both the individual and structural levels. Those "isms" are not only alive and well in higher education and post-graduate education but often bred and reproduced in those same spaces.

Indeed, researchers have spent many years documenting the daily and institutional practices that work to marginalize, demoralize, and silence graduate Students of Color, in particular, in and beyond academia. Black students, specifically, have a long history of dealing with racist policies and practices as well as what are called *racial microaggressions*. In the 1970s, psychiatrist Chester Pierce and his colleagues identified these as "subtle, stunning, often automatic, and nonverbal exchanges, which are 'put downs' of blacks by offenders."[7] According to legal scholar Peggy C. Davis, over time, these seemingly innocuous and "unconscious attitudes of white superiority constitute a verification of black inferiority."[8] These often unconscious and subtle forms of racism, as education scholar Daniel Solorzano and his colleagues argue, are pervasive, leading Black students to feel ignored and invisible, particularly in the course curriculum, as well as "'drained' by the intense scrutiny" they receive every day, especially about their supposed lack of qualifications for being at the university. The same students reported sensing low expectations from faculty and their peers, exacerbating self-doubt and feelings of being personally diminished. "Whether inside or outside the classroom, racial microaggressions within academic spaces are filtered through layers of racial stereotypes," Solorzano and his colleagues write.[9]

Psychologists Claude Steele and Joshua Aronson have shown that the cumulative effects of racial stereotypes are also detrimental, significantly impacting Black students' performance on standardized tests. Steele and Aronson argue that, while Black students do not necessarily internalize the negative messages, the "threat of possibly being judged and or treated stereotypically" depresses their performance.[10] These experiences, in turn, have detrimental effects on students, resulting in dropping classes, switching majors or schools, or leaving the institution altogether, as well as higher levels of stress, anxiety, and mental health issues. As Solorzano and his colleagues note, "even at high levels of accomplishment (i.e., at elite undergraduate universities), where educational conditions might on the surface appear to be equal, inequality and discrimination still exist—albeit in more subtle and hidden forms."[11]

Researchers find that, like Black students, Latinx students face racial microaggressions within interpersonal and institutional contexts. Education researcher Tara Yosso and her colleagues have demonstrated how Latinx students experience interpersonal microaggressions directly from faculty, students, and others who marginalize and diminish their abilities on a daily basis. Institutional microaggressions, in contrast, are built into the "structures, practices, and discourses that endorse a campus racial climate hostile to People of Color." These assaults, Yosso continues, "appear to be 'collectively approved and promoted' by the university power structures[.]"[12] Racial jokes, which Yosso and colleagues also document, are an altogether different phenomenon. They are "offensive verbal remarks with questionably humorous intentions expressed in social contexts in the company of, or directly to, Latina/o students."[13] Unlike interpersonal and institutional microaggressions, racial jokes are undeniably intentional, leaving the Latinx student feeling belittled, marginalized, and stressed over how to handle such incidents, especially when they come from people they know who later claim unconscious ignorance. These "racially assaultive 'words that wound'" served as "constant reminders of their subordinate status in the social/racial hierarchy of the university."[14] The impact of the negative racial climate and racial environment contributes to "poor academic performance and high dropout rates" as well as alienation, self-doubt, and discouragement.[15] These experiences, in turn, can lead to extreme environmental stress and to what William Smith calls "racial battle fatigue," hindering achievement and exacerbating mental, emotional, and physical stress.[16] Given the minefields Latinx, Black, and other nontraditional Students of Color navigate in higher education, it is crucial to learn how to identify these challenges before encountering them so that you recognize them and know how to handle them.

A student's sexuality and gender identification also impacts their experiences in graduate school. Students who are part of the LGBTQ+ community often face overt and covert microaggressions and do so throughout their lives.[17] Similar to racial and ethnic minorities, lesbian, gay, bisexual, transgender, and queer students are susceptible to what are called *homonegative microaggressions,* which are "the everyday verbal, behavioral, and environmental slights aimed at sexual minorities."[18] Researchers have found that those who experienced homonegative microaggressions reported lowered levels of self-esteem, increased negative feelings, and difficulty with their identity.[19] Unfortunately, heterosexism, the system of oppression marginalizing lesbian, gay, bisexual, and queer people, is alive and well on college and university campuses, negatively impacting LGBTQ+ students.[20] A 2014 campus climate survey conducted by the University of California on its ten-plus campuses found that more than three-quarters (or 78 percent) of genderqueer and three-quarters (or 76 percent) of transgender respondents, including faculty, staff, undergraduate, and graduate students, who reported exclusionary conduct, indicated that the conduct was based on their gender identity.[21] The survey found even more dire outcomes at the University of California, Santa Barbara (UCSB), an institution familiar to both authors of this guidebook. At UCSB, genderqueer respondents not only experienced higher levels of "exclusionary conduct," as did ethnic and racial minorities, but also "were least comfortable with the overall climate" as compared to racial and ethnic minorities. Genderqueer people were also less comfortable in their department, work or academic unit, college, school, and/or clinical settings than were other groups.[22]

Negative interactions in these educational and work spaces, in turn, leaves LGBTQ+ graduate students, particularly graduate Students of Color, who have even fewer systems of support, with limited options for finding or choosing mentors who share similar experiences or are comfortable with openly disclosing them. Queer Students of Color often have to do the work of identifying the climate of a campus and program to determine if it is a safe or hostile or lukewarm space for them. This often includes finding resource centers or support spaces or meeting potential LGBTQ+ femtors or Mentors of Color who respect and understand their needs. They also have to determine how much of their queer identity to disclose, whether it is in the classroom, campus community, or beyond.

Like LGBTQ+ students, those with disabilities—both mental and physical, visible and invisible—have to deal with a host of issues as well, which are often not recognized by institutions or administrators as well as faculty or staff. For instance, disabled students with physical disabilities and mobility aids must navigate not only gaining access to campus buildings but also online classes, websites, and other digital resources that are often not available. Neurodivergent students, students with mental health issues, and students with learning disorders must secure medical documentation and work with disability or accessibility services offices to request classroom and workplace accommodations from professors who may be unfamiliar with this process or skeptical of its purpose. Campus services for students with disabilities do provide an array of resources, everything from exam accommodations and notetakers to advising you on which modifications to expect and which ones to demand if they are not forthcoming. Many disabled students also struggle with gaining respect and appreciation from their professors and peers as equals and recognition for the intellectual and social assets they bring to academia. The 2014 University of California survey found that respondents with a disability were less comfortable than respondents with no disability with the overall climate, the climate in their classes, and the climate in their work units or departments.[23]

Similar to students with disabilities, parenting students must negotiate the post-graduate school landscape with the needs of the household unit in mind. If you are a parent who wants to return to the university to fulfill a life-long dream of earning a PhD or to demonstrate to your children what it takes to achieve your educational goals, you must find new ways to negotiate your family and graduate student life. If you were a parent as an undergraduate, you already know the challenges and rewards of pursuing an education. According to the National Center for Education Statistics, "college students who have children are 10 times less likely to complete a bachelor's degree within five years than students who do not have children, even though student-parents on average have higher GPAs."[24] Despite the lack of supportive structures and resources, parenting students persist because of the potential gains. Indeed, higher levels of education, writes Claire Wladis, "can improve both the educational outcomes of their children and their own parenting behaviors. Students who earn a bachelor's degree in the United States earn 68 percent more and are half as likely to be unemployed as those students with just high school diplomas, so their families are less likely to be in poverty."[25]

Be aware, however, that the prevailing ideology in the academy is not the cultivation of a nurturing space for individuals and families, as is often advertised or described on websites and in brochures. Rather, childlessness, especially for female academics, is often the unspoken rule. As the research demonstrates, women, especially mothers, in academia receive less pay than men, particularly fathers. Sex and gender discrimination is at the heart of the disparity, including the belief that women are less productive over time because of their potential to interrupt their careers to have children. Men and fathers, in contrast, are rewarded not only for their male privilege but also for the assumption that, as the "head of the household," they should be entitled to a "family wage." An early-twentieth century construct, the family wage identified men as the primary income earners who needed extra means to support an entire unit and, effectively, discounted and diminished women's ability to compete in the marketplace. And, researchers argue, it continues to influence hiring practices today. In these ways, childlessness— foregoing a family or obscuring family responsibilities that might detract from work—is expected among women and discouraged among men. A wide range of institutional barriers continue to impact a studentparent's ability to succeed in graduate school and at the professoriate level, should they choose that career path. Institutional barriers in academia include "(1) poverty-level stipends for graduate students, (2) exploitative wages for adjunct faculty, (3) unstable contingent employment, (4) little to no financial resources for childcare, (5) numerous unpaid service obligations, (6) conference presentation in non-child-friendly locations with expensive registration and travel fees, and (7) the expectation to attend professional networking events that often conflict with childcare and school hours."[26] These challenges are common not only among faculty but also graduate students.

Most colleges and universities will argue that they provide a wide range of support mechanisms for graduate students, allowing parenting students to maintain a level of involvement with their children. Some graduate schools or divisions, for instance, provide lactation accommodations, childcare services with tuition subsidies for low-income families, financial assistance in the form of grants for childcare, subsidized family housing, and extensions on time-to-degree for parenting demands during the first twelve months after the child's birth or placement in the home. Graduate students who work as research assistants (RAs), graduate student researchers (GSRs), or are employees at the university are sometimes eligible for leave options related to parental obligations. Unfortunately, these support options are not guaranteed at all institutions. Additionally, support for medical insurance or continued assistance for childcare after the initial six months may be lacking, forcing new parents to find ways to cover those expenses.

Even with some campus-wide support systems in place, parenting while in graduate school can be a daunting prospect. Communicating your status as a parent and providing details of your children on the first day of the semester can work for some but not for others. Get to know the culture of the department or campus before revealing details that others may assume relate to your productivity as a graduate student. Whether new parents or not, students with children of all ages face the pressure of having to attend to their demanding academic responsibilities while meeting their personal and family needs. While it might seem unconventional to talk to your advisor about your needs as a parent, consider doing so. Certainly, not all advisors are sympathetic or have any clue as to what it means to be a parent as well as a student, and we would not suggest approaching such individuals, but more and more these days faculty advisors and administrators are willing to concede the unique challenges of taking on an intensive course of study while juggling family or other similar responsibilities. We recommend talking with femtors and mentors who will support your journey and to academic counselors outside of your department (potentially in the graduate school or division). If possible, prior to applying or accepting an offer of admission, discuss with these people campus and departmental-level policies and practices on parenting while in graduate school. A conversation about flexibility afforded to parenting students in graduate school will help relieve any anxieties around having to separate your family life from your work space.[27] As Lynn Lewis argues for undergraduate student-parents, "If more colleges and universities could widen their vision of who their students are—and who they could be— that number [attrition] could change, preventing millions from having to decide between going to college and raising a family."[28]

Parenting students in graduate school may also face the reality of being a nontraditional student rather than one who went straight through from undergraduate to graduate school. Those in their thirties, forties, fifties, and beyond may face ageism in various guises, including being confused for a professor, staff person, or parent of a current student. Ageism works both ways and also impacts younger students, especially women and women of color in particular, as they may also experience incidents where they are mistaken for undergraduates. Indeed, ageism can play out in a wide range of ways, including, for instance, when older students are left out or excluded from social and cultural events organized by the younger set of the cohort or when younger students are infantilized and made fun of by the seemingly more mature students. No matter where you fall within your cohort's age group, be on the lookout for incidents of ageism and do not forget the level of maturity, insight, and fierceness that you bring to the classroom that is difficult to replicate among those with different experiences.

Similar to nontraditional students are what we call *re-entry students,* or students who are returning to college after a prolonged absence from school. They will have to grapple with how to readjust to academic life after being out of school for a while. The impact of going back to school, especially a graduate program, can be profound, given the fast and intense pace as well as the expectations of a master's or doctoral program. Most programs will require a mix of coursework, a teaching assistantship or other means of support if no fellowship was provided, internships, preparation for written and/or oral exams, writing an academic proposal or prospectus followed by a thesis or dissertation, and otherwise meeting all the requirements for your master's and/or doctoral degree. Certainly, the specifics of your program depend on your field and its practices. Overall, though, we know that launching a successful graduate student career and attending to your personal and familial needs is a lot to consider, especially if you are, for instance, disabled and need assistance accessing classrooms or offices as well as virtual spaces such as online classes and resources. All re-entry students must learn to navigate the academic ropes quickly.

Remember, you have many resources at your disposal to make this happen. It begins with seeking assistance in your department, graduate school or division, and campus resource centers. They all have a mission to assist you and are waiting to hear from you. If those options are not available or do not seem viable, talk to your advisor or the graduate staff advisor or, better yet, to second- and third-year graduate students about campus resources. Find ways, too, to connect with your peers, even if they seem distant from your concerns as a nontraditional student. You are each other's best advocates. In many cases, particularly if you find colleagues with similar backgrounds or identities as your own, you will make strong connections and, as in our experiences, remain friends after having gotten over all the hurdles you faced in graduate school.

An equally important facet of your graduate school career to consider is the political climate of the university's regional setting, as it may directly impact your physical safety and emotional health if you are non-white and/or nontraditional. The racially motivated white supremacist assaults against Black people and non-whites in 2017 in Charlottesville, Virginia, for example, severely impacted the summer program and graduate school decisions of students that Yvette, in particular, had worked with in the past. A student who was accepted into a highly competitive summer research program at the University of Virginia, for instance, turned down the opportunity out of fear over personal safety. Many Students of Color, as we know from experience, will not apply to regions across the United States that they find to be unwelcoming because of their history with racism, white supremacy, and homophobia, among other threatening power differentials. While an institution of higher education will not necessarily reflect the values of the local community, it must take into account the ways that its regional context may affect the diversity of its student body. Colleges and universities must work with potential students to ensure they feel welcome and, more importantly, to see to it that they are reflected in the curriculum as well as among the staff, faculty, and current student body. Before applying and especially accepting an offer of admission, investigate the campus's climate for first-generation, low-income, LGBTQ+, and disabled students as well as Students of Color more generally. Run online searches about the university's history with these climate issues and, if possible, talk to current students and alumni.

Students of all backgrounds would do well to also learn the key cultural norms of academia even though academic spaces have yet to make a genuine effort to understand and make accommodations or changes for its newer and still changing student population. When a student is of a different race and ethnicity than the majority of their classmates in college and graduate school and comes from an environment where higher education is not understood or transparent, they face particular difficulties in navigating the expectations of graduate school. For instance, students raised in an environment where direct eye contact is considered disrespectful, and neurodivergent students who may have difficulty maintaining eye contact, may struggle to be read or understood—by their professors and/or peers—as being engaged. Their actions may appear too deferential or aloof. For others raised in a culture where humility is expected, accepting praise may induce stress and their reaction may appear to be disengaged. These culturally diverse and neurodivergent students may not feel comfortable or encouraged to participate in class discussions, attend office hours, and speak up when they have questions or concerns, through no fault of their own. These spaces have yet to be as inclusive or responsive as institutional administrators have professed in recent years.

It is important for you to understand that we are not encouraging academic "assimilation," that is, adopting the dominant cultural norms and values of academia to succeed, for we know that the academy reflects the white, male, able-bodied, straight, and cisgendered norms of earlier Western philosophers and intellectuals as well as the institutional founders. Rather, we believe it is crucial for you to know and recognize these customs and practices in order for you to consider which are in your best interest to follow and which are not. We support efforts to resist or push back on these meta-narratives in the pursuit of altering university policies and practices to make it a welcoming and inclusive space. Universities, we argue, have a lot to learn and gain from their evolving student population. In advocating for yourself and your community while you are a student, you have the opportunity to make impactful systemic change within academia and outside of it too. At minimum, Solorzano states, a positive racial climate should include "students, faculty, and administrators of color," a "curriculum that reflects the historical and contemporary experiences of people of color," "programs to support the recruitment, retention and graduation of students of color," and "a college/university mission that reinforces the institution's commitment to pluralism."[29] In contrast, a negative or non-supportive campus climate is associated with poor academic performance and high dropout rates.[30]

In addition to understanding the norms of academia, a student must be aware of how citizenship status will also impact their options for where and how they pursue graduate study. Graduate students with US citizenship have access to nearly the full array of academic, material, and cultural resources available on campus and, when they cannot find the support they need, they usually have the opportunity to ask and, in many cases, obtain it. Students with US permanent residency, that is, foreign nationals with the permanent right to live and work in the United States, have similar advantages but must be aware of potential pitfalls. Given the increasingly restrictive nature of US immigration laws since the early 1990s, permanent residents, or "green card holders," are vulnerable to the threat of possible deportation if they engage in a number of ill-defined activities that make them eligible for removal. According to the Georgetown Law Library, those at risk for deportation are those with a "conviction of fraud, conviction of a crime within five years of admission with a conviction and sentence of at least one year imprisonment, conviction of a crime of moral turpitude, or commission of an aggravated felony."[31] While most of these incidents are self-evident, a "crime of moral turpitude" remains a vague designation but is generally seen, according to immigration lawyer Ilona Bray, as "one that was done recklessly or with evil intent, and which shocks the public conscience as inherently base, vile, or depraved, contrary to the rules of morality and the duties owed between people or to society in general."[32] The law covers spousal abuse, child abuse, and animal fighting.

Aggravated felonies committed by noncitizens also require further insight. They are neither aggravated nor felonies but are a particular class of offenses making permanent residents and undocumented individuals ineligible for any kind of immigration relief, including asylum. When Congress first established such crimes in 1988, it narrowly defined aggravated felonies as murder and drug and other forms of trafficking. Today, aggravated felonies are much more expansive and include, according to the American Immigration Council, "more than thirty types of offenses, including simple battery," resulting from a domestic dispute, "theft, filing a false tax return, and failing to appear in court."[33] As such, noncitizens are vulnerable to losing their status and eligible for deportation for a wide range of seemingly minor infractions. Be sure to learn about and know your rights.

Undocumented students, who do not have US citizenship, permanent residency, or a temporary visa, must navigate their higher educational career path even more carefully. Fortunately, as of 2021, seventeen states, including California, Florida, Illinois, New York, and Texas, and the District of Columbia, as well as an additional seven state university systems, offer in-state tuition to undocumented students. According to the National Conference of State Legislatures, these provisions "typically require attendance and graduation at state high schools, acceptance at a state college or university, and promis[e] to apply for legal status as soon as eligible."[34] States such as Alabama, Arizona, Georgia, and Indiana, however, bar unauthorized students from in-state tuition benefits as well as state financial aid, while two states, Alabama and South Carolina, forbid them from enrolling in any public postsecondary institution. Every state and campus will have a different approach in working with undocumented students. The best advice we have found is to find universities that have an undocumented student services office and reach out to a counselor, as they can provide specific information about what benefits and support services are available.

As in the larger society, undocumented students must learn to navigate a sometimes inhospitable environment in higher education, especially if they reside in parts of the United States that have been hostile and, in some cases, violent towards noncitizens. The UC-wide climate survey of 2014 found that "undocumented Residents were less comfortable than U.S Citizens and non-U.S. citizens with the overall climate, the climate in their classes, and the climate in their work units/departments."[35] Fortunately, today, many academic spaces are increasingly welcoming and inclusive, working with you to navigate your educational path and providing information on resources available to students who are noncitizens. Certainly such services will not cover all your needs and you will find it more challenging than a documented student to gain access, but you will likely have the opportunity to pursue and obtain your educational goals. Reach out to staff and faculty as well as to current undocumented graduate students who are willing and able to share their insights and experiences of navigating immigration laws as well as about their educational career. Research the environment of the college or university before you apply if possible, and certainly before you go.

Whether undocumented, permanent resident, or US citizen, many first-generation, low-income, and/or nontraditional Students of Color have faced a circuitous route to higher education. Many times, as we know from the students with whom we have worked, this path has included involvement with the juvenile justice and foster care system. We have femtored and mentored undergraduate and graduate students who, as children, were exposed to poverty, homelessness, the criminal and juvenile justice systems, as well as alcohol, drugs, and gangs. For many, these experiences have meant not being able to finish, their studies in middle school, let alone high school. Some have been expelled and sent to continuation programs, while others have faced detention and incarceration until they reach majority age. For these students, the rewards of research that come with higher education and post-graduate education is often an inaccessible hope and dream. Yet, as we have also seen, with the right mentorship, networks, and resources, these students can find their way to community college where, after two to three years of intensive study, they can matriculate to four-year state colleges and universities and onto graduate programs. Such was the experience of Rosie B., who is currently an assistant professor at a leading research university. She writes,

> As a child growing up in a single motel room with three siblings and a single mother, life was difficult. My father had passed away from alcoholism at the age of thirty-six, leaving a young wife and four young children

behind. During my adolescent years, I led a life of criminal activity, and drug abuse, which led to my incarceration as a juvenile. Education was the farthest thing from my mind, and I dropped out of school in the eighth grade for almost two years. I did not have examples of economic or educational success in my family. I went back to school as a condition of my probation and ended up in a continuation high school in South Central Los Angeles for 'at-risk' youth. There were moments in my life as a young Chicana that I thought I would not graduate from high school. No one in my immediate family had excelled academically; this was a direct result of poverty. I did not have any models of academic success, but it was heavily stressed in my home. My mother believed that through education the cycle of poverty could end in our family. I didn't have much hope when I went back to school; I figured this would just be another poorly funded continuation school with teachers that could care less about the students. I was wrong. It was there that for the first time a teacher showed me that they genuinely cared about me and more importantly believed in my abilities. This experience would resonate with me throughout my educational journey. As I continued on to community college and to the university as an undergraduate and graduate student, I have received an amazing amount of support and extremely vital mentorship.[36]

Students with similar profiles can and do find support groups on campuses. Today, groups such as the Underground Scholars Program and Initiative, which works with formerly incarcerated students, assist students in navigating the prison-to-school pipeline via recruitment, retention, and advocacy work that includes support for successfully applying to graduate school. Institutions of higher education have not always been responsive to the needs of formerly incarcerated students in particular, but those working within the institution who have been formerly involved with the justice system have carved out spaces to address the needs of individuals like themselves. With supportive staff, faculty, and administrators, these individuals have laid a path for others with similar experiences.[37]

Finally, we encourage all of you to gather your reserve, as did Rosie B. and Jamaal Muwwakkil, an accomplished former doctoral candidate (now PhD) in linguistics at UCSB, who took a ten-year circuitous path from community college to UCLA, to connect with those who offer their support. In discussing the ways he has benefited from networking, he shared, "That's the strategy that I've taken. . . . I take people at their word, they say, 'shoot me an email, I'd love to talk to you,' I'm shooting an email today. I'm going to set up a meeting, I'm gonna connect with you. And I've done that with everybody. Every class I've taken at UCLA, I went to every grad students' office hours, etc. With every professor's office hours . . . I asked about stuff that I hadn't known, that I could not know, and that I did not know that [I] needed . . . help."[38] We urge you to do the same: to reach out, find support, or create your own support systems, as you navigate your own graduate school journey.

Deciding whether graduate school is right for you takes a lot of thought and, as we discussed in this chapter, involves many conversations with people who can offer support or first-hand accounts of what to expect, including the challenges and rewards of higher education. We believe that this approach will work to debunk the myths and misconceptions of graduate school and help you to avoid attending graduate school for the wrong reasons. If possible, seek out those who have an understanding of how your life and career stage as well as your intersectional identity, that is, your identity and experience as a first-generation, low-income, and/or nontraditional Student of Color, will influence your path to a graduate education. In full disclosure, we will say that, even though we were both in top graduate programs, we struggled from the first day with believing we had the ability to remain in spaces that seemed so isolating and foreign. Quite simply, for a long time, we felt we did not belong. As native Spanish-speaking, working-class Chicanas, we did not see ourselves reflected in the curriculum or in the classroom. It remains a dismal reality that, as you ascend the academic pipeline, the number of members of marginalized populations—Black, Indigenous, People of Color, Women of Color, queer, trans, nonbinary, undocumented, disabled, and/or neurodivergent—diminishes. With time and the support of many individuals and institutions, we found our way and made it our mission to carry out the research, teaching, and service work we had set out to accomplish. Whether you do this right after your undergraduate career or years later, it is never too late to keep learning, growing, and building a path for you, your family, and your community.

KEY TAKEAWAYS

- We discussed the common reasons not to pursue a graduate degree.
- We acknowledged the ways that your life and career stage—as well as finances and employment options—may impact your graduate school decision.
- We offered examples of how people with varying intersectional identities—including Black, Indigenous, People of Color, Women of Color, queer, trans, nonbinary, undocumented, system-impacted, disabled, and/or neurodivergent—face distinct challenges in graduate school.
- In light of these challenges, we also shared the importance of understanding academic norms, not to assimilate, but rather to make informed decisions and build support systems to help you navigate your campus climate.

3

MYTHS AND MISCONCEPTIONS OF GRADUATE SCHOOL DEBUNKED

AS WE HAVE SEEN, prospective students often allow fears of inadequacy, unpreparedness, and financial distress to get in the way of applying. Certainly, these concerns are rooted in material circumstances: it's not "all in your head," as we are told by those outside of our communities who don't understand the struggles of first-generation, low-income, and/or nontraditional Students of Color. Unfortunately, we do not have the funding or cultural or educational resources often available to white, middle-class, and second- and continuing-generation students, that provide tuition and housing expenses or the confidence to step onto a college or university campus and feel that we belong. In this chapter, we tackle common myths and misconceptions about graduate school and provide you with real-world knowledge about the expectations of graduate school admissions committees.

DEMYSTIFYING COMMON GRAD SCHOOL MYTHS
AND MISCONCEPTIONS

Fears and concerns about going to graduate school have led to many myths and misconceptions about post-graduate education. You may be concerned that you are applying the wrong way, you are not meeting academic expectations, you have little research experience, or you have inadequate financial and cultural resources to complete a graduate program. Reviewing these and other common myths will not only help debunk them but also teach you that you have more options for pursuing graduate school than you realize.

I have to get a master's degree before applying to a doctoral program.
Contrary to popular belief, you do not have to get a master's degree to pursue a doctoral program. Some doctoral programs may require a master's degree, but some will not and will provide the option to earn one along the way. These are typically known as MA/PhD programs. Some doctoral programs do not offer the master's degree unless it is a terminal master's. In such instances, a master's, rather than the doctorate, is given if you plan to leave your program and not continue on with the PhD. Yvette, for example, was admitted into a PhD program that did not require a master's degree and did not offer one, except for a terminal master's. To this day, she does not hold a master's degree but does have a PhD. She was considered competitive enough for a doctoral program due to undergraduate research experience and academic profile, which included a senior thesis, awards, and conference presentations. Not all programs operate similarly. As such, we strongly recommend that you look into the educational requirements of the programs of interest to determine if a master's degree is required.

I don't have a competitive enough GPA [grade point average] or GRE [Graduate Record Exam] score to get into graduate school.

Many students have come to Yvette over the years with significant concerns about having a low GPA and low GRE as well as having a gap or dip in their transcripts, indicating a lapse from schooling or temporary struggles with performance, respectively. The students have an impression that, if you do not have a perfect GPA or GRE, your chances of attending a graduate program are close to none. This is not true. While some programs do require or recommend a particular GPA or exam score, not all do. More and more graduate programs are moving away from GRE scores, in particular. This shift away from standardized tests has happened largely as a result of recent studies, explains Katie Langin of *Science,* "showing little correlation between GRE scores and success in graduate school" and, meanwhile, "the concern that the test puts underrepresented groups at a disadvantage."[1] Pay attention to the program's GRE requirement, as not all are the same. We advise students who are concerned with their scores to consider attending a postbaccalaureate program or master's degree program before they embark on the path to the doctorate and to do so not only to boost their scores but also to demonstrate additional preparation and expertise. Another option is to apply for a combination master's and doctoral program. Ensure, too, that you have strong research and personal statements as well as letters of recommendation. And do not be afraid of asking your recommenders if they are able to write you a *strong* letter of support, one in which the recommender says specific things about your academic abilities and personal motivation to pursue higher education.

If you have a particularly close relationship with your letter-writer, you might ask them to address any glaring issues with your GPA or coursework and explain what accounts for any decline in your performance, why you switched majors multiple times, and why your classes don't align with your intended field of study. Letters like these can often help persuade committees to empathize with an applicant who has had a bumpy educational journey, since many faculty use transcripts to gain insight about your preparedness and training in the field of interest. Fortunately, more and more these days, graduate admissions committees review applications holistically, taking into account all parts of the applicant's materials, including personal attributes, not just exam scores or previous educational history, with the ultimate goal of promoting an inclusive, equitable, and rigorous graduate application review process.[2]

It's too expensive for me to attend graduate school. I can't afford it.
We hear the phrases "graduate school is too expensive" and "I can't afford graduate school" all the time. And, to be frank, graduate programs are expensive and, yes, if you come from a working class or low-income background and had to attend a two-year community college before transferring to a four-year institution, you will have to work hard to secure funding so that you do not pay out of pocket. As Amanda Peña, a nontraditional student, confided on the Grad School Femtoring Podcast, she waited to get her master's degree because she knew they were pricey. "I didn't want to pay out of pocket for it if I didn't love it," she said. "I think, as you go to graduate school, you have to understand that it's an investment in yourself."[3] We wholeheartedly agree with Amanda. And, yet, the point we want to make is that the cost of graduate school should not prohibit you from pursuing a degree because funding opportunities are also available. Indeed, doctoral programs provide more chances than master's programs to secure full funding where the bulk of your tuition and personal costs are covered. But we know many master's students who have avoided debt because of scholarships, fellowships, teaching assistant positions, and other opportunities they have secured. Contact the graduate advisor in your department and the campus's graduate division and ask about funding earmarked for first-generation, low-income, and/or nontraditional Students of Color. The department or program may have already considered or nominated you for those opportunities, but it is always a good idea to advocate for yourself or find those who are willing—and whose job it is—to do so on your

behalf. Finally, if necessary, do what some folks have done to get by: take a part-time job in or outside of academia, preferably in an area related to your studies or skills. We have known individuals who worked in staff positions at the same university where they pursued their degrees. While it might slow you down, it will help alleviate financial stress and, in some cases, provide you with health and other benefits and keep you connected to the educational environment.

I did not carry out any or enough research in college to get into a graduate program.

Not all graduate programs require extensive—or any—research experience for admission. Postbaccalaurate and master's programs, for instance, exist to provide you with the training needed to either go straight into the workforce or continue on with a doctoral program. It is possible to get into one of those programs with no prior experience so long as you have a clear idea for what you plan to study and what you seek to gain. If you have some research experience, it is also worth the effort to apply to a combination of master's and doctoral degree programs. Many doctoral programs will inform you if they believe you are a better fit for their master's degree and, in some cases, may admit you into that program. Both of us have seen that happen to several candidates, giving them the chance to gain the skill set they would need for a doctorate. In some cases, too, where individuals decide to pivot in their major field of interest, yet have no research experience in their new area, they can rely on their previous experience. The earlier research experience works in their favor, demonstrating their multidisciplinary strengths and ability to diversify the program of interest.

To be competitive, I must go straight from undergraduate to graduate school. A nontraditional path will hurt my chances of getting in.

Many students worry that if they do not go into graduate school immediately after finishing their undergraduate degree, they will be less competitive than those who do so. They may also worry that after graduating, they will lose access to university resources and mentors, which will decrease their chances of applying in the future. Some of them wonder if and how it will be possible to ask for letters of recommendation from professors after having graduated so many years earlier and if these individuals will even remember them. And they are concerned about how they will make time for a graduate program after having been away from a formal educational environment for so long. Remember, not everyone follows a similar path to graduate school or has the same relationship to their education. Indeed, many undergraduates that we have worked with have decided not to seek a postgraduate education right after graduation as a result of burnout and needing a break, especially from the isolating online learning environment demanded by the conditions of the COVID-19 pandemic. We cannot dismiss, too, the physical and mental anguish communities of color, particularly Black communities, have faced as a result of the broken white supremacist criminal justice system that murdered George Floyd, Breonna Taylor, Michael Brown, Trayvon Martin, and countless others. We must recognize that these and similar events severely impact our ability to navigate our everyday lives and plans for the future, including higher education.

Whatever the reasons for taking a break from formal education, you must consider the many potential benefits you gained during that time away. Many individuals earn valuable hands-on experience in the workforce or in internships and volunteer opportunities. Sometimes they discover or learn more about a potential subject or topic they wish to explore or research in graduate school. Dr. Angela Crumdy, the creator of Grad Girl Wellness, a platform designed to inspire and encourage Women of Color to prioritize their overall health and wellness while pursuing higher education, had such an experience in her journey to the doctorate. She had not been accepted to any graduate program, so she pursued her backup plan, Teach for America. After teaching English for two years in a high school in Dallas, Texas, an "an amazing experience," she re-applied and was admitted to graduate school, where she not only received full funding but also developed a project on teachers that grew from her experience. In retrospect, the two years away were "a necessary detour," she said. Angela learned about her love for teaching, despite the "rough" challenge of working with students only four years her junior. "It was an absolute whirlwind. I have so much respect for teachers."[4]

These experiences gained outside of school can and will help you with graduate school applications, particularly in applied programs. In some cases, going to graduate school soon after graduating from college is the right decision, but it is certainly not the only option. Increasingly, many master's and especially doctoral programs will seldom admit applicants without some kind of real-world experience outside of the university context. A gap in your resume—whether between high school and college or between college and graduate school—does not reflect poorly on you if you are intentional about how you use that time and how you frame it in your graduate application essays.

My undergraduate degree does not align with my interests in graduate school. I'm not prepared. They won't admit me.

While switching fields from undergraduate to graduate school may not be easy, it is also not impossible and becoming increasingly common. A 2014 study by the Federal Reserve Bank of New York found that only 27 percent of college graduates worked in a field related to their undergraduate major. And, according to the 2022 Bureau of Labor Statistics News Release, almost 50 million US employees voluntarily separated with their employer that year, leaving a large population in the midst of career transitions of their own.[5] If you are among the many individuals who are pursuing graduate school as a way to pivot in your career, then you will need to understand the requirements of the new field. If it includes firm requirements for your graduate program (such as required math courses, a portfolio, and/or a particular exam score) then you will need to plan for gaining that experience or meeting the criteria prior to applying. If no firm requirements exist, you will want to be mindful about framing your current skill set in a way that complements your new program or discipline. Nowadays, more programs are seeking to diversify their student body and this comes in many forms, including the disciplinary background, skillset, and dis/ability of the incoming students.

I don't want to be a professor so I shouldn't attend graduate school.

Graduate programs are not only for individuals seeking to pursue a career in the professoriate. The reality is that most PhDs will *not* find tenure-track positions but, rather, find other forms of employment. Indeed, for nearly four decades, the numbers of recent PhDs landing such opportunities has declined significantly, despite rosy predictions of a great wave of faculty retirements followed by a steep uptick in hiring. That prediction never came true. Recent doctorates have failed to land tenure-track jobs not because they did anything wrong, but rather because these positions are rare and continue to decline. Recent doctorates will struggle to escape the clutches of what Leonard Cassuto describes as the "adjunctification of academia: the rise of a new generation of contingent faculty working full and part time in non-tenure-track positions."[6] Admittedly, many, if not most, highly competitive doctoral programs work under an apprenticeship model where you will be trained to pursue an academic career. If you are interested in a career in research or as a professor, a doctoral program in an "R1" or *Research I institution,* that is, a university with high research activity, is the main option. This would include institutions in the University of California system. If you are in California and interested in a career in teaching or counseling or any kind of applied work, however, campuses in the California State University system may be a better fit. Lastly, if you are interested in a vocational career, attending graduate school is not necessary and, instead, taking courses at a community college or a vocational school to learn specific skills might be the best option. Be aware that universities across the United States come with their own missions and models for higher education as well as criteria for admission and tuition costs.

Do not assume, however, that graduate programs will teach you specifically the practical, day-to-day skills you will need in your career or profession. In a research-intensive university in the 1990s, Miroslava found that her program offered only minimal teaching experience and it was usually attached to teaching assistantships, which are quite different from preparing and leading your own course. Students in her program received little training, too, in curriculum development or pedagogy, much less on issues of diversity, inclusivity, or equity in the classroom. Today, colleges and universities are more in tune with enhancing teaching and learning skills for diverse populations, offering a variety of training opportunities to graduate students and faculty. Graduate programs also have a wide range of applied, practical, and hands-on options that can provide valuable networking, internship, and skill-building opportunities that may help you land a job in your field of interest. Take advantage of as many chances as possible to develop your professional skills in and outside the classroom.

I cannot attend graduate school since no one in my family has done this before.

As a first-generation student, you are a trailblazer. You are among the first in your family to attend college and, similarly, you are also likely the first to attend graduate school. That fact should not be an obstacle holding you back from pursuing graduate school if that is what is right for you. Instead, we hope it will embolden you. Certainly, cultural and familial considerations will be necessary to navigate for you and your family. But know that you are not alone. Today, about 40 to 50 percent of undergraduate students at colleges and universities across the United

States are first-generation, though highly selective institutions tend to have a smaller proportion than do their less selective peers.[7] As you may well know, first-generation students often struggle and/or are pushed out of institutions of higher education. Studies have shown that first-generation undergrads are less likely to graduate than non-first-generation students, regardless of parental income. At the graduate level, the proportion of first-generation doctoral students—those who are the first of their generation to both complete a bachelor's degree and pursue a doctoral degree—is smaller, at about 30 percent, though no less significant.[8] Many colleges and universities have responded to first-generation students and their needs at the undergraduate and graduate level with on-campus resources, programs, and fellowships. And, as a first-generation student, it may help to remember that you are paving the path for someone to follow in the future.

I don't have the time to complete a graduate program.
Sometimes nontraditional students who have developed full careers come to the realization that they would like to attend graduate school, but do not do so because of the time it takes to complete a program. They often wonder how they can run a household, shuttle children to and from school, assist aging parents, and/or commute, and still find the time to be present in the classroom and complete their assignments. They may fear not being able to achieve balance—or, as Yvette says, harmonize or cycle—between multiple familial and financial responsibilities. They may also have concerns over ageism in the workplace, especially if they hope to enter a new field and apply to entry- or mid-level positions, working or competing with potentially younger candidates. These concerns are real, and yet plenty of individuals have successfully switched careers or returned to school despite nontraditional pathways. If you decide to pursue a graduate program and have household or caregiving responsibilities, it will be necessary for you to enlist the help of family and friends to give you the physical and mental

space to focus on your academic work. We also recommend setting firm boundaries around your personal life, work, and education. If you are concerned over ageist beliefs that might hold you back, showcase what you bring to the table and continue learning new skills to make yourself a competitive candidate in your field. We both have learned some of the most important lessons in graduate school from peers who have navigated nontraditional careers. They are usually among the most prepared and focused. And, as Miroslava has seen in her work, they often finish quicker than others.[9]

All graduate students are highly intelligent and I am not. I am an impostor.
This concern is all too common, especially among those of us who are first-generation, low-income, and People of Color. Unlike our classmates, who may be multi-generational, middle-class or wealthy, and white, we do not carry the same privileges and resources that enable others to understand the hidden curriculum of academia. As such, it can be easy to feel like we do not know enough. Indeed, on Yvette's first day of graduate school she felt like her classmates were speaking a foreign language because she had switched disciplines and had not yet learned the disciplinary jargon in critical theory and performance studies. Little did I know, most of my cohort mates had master's degrees and/or had parents who themselves had advanced degrees. One of them even had parents who were professors. If I had known this, I would not have assumed that everyone but me was highly intelligent or that I was admitted into my graduate program by mistake. And, to be clear, not all graduate students are gifted. You do not need to be a "genius" to obtain a graduate degree. Instead, you need to be committed and consistent as well as resilient and motivated in your work to follow through on completing your program requirements. As Yvette has told her listeners, "at the end of the day, [it's] about dedication, about perseverance, [and] about hard work. It's not about how smart you are. . . . Yes, you will have a couple of exams in graduate school,

but you will have more than enough time to prepare for [them]. Again, it goes back to all of your hard work."[10]

My school [undergraduate institution] was not prestigious, I'll never get in.
Talk to anyone about graduate school admissions and the first thing they'll say is that one of the most important components of the application is the prestige of your undergraduate institution. Sadly, this remains true in many situations, given that implicit bias remains prevalent in the academy. Without even realizing, faculty are looking to reproduce themselves and gravitate towards those applicants they know and recognize. Miroslava will admit to doing the same. After reading work done by Julie Posselt on the role of implicit bias in graduate admissions and graduate school, she realized that she too was looking favorably at applicants who had attended colleges and universities that sounded familiar or that she had attended herself.[11] She read with eagerness letters of recommendation from professors who held a lot of power and prestige in their fields. Fortunately, these practices are coming under increasing scrutiny and faculty are paying much more attention to the application's substance and promise, not just the window dressing. And Miroslava has seen students from small and under-resourced institutions bloom into magnificent, critical, and engaged thinkers. We believe that, with the continued education and the commitment of faculty, staff, and administrators to diversity, equity, and inclusion, real change can and will come about, albeit incrementally.

Applying to graduate school is just like applying to college.
Lastly, we want to stress that applying to graduate school is very different from applying to college. Whereas in college, you could apply to multiple schools through a single portal, in graduate school, you are applying to each program individually. And while for an undergraduate degree, your application went to one admissions office, in graduate school your application is first directed to a graduate division office and

then directed to the particular program or department of interest. The departmental admissions committee, which could change every year, determines who gets admitted to their graduate program. On a related note, sometimes students worry that they need to get involved in a wide range of extracurricular activities to make them stand out as an applicant, much like they did for undergraduate admissions. But in reality, if you are involved in too many activities that do not seem directly related to your research, graduate school interests, and career trajectory, it could hurt your application. Fewer and more focused experiences will benefit you in graduate school applications than many seemingly random experiences.

Given all the myths and misconceptions about graduate school, making the decision to apply and attend can be nerve wracking. Sadly, these and other similar graduate school myths have played a role in holding people back from pursuing higher education, which is why it is important to demystify and debunk them. While we acknowledge that graduate school is not the right option for everyone, if it is right for you, you should go in with a clear understanding of what you have committed to do.

GRADUATE SCHOOL ADMISSIONS COMMITTEES' EXPECTATIONS

We turn now to what graduate programs *do* expect from you as an applicant, as well as some of the challenges you may face during the process. We will review each component of your application and the ways in which an *admissions committee*—or the groups of people assigned to review your application, including faculty, administrators, and, sometimes, other graduate students—determine if you are a good fit and competitive candidate for their program. We begin with a focus on your research agenda and academic preparation, which you will demonstrate via your statement of purpose, personal statement, and letters of recommendation. We will go into more detail defining and explaining how to write a statement of purpose and personal statement in part 2. When you submit your materials to an admissions committee, they may review them with the following questions in mind: Does this candidate meet the minimum requirements and did they submit all the required materials? Do the candidate's interests align with those of our program? Most importantly, what evidence does this candidate showcase to prove that they are prepared and will be successful in our program?

Academic Preparation and Research Experience

In considering a candidate's academic preparation and research agenda, each program may have a baseline. In some programs, this could mean having a particular grade point average, while in others it could be demonstrating some research experience or having practical or work experience in the field. Whatever the case, you can determine a program's minimum requirements by reviewing the department's website, the university course catalog, or reaching out to a graduate advisor or staff member of that department. Another way to research expectations that may be a little less formal is to contact current graduate students in a program and ask for their input and advice. If you have trouble locating the contact information for graduate students in any particular program, you can also send your query directly to the graduate advisor or another staff member and have them forward it to their graduate student email listserv. Yet another way to determine what admissions committees are looking for in an applicant is by communicating and/or meeting with professors in the program and asking them what they typically look for in a competitive or successful candidate. We strongly urge doing this, while also doing your homework to prepare yourself for these meetings with professors. We will admit that it is not always easy to get in touch with professors. Not all respond to "cold" emails—or to emails, period. We suggest, whenever possible, having a third party introduce you via email to the professor of interest. You will have a much better chance of receiving a response. If they do not respond, try other faculty in that or other departments or programs. Do not wait around for a single response. Cast your net widely. (We will cover how to ask for a meeting via email, what to do to prepare for meetings with professors, and what questions you can typically ask in chapter 4.)

The next questions an admissions committee member may ask is whether you are prepared for graduate school and whether you are likely to be successful in their program. To answer those queries, they will look for research experience derived from a number of sources. These might include participating in undergraduate and summer research programs, writing an undergraduate thesis, publishing a research-based paper, taking research- or methods-based courses, having a master's degree, having internship, work, or volunteer experience in the field or a related field, and so on. For doctoral programs, admissions committees expect the applicant to have a research agenda. Applicants should be able to showcase research experiences and articulate the connections between the former work or previous research they have done and the specific project they plan to undertake at the doctoral level. If you participated in programs designed to expand the pipeline of first-generation, low-income, and underrepresented students, such as the Ronald E. McNair Scholars Program or the Mellon Mays Undergraduate Fellowship Program, odds are you have already carried out some kind of investigation and have written up your findings. It is crucial for you to connect your undergraduate research as well as your other experience with the specific subjects you wish to study in a doctoral program.

If you are a returning student and have spent years in the field of social services, healthcare, or childcare, for example, it is likely you have strong skills with communication, accountability, and empathy. Use your application to provide examples of how you successfully used your talents in advocating for your clients' special needs and provided them with the resources they needed to lead a healthy and happy life. If you have a master's degree as an architectural historian and have many years of experience in the field and want to obtain your doctorate to enhance your career opportunities, you will be well prepared and versed to talk about the practical applications of historical work. Cite projects where you provided the historical and cultural context needed to make an argument about its necessity as a historical landmark. As difficult as it may be for us to talk about our assets and strengths to a committee of faculty and staff, given that many of us come from cultures that do not always encourage us to sing our own praises, now is not the time to hold back. Identify your skill set and let the committee know about the strengths you bring to the program.

In addition to highlighting your skills, it is critical that you identify faculty who will be potential advisors, specifically those whose research aligns with your own. We would strongly advise you to reach out to them before you apply, and determine if they might or might not be taking any students at the moment. You can email them directly or see if you can find someone (such as the graduate advisor) who can introduce you and advocate on your behalf. This does not always mean that this person will become your permanent advisor or will be your femtor, but it does help to demonstrate the connection between your interests and the faculty's, showing that you will be able to find advisors and committee members there.

GPA and GRE Matters

When it comes to discussing a "strong" grade point average, the number varies widely across disciplines. In Yvette's experience, after advising hundreds of students through this process, you cannot predict whether someone will get into a graduate program from a grade point average alone. She has seen students with 4.0s not get admitted into any graduate program and students with GPAs below a 3.0 get into top graduate programs in their field. Some disciplines, particularly in certain STEM and quantitative social sciences, will share minimum GPA requirements or the average score of their incoming students. This can give you an idea of how competitive your own GPA may be for that discipline. Having a strong GPA can also be helpful in that it could qualify you for competitive institutional and national merit scholarships and fellowships. In other disciplines, the GPA expectations may be less clear. You can reach out to femtors and mentors in your own discipline to ask what a competitive GPA is in your field, but do not let this information discourage you if your GPA is lower than what they mention. In fields with no minimum GPA requirement, you can expect your application to be measured holistically; your GPA will not make or break your application, especially if other parts of your application are strong and you articulate your personal strengths.

Like the GPA, the GRE score can sometimes become a barrier that holds a student back from applying for fear that a poor performance will automatically lead to rejection from a graduate program. The GRE, however, as noted earlier, is becoming less common as a requirement but is still worth noting. As briefly mentioned earlier, the GRE or *Graduate Record Exam* is a standardized graduate admissions test that attempts to measure your reading comprehension, writing, and math abilities. The GRE also includes subject tests for areas including Chemistry, Math, Physics, and Psychology. The GRE is meant to provide graduate programs with a common measure of comparison between applicants. Unfortunately, this test does not provide a fair comparison as it is not financially accessible to all. This standardized exam comes at a financial cost to anyone taking it, and while there are income-based fee waivers available, they do not typically waive the full cost. This makes the exam inaccessible to working-class and poor students, who may already struggle due to the inability to afford test preparation courses, tutors, and study materials. Though recently shortened from four to two hours in length after increased scrutiny of the exam, the

GRE remains an example of institutionalized classism and a graduate school barrier to students who cannot afford it. Studies have also shown that the GRE does not accurately predict academic performance. Having realized that scores on this test offers little correlation with graduate school success, many—arguably an increasing majority of—graduate programs no longer require the exam. Ask the graduate admissions office if the exam is required for your field.

When students have asked Yvette for advice regarding the GRE, she asks them to create a graduate school list and determine if any of the programs on their list require a GRE score to apply. If so, then they will need to register, study, and take the exam. It is important to register for this test early, ideally a few weeks in advance, and for subject tests (which have fewer annual testing dates) a few months in advance. You will also want to find out if those programs have a minimum GRE score requirement. After that, it is useful to take a practice test to get a sense of your baseline score. There are several websites like ETS, Magoosh, Kaplan, and Princeton Review that offer the opportunity to take a practice test for free. Finding out where you score without studying and what score you are aiming to get after studying will help determine how much time to dedicate to preparing for this exam. If you are in the fortunate situation where none of your programs require the GRE score, we do not recommend you take it. The test will cost you money and time that could be better used to strengthen other components of your graduate school application.

Letters of Recommendation

With similar misgivings about their readiness for graduate school, we have witnessed students not apply to programs because they believe they do not know enough faculty or other professionals who will write and submit strong letters of recommendation on their behalf. In many cases, potential applicants are simply unaware of who they can ask for letters of reference and how to do so. We will cover how to secure strong recommendation letters in chapter 7, but, for now, we want to note that admissions committees review closely letters of recommendation because this is an area where they get to learn about you from the perspective of a colleague, a peer, or another professional who has assessed you as a student, researcher, or employee. Letters of recommendation provide little-known professional and personal insights about an applicant and are an opportunity for a recommender to explain and justify any gaps or weaker components of a student's academic profile. Normally, strong recommendation letters from a respected and/or established colleague in the field will carry greater weight than a letter from someone outside of that discipline or someone less established in their career. For example, a letter from a faculty member at the rank of "professor" or "associate professor" will typically hold greater weight than a letter from an "assistant professor," since the latter are not tenured and may not have as strong a research profile, mentoring experience, and academic network as more senior colleagues. However, letters from assistant professors, faculty who are "tenure track" and who have been hired with the potential for near life-time employment, are given greater weight than those from non-tenure track employees, including lecturers, adjunct professors, visiting professors, and teaching assistants. Letters from a femtor or mentor who has worked with you for more than one year tend to be stronger than letters from someone who was your professor for one course, one quarter, or one semester. As noted earlier, a letter will not hold weight—no matter who writes it—if it does not include specific examples or details about your work and your potential. Letters of recommendation serve as a reminder that the professional relationships you form or formed in college matter and reflect your readiness and preparedness for the next steps. Reading a letter of recommendation alone can indicate to the admissions committee what type of student you are, what research you have conducted, what achievements you have earned, what personal hurdles you have overcome, what your long-term goals are, and why you are a good fit for the program.

Challenges of Self-Perception and Negative Feedback

In addition to the application materials, prospective first-generation, low-income, and/or nontraditional Students of Color who plan to apply to graduate schools might face other challenges, including self-perceptions that are conditioned and/or reinforced by negative feedback. Among the most common that can hold students back from applying to graduate school are impostor phenomenon, family achievement guilt, and feelings of doubt. *Impostor phenomenon* is a term that has recently supplanted the misleading term *impostor syndrome*, which individualizes beliefs or thoughts of personal inabilities or shortcomings, rather than attributing them to systemic, institutional barriers. It refers to the phenomenon of a high-achieving person who perceives herself as a fraud, or believes that he cannot meet expectations regardless of experience, skills, or other qualities. Issues of impostor phenomenon often get further compounded if you identify as having multiple intersecting marginalized identities. Disabled people, for instance, are well aware of the ableism pervasive in academic culture, as academia relies on and demands productivity to reproduce and sustain itself. Attempts to redefine productivity—such as extended periods of time needed to complete assignments—are often met with resistance, creating stressful situations for students. While many college campuses are compliant with accessibility mandates for physical space, observers suggest that, "in many cases, compliance with accessibility for digital and web-based technologies have fallen behind. Since these technologies are now vital to education, these laws governing disability access apply."[12] Students with vision, hearing, and speech disabilities cannot always depend on colleges and universities to provide them with equal access to online courses and websites.

In contrast to higher education, the K-12 educational system must provide students diagnosed with a disability the right to state-mandated Individualized Education Plans, or IEPs, which allow them access to therapies, counseling, and other resources. Once that same person steps onto a college campus or university, the IEP is gone. Instead, disabled students must navigate a disability or accessibility services office and provide the physical health and mental health documentation necessary. For Black individuals, who have higher rates of disability than any other racial or ethnic group, the implications are stark, suggesting that not only will they need to navigate systemic racism and classism but also ableism to a greater degree than non-Black folks in academia and beyond. Moreover, as researchers have found, "disability is both a cause and consequence of poverty and poverty and disability reinforce each other, contributing to increased vulnerability and exclusion."[13]

As we know from personal experience, not all medical providers, however, are willing to sign off verifying a disability, especially when they are dealing with disorders that look different across diverse populations or that are invisible to the naked eye, such as chronic pain or depression, leaving students with little recourse. What "counts" or is defined as disability varies across sectors, as well, with some disability-related programs having stricter definitions than the Americans with Disability Act (ADA).[14] The differing interpretations of disability is especially challenging for graduate students, for studies show that they are six times more susceptible to mental health issues like depression and anxiety than the general population.[15] LGBTQ+ graduate students are even more vulnerable to mental health issues than non-LGBTQ+ students. Researchers have noted that "transgender and gender-nonconforming graduate students, along with women, were significantly more likely to experience anxiety and depression than their cisgender male counterparts."[16] Alarmingly, half of the graduate students who reported high levels of depression and anxiety also reported poor mentorship and poor support from their advisors, contributing to feelings of impostor phenomenon. To create a welcoming space, researchers advocate a "shift in the culture within academia to eliminate the stigma [surrounding mental health issues] and ensure that students are not reluctant to communicate openly with their faculty advisors." Maintaining work-life balance is critical, the researchers continue, yet they know it is "'hard to attain in a culture where it is frowned upon to leave the laboratory before the sun goes down,' especially in an ever-competitive funding environment. Faculty and administrators must nevertheless 'set a tone of self-care as well as an efficient and mindful work ethic' to move the dial."[17]

These findings can make graduate school a minefield for first-generation, low-income, and/or nontraditional Students of Color, for many of us fear that our supervisors—whether employers or advisors—will think we are "gaming" the system or committing fraud. Such thinking, in turn, stops us from advocating for ourselves and reinforces the impostor phenomenon. Even while our employers or advisors may agree to the accommodations, they remain cold and indifferent to any additional requests. The last thing we want is to bring attention to ourselves, much less negative attention. Rather, the impostor phenomenon drives us to ignore our health and mental health needs to prove that we belong in the academy.[18]

While the impostor phenomenon is prevalent among first-generation, low-income, and/or nontraditional Students of Color, anybody can experience it. Impostor phenomenon comes in many forms, including:

· self-sabotaging yourself by not applying to an opportunity for fear of rejection,

· overachieving, overworking, and overpreparing for fear of doing something wrong,

· attributing your success to external factors like luck or even someone's mistake.

If you find yourself battling impostor phenomenon, know that you are not alone. It is a common experience, though it need not continue forever. In this book, we provide many strategies to combat it. For instance, a useful approach includes reframing your thoughts about feeling like a fraud. Rather than passing up opportunities like applying to graduate school because you think you're not "smart enough," why not apply and let them tell you where you stand? Rather than overachieving and overworking, which can often lead to burnout, why not consider what "good enough" work might look like or what kind of workload is sustainable for you? And, rather than attributing your success to luck, why not reflect on how far you've come and how you did that? Or, ask loved ones about your successes, that is, ask them to provide an assessment of what you have accomplished. This gives you the opportunity to see yourself from someone else's perspective.

Samantha González, a guest on the Grad School Femtoring Podcast, had similar words of advice. Battling what she refers to as the "impostor syndrome," she said, "has a lot to do with your support system, who you surround yourself with. And just knowing that to dream big, essentially, that's something that first-gen students are great about, [they] aim high." Speaking from her personal experience, Samantha continued, "that is . . . the aspirational capital that we hold. And that is the counter message to impostor [phenomenon] . . . constantly reminding yourself of who you are, what you bring to the table. And, don't focus on what you're not, you'll get there eventually." Working on your mindset, Samantha reminds us, is just as important as working on your writing for crafting a strong graduate school application because it will help keep you motivated, honest, and brave throughout the process.[19]

As we know from personal experience, the impostor phenomenon is hard to shake, even for someone like Miroslava who has spent nearly twenty-five years in academia and is a full professor with several books under her belt. In 2015 her former student Ishman Anderson, a young Black man who was then a doctoral candidate in the San Francisco State

University Educational Leadership Program, asked if she battled the impostor phenomenon. He asked this question because he knew that she had grown up in the *barrio* of East San José and was a Chicana scholar in the academy. (Ishman, too, grew up in an underserved neighborhood, West Oakland, and now has his PhD.) "All the time," she replied, "but I don't care anymore," which she knew was a lie as soon as she said it. "But if I no longer cared," she continued, "then why would I have published my third book before many of my white colleagues had yet to publish their second book?" "I do pressure myself a lot," she confessed to Ishman. "And it's probably because of my need to overcompensate, as I've never felt 'good enough' or 'legitimate' in academia." These beliefs, she told him, "hurt us in so many ways."[20]

Though the impostor phenomenon stays with us along our journey, we can find ways to put it to rest. "Well, unfortunately," Samantha González astutely observed in the Grad School Femtoring Podcast, "there's no threshold that you're going to reach that's going to completely stop impostor [phenomenon]. That would be amazing. Some people may think it's like a six figure salary. And suddenly, I'm not an impostor, right? Suddenly, I've made it. But unfortunately, no. . . . It's being kind to yourself as well as surrounding yourself by a group of people that is supportive." She continued, "because, you know, there's that impostor in you, that's telling you that you can't do it. But your family, your friends, your partners, they don't see that impostor, all they see is all that you've done." We need to reframe the way we think, Samantaha reminds us, and return to those rituals that uplift us. "Whether it's prayer, whether it's therapy, whether it's mirror talk [with] some mantras in the morning, but it's just realizing that . . . you can't let yourself be afraid of failure, because . . . [you are] getting one step closer . . . to the achievement . . . you hope to have."[21]

Family achievement guilt is another common obstacle that first-generation, low-income, and/or nontraditional Students of Color may face. This refers to the guilt and discomfort students may feel for having more educational opportunities and college success than their family members. Students who experience family achievement guilt also tend to minimize their academic achievements, such as earning a scholarship or participating in a research program, when they are around their parents, siblings, or extended relatives, for fear that they will be read as showing off (*presumida*) or trying to look better than them. Dealing with family achievement guilt can also affect a college student's mental health and put them at an increased risk of depression if their guilt comes with negative side effects. Family achievement guilt can have many facets. For instance, some students may experience guilt for violating a family norm by being the first in their family to move away from their home or for leaving their family in their pursuit of formal education. Others may feel a greater sense of responsibility to do well academically and to financially support family members due to the privileges afforded them in college. More broadly, many students who feel family achievement guilt experience conflicts between their school and home environments. If this sounds familiar and you think you have experienced (or continue to experience) family achievement guilt, become aware of it in theory and in practice. We believe that, in doing so, you will go a long way towards managing it.[22]

When it comes to applying to graduate school, we would like to offer a few strategies to help you manage *feelings of doubt* and increase your sense of confidence. When you are the first to do something, it is not uncommon to doubt yourself. Self-doubt can manifest itself in cycles of impostor phenomenon, self-sabotage, and even indecisiveness. To combat feelings of self-doubt, it can be helpful to practice self-compassion; this means reminding yourself that you do not have to be perfect to achieve your goals or achieve them on your own. You are also not obligated to do things in the same way that others have done. We urge you to reflect, too, on how far you have come to get to this point in your educational journey. What major milestones have you achieved? What major hurdles have you overcome and how do those compare with continuing your education? Think of all the individuals who have supported and believe in you. Who are they? What did they do for you? How have you, in turn, helped people like yourself?

Certainly, we are not suggesting that the challenges are "all in your head"—as we know many of us have been gaslit with these messages that structural racism, sexism, homophobia, ableism, and ageism are not real barriers. We know they exist. The research proves they thwart the efforts of first-generation, low-income, and/or nontraditional Students of Color in their quest for higher education and post-graduate degrees. Yet, we also want to remind you that you are not alone. Keep asking for help at each stage of your educational journey, whether that's via a femtor, mentor, academic and career coach, family member, or friend. And avoid comparing yourself to others in your surroundings or on social media because we all have our own experiences, circumstances, and trajectories. The person next to you may have more or fewer privileges, resources, and hurdles than you. Unfortunately, we do not start on a level playing field. Therefore, it may be more helpful to focus on identifying your own markers of growth and success rather than on comparing yourself to those around you.

Remember, too, that graduate programs will look at key elements of your application and weigh them within the context of your larger portfolio. No one criteria, however, will eliminate your chances. Keep that in mind. As discussed, committees will pay attention to your academic preparation and research experience; grade point average and, if required, GRE score; and letters of recommendation (we say more about other essential components in part 2). Spend time strengthening all these components as much as possible, preferably months before you apply, for you need the time to engage in research, prepare for the GRE if necessary, and contact professors who will write you strong letters.

Finally, we highly encourage you to minimize or, ideally extinguish, the impostor phenomenon and to remove yourself from any negative talk, whether that is self-talk or talk of others, even from family and community members. Many times that talk manifests itself as family achievement guilt, which can hold you back from pursuing your dreams and desires. As people who have survived the many challenges thrown our way, including poverty, under-resourced schooling, limited choices and opportunities, and the necessity of work, we know how to survive and thrive in inhospitable circumstances. Certainly, academic culture reifies structural forms of oppression such as white supremacy, racism, sexism, homophobia, classism, ableism, ageism, and more. But don't let that stop you. We invite you to join in the struggle to create more inclusive, diverse, and equitable spaces where more individuals from our communities can enjoy the fruits of the labor that our ancestors helped build for future generations.

KEY TAKEAWAYS

- We began the chapter identifying and debunking some of the most common myths about graduate school to empower you to commit to applying if grad school is right for you.
- You don't need a master's, you don't need to have a perfect or near perfect grade point average or Graduate Record Exam (GRE) score, and you don't need extensive research experience to get in.
- You also don't need piles of cash or extensive lines of credit—though these always help!—to finance your education.
- Nontraditional paths are not dealbreakers, nor are interests outside of academia. Not everyone wants or needs to, or will become, a professor.
- Main elements that admissions committee will balance are research experience, grade point average and/or GRE, if applicable, and letters of recommendation, among other components discussed in part 2.

- If you are struggling with the impostor phenomenon, family achievement guilt, and feelings of doubt, know that you are not alone and that there are strategies you can implement today to manage these challenges.

- Every applicant brings a unique set of assets, achievements, and experiences that can and will allow them to gain admission to a graduate school of their choice.

PART TWO

THE APPLICATION PROCESS

4

GETTING ORGANIZED AND CREATING THE GRAD SCHOOL LIST

IF YOU'VE READ UP to this point or jumped to this chapter, chances are that you are ready to start the graduate school application process. We want to ensure that you set yourself up for success; therefore, we will first introduce some time and task-management as well as accountability strategies to help you prepare for the upcoming application cycle. After that, we will review three parts of an organizational system you can set up now to help you work smarter, not harder, and follow through on applying without burning yourself out. These steps are to assist you with setting up what is called a *foldering system* as well as with implementing standard operating procedures and using templates whenever possible. Finally, we will share a sample application timeline to give you an idea of the tasks that will come up and suggest how to use it, modify it, or create your own. Why do we ask that you spend some time assessing your strategies, getting organized, and planning? The more work you do to set yourself up for success early on, rather than later, the better off you'll be when it comes to meeting your graduate school application deadlines.

ASSESSING YOUR TIME MANAGEMENT, TASK MANAGEMENT, AND ACCOUNTABILITY STRATEGIES

First, we want you to take stock of what you currently use to manage your time and work. Do you keep track of your work with a digital or printed calendar and planner? Do you handwrite your "to-do" list or use apps (applications or software installed on a device) to help you keep track of your tasks? For instance, Yvette manages her time and tasks by using a combination of a project management tool (such as Trello, Kanbanflow, Asana, Monday.com) and a digital calendar (such as Google Calendar, Microsoft Outlook Calendar, Apple Calendar). She keeps track of a running list of to-dos online and organizes them in different columns by priority based on major goals, urgency, and time frame. She asks herself: Does this need to get done today? Tomorrow? This week? Next week? Does this need to get done at all? And she adds the task to her task-management tool accordingly. Organizing tasks or to-dos by column is a common practice within the *kanban* method of productivity, or a visual system for managing your work that shows your tasks as they move through a process.

Aside from using a task-management tool that helps organize tasks by goals and urgency, Yvette uses an online calendar. That means that, after tasks are added to the task-management tool, she adds the top priority tasks for the week—those that will help make the most progress on her major quarterly goals—to the online calendar along with other personal and professional obligations, such as meetings, appointments, and workshops. To ensure that she gets her high priority tasks done, she likes to schedule them into her calendar during a time when she is most focused. That might be early morning for the early risers or evening for the night owls. She also likes to practice *time-blocking* and *monotasking*.

Time-blocking is the act of defining and assigning certain periods of time on a calendar to a predetermined type of task. For Yvette, time-blocking means dedicating a certain set of hours each day for meetings, reading, writing, and editing, as well as two small blocks of time a day to check emails. Monotasking, unlike multitasking, happens alongside time-blocking and refers to the practice of focusing on one task at a time. Time-blocking and focusing solely on one task at a time helps maintain focus, which ultimately allows Yvette to meet deadlines and reach her goals with less stress and anxiety. Identify days and times each week specifically that you might block out to dedicate time towards completing your work. Figure out, too, how you ensure that you are monotasking while working on your applications. That might include turning off your phone or other devices, or muting them. Or, as we have done, put a "do not disturb" sign on your door or work space so that family members or colleagues know you need time to yourself. We can't guarantee those approaches will always work, but consider what you need to take advantage of those precious hours.

As you prepare for the upcoming graduate school applications cycle, keep in mind how your obligations will be impacted by the time you spend on your materials (such as statements or requests for letters of recommendation). Consider, too, whether you can put any of those responsibilities on pause or say "no" to them during this period of time. Remember, when you say "no" to one thing (like joining a book club or assisting in building a website), you're saying "yes" to another (advancing your applications). Whenever a new opportunity is presented to Yvette, she takes a look at her current goals and obligations and assesses if it is manageable to add it to her current projects. She also considers how it might impact other areas of her life. How might adding the task of applying to graduate programs impact your schedule? What will you sacrifice to make time for this? And how will you hold yourself accountable to setting aside time each week to dedicate towards your application process?

Assuring that you have some accountability set up within your grad school application planning process is essential to taking responsibility for your goals and increasing your chances of success. Staying focused can present itself in a variety of ways, including personal, financial, and identity-based approaches reminding you of your commitment. Some folks may benefit from personal check-ins that come from forming study groups or a buddy system to work on applications alongside others. Others may prosper from making a financial pact with someone or hiring a coach or editor to assist them. And some might flourish through an identity-based method where the mere act of identifying as a prospective graduate student, a nascent scholar, or a soon-to-be doctor will motivate them enough to get them to apply. Whatever the case is for you, we want you to be intentional in developing an effective time and task-management system as well as strategies for productivity and accountability that work in helping you manage the application process.

SETTING UP A SYSTEM TO WORK SMARTER, NOT HARDER

If you are applying to multiple graduate programs, keep in mind that each application requires several components: biographical information, essays, a curriculum vitae or CV, transcripts, letters of recommendation, writing sample, test scores, and more. It may become more difficult to keep track of all application materials if you do not have a foldering system set up to keep yourself organized. One common foldering system that Yvette has seen students use successfully over the years is setting up computer desktop folders and subfolders for each graduate program and backing them up with an external hard drive. Another option is to save everything to a cloud storage system such as Google Drive, DropBox, or Box. Assuming that you are applying to ten programs, for example, this means you will have one main "Grad School Apps" folder and within that ten sub-folders, each with the title of the university and program on it ("Boston College MSW," "CSU Northridge MSW," "UC Berkeley MSW," and "U Michigan MSW"). Inside the main "Grad School Apps" folder, you can keep a copy of your graduate school list and your general application materials. Inside each sub-folder, you store application materials that you have tailored for each program and any other information for each program. You can also create a separate checklist for each program and save it in the relevant subfolder. The key is to keep anything that is important for each application within its folder. You can even retain important email communication or website information by saving it as a PDF and adding it to the folder. The main thing to remember is to establish a system that is easy for you to use and that makes it simple for you to store and find information in the future so that you're not having to dig through multiple emails or keep using the search bar to find materials. Another important reminder is to ensure that whatever method of storing information you are using is backed up via an external hard drive or a cloud system. We do not want you to ever be in the position where you lose a document to a computer crash or to an overly complicated foldering system.

CREATING STANDARD OPERATING PROCEDURES

Establishing a foldering system may take some time, but you will more than make up for that time and even save more in the future by easily locating materials. Similarly, another time-saving strategy that will help you work on your applications in a more efficient way is the act of creating standard operating procedures. A *standard operating procedure* refers to a set of instructions that lays out the step-by-step process for carrying out a process, task, or project. An example of a standard operating procedure may look like logging into an application portal, then reviewing the site to get a sense of the layout of the site and materials needed for submission. Then on a separate document, you can type up notes that include the website URL (so that you do not have to keep searching for it in a search engine), your username and password or password hint (alternately, you can save your passwords by using a password manager website, which tend to be more secure), and any steps you have to take for this application that are unique or different from the rest. Please note that this document is separate from a checklist in that it has pre-written instructions. This could also be a place to indicate if a graduate program requires that you submit your application before they send your recommenders a link to upload their letters of recommendation. (We'll talk more about how to manage the letter of recommendation process in chapter 7). If you want to keep your standard operating procedures simple, you can type up instructions that you will follow for every program and in what order you'll complete them. Here is an example:

1. Fill out application form
2. Send GRE scores, if needed
3. Upload transcripts
4. Update and upload curriculum vitae
5. Draft, revise, edit and upload statement of purpose and/or personal statement
6. Draft, revise, edit and upload diversity statement, if required
7. Send email reminder to recommenders
8. Verify fee waiver submission or pay full application fee
9. Submit application

You get to decide in what order you'll submit your materials, but the more you can systematize the process the easier it'll be, especially if you are applying to multiple programs. You may also find that, with a standard operating procedure, the submission process becomes less difficult to navigate over time because you will know what to expect and in what order to complete requirements.

HOW TO USE TEMPLATES EFFICIENTLY

One last time-saving strategy we want to introduce is the act of creating templates for similar and repeatable tasks. A *template,* in this case, is a predefined document with a layout and text that you can modify and reuse each time you need to work on a similar task. For instance, you will notice that in this book we provide you with email templates for certain components of the application process. If you will be emailing several professors and graduate students before submitting your applications, it can be helpful to have templates that you can then tailor and modify to help you save time. Perhaps you also plan to email graduate advisors to ask them if the GRE exam is required, if the information is not available on their website. Having an email template you can use to send to multiple graduate advisors can be helpful. If you plan to reach out to graduate admissions offices to check if they have received your test scores, again, a template may come in handy. In any case, we do recommend that you spend some time tailoring emails with people's names and an explanation as to why you are reaching out to them. This extra step will ensure your messages do not come off as generic, inattentive, or rushed.

Another example of a template that you can create focuses on your application essays. If you decide to draft a general statement of purpose that you will then modify for each of your programs, you have created another template. Some applicants choose to write a longer statement of purpose that they then cut down to meet varying page and word limits per program. Sometimes applicants decide to create three essay templates to have at their disposal: a statement of purpose, a personal statement, and a hybrid to be used if a program does not ask for a personal statement. We will discuss more about how to write these application essays in chapters 5 and 6. For now, we want you to consider how you might be able to create multiple templates that you can reuse and tailor to help you save time and work smarter, not harder.

GRADUATE SCHOOL APPLICATION TIMELINE

In the following chapters, we will review the different components of your graduate school application, which will include essays (the statement of purpose, personal statement, and diversity statement), letters of recommendation, the curriculum vitae, the GRE (Graduate Record Examination), your transcripts and your grade point average or GPA, the writing sample, and other miscellaneous application materials you may be asked to submit. Before we go into detail on each application component, we are sharing a timeline to give you an idea of when you can begin working on each component. A timeline is another productivity and organizational strategy that will help you get from point A (getting started) to point B, C, or Z (accepting a grad school offer). It will also ground you in the reality of how much time you have to get work done and alert you when you are either ahead or behind with meeting deadlines. Below is an example of a PhD application timeline or calendar and examples of monthly tasks during the fall application season. A master's program timeline will look similar except that the application deadlines will be extended a few months later into winter and early spring. If you are reading this in fall or winter, do not fret. So long as the application deadlines have not passed, you still have time to apply. But depending on when you start this process, you'll need to dedicate a bit more time initially to catch up on the tasks that are included in the previous months.

While it might seem that this talk about the minutiae of graduate school applications is overstated or obvious, we want to reiterate the significance of completing the tasks. If you have a missing statement of purpose or letter of recommendation, your application will not advance, that is, the admissions committee will not review it. Some institutions will contact you about a missing letter of reference, but most won't. They just won't have the time or the system to do so. Again, staying organized and planning to submit your materials in advance will help to minimize the chances that you'll run into these setbacks.

Sample Graduate School Application Timeline

JUNE

- Decide to apply (or not) to graduate school
- Create the graduate school list
- Study for the GRE, if required

JULY

- Begin drafting the statement of purpose
- Begin drafting the personal statement
- Contact faculty and graduate students from your graduate school list
- Identify external funding opportunities

AUGUST

- Take GRE, if required
- Create and/or update your CV
- Finish first draft of the statement of purpose
- Secure three or more writers for letters of recommendation
- Follow up with faculty and graduate students from your graduate school list

SEPTEMBER

- Work on recommendation packet for letter writers
- Apply for external funding opportunities
- Register and/or log into online graduate school application portals and review criteria

- Apply for and obtain fee waivers
- Again, follow up with faculty and graduate students from your graduate school list

OCTOBER

- Finish first draft of the personal statement
- Work on the writing sample, if required
- Give recommenders packet of information
- Keep applying for external funding

NOVEMBER

- Revise and edit the writing sample, if required
- Order official transcripts
- Send GRE scores to schools, if applicable
- Begin submitting graduate school applications

DECEMBER

- Continue submitting graduate school applications
- Send reminder emails to letter of recommendation writers
- Ensure transcripts and/or GRE scores have been delivered or sent before winter holidays

JANUARY

- Finish applying to graduate programs
- Fill out FAFSA (Free Application for Federal Student Aid)

- Review MA/PhD admissions timeline
- Begin receiving admissions notifications
- Begin preparing for interviews and open houses or preview days

FEBRUARY

- Continue receiving admissions notifications
- Attend interviews and open houses

MARCH

- Continue attending interviews and open houses
- Create a graduate school budget
- Negotiate funding offers
- Meet with faculty and graduate students

APRIL

- Decide on graduate school and sign registration forms
- Plan for the transition to graduate school

MAY

- Look into housing options and plan for the move
- Ask your department when you should expect to receive your first funding payment
- Secure a summer job to save for the move
- Take care of yourself and celebrate!

THE GRADUATE SCHOOL LIST

Creating a graduate school list takes time and effort. The goal is to develop a list of schools that are best suited for you and your career goals. Be sure to have a strategy. While some students will choose the top ten programs in their field and call it a day, we do not recommend that approach. Yes, a program's ranking and graduate success rate plays a role in your decision to apply, but an even more significant considera-tion is ensuring that you're applying to programs that are a good "fit" or match. By fit we mean institutions that have the best resources and opportunities for you. If your goals and the program's goals do not align, or if a program has no faculty member who is well suited to advise you, we recommend giving that place a second thought. Cer-tainly, it is not always possible to know what you're getting yourself into in terms of the cultural norms or climate (as it relates to race, eth-nicity, sexuality, etc.), as institutions and individuals are often good at feigning a collegial environment when, in reality, it is in short supply. If you do get admitted to a program you find does not meet your needs, you are within your rights to decline the offer or, if you do enroll and then encounter an inhospitable and hostile environment, you can cer-tainly create an exit strategy with the assistance of a femtor or mentor. The graduate school list prepares you for what to expect in a program and as such we recommend, again, taking the time to build it and update it frequently.

Typically, the graduate school list looks like a spreadsheet you create with a list of programs and some critical information about them. We recommend including the following points in separate columns:

- Application deadline
- Name of the program
- What type of program it is (postbacc, master's, PhD, etc.)
- Names of professors you want to work with (2 to 3 per program)

- Location (city and state)
- Application opening date (if available)
- Application materials required (statement of purpose, personal statement, diversity statement, CV, writing sample, recommendation letters, etc.)
- Graduate advisor and faculty advisor contact information
- Link to application portal (save your passwords)
- Application fee
- Fee waiver application deadline, if applicable

If you are just getting started, you are probably staring at a blank document—we recommend an Excel or Google sheet—with many empty columns. Just know that the graduate school list, however daunting or intimidating, is an excellent tool to help you get started. The list doesn't have to include all the points of information we mentioned, especially if it is overwhelming, but it should include critical components that will be useful for you to access throughout the application period. Some students create separate sheets, one with all the columns we mentioned above and another smaller sheet that only has the names of the programs and their due dates. Yvette has even seen a student who included pictures for every professor they wanted to work with. It helped them put faces to names, which facilitated their ability to remember the professors when they met them. Once you have the template, you can get started identifying programs using a few strategies we suggest below. These will help you determine if the programs are right for you. The following are strategies for creating a grad school list:

Strategy #1

If you are a current or former student who has conducted research, take a look at the scholars who keep coming up in your work. Who are they? Where are they currently working? Where have they worked prior to this institution? Where did they receive their training and complete their graduate work? Who was their advisor? Who are their students? This information can give you an indication of the potential programs and universities to look into because this person has experience conducting research in your area(s) of interest and likely also has ties to individuals doing work that you'd be interested in as well.

Strategy #2

Another strategy to consider is to consult with your own network. Reach out to your femtors, mentors, faculty, and graduate students that you know in your field or the field for which you are applying. Similarly, conduct informational interviews with people who hold your dream job or have pursued your ideal career. Ask them for suggestions for programs that you can further explore. It's even better if they can offer a referral or connect you with a colleague who you can communicate with or meet to learn more about the program.

Strategy #3

A popular strategy, which isn't always the most effective or efficient, is to take a look at the *US News and World Report* rankings for "Best Graduate Schools" in your field and identify the top ten to twenty programs, then search their faculty websites to find individuals of interest. We say this is neither effective nor efficient because it leaves out many other programs with faculty who might be a better match for you. The rankings are also not focused on your needs but are based on *selectivity*— that is, how many applications were accepted from among those who applied. The smaller the figure, the more prestigious the institution, which is what colleges and universities look to achieve. Using the report can also be tedious, as it involves reviewing many websites and faculty directory pages in the hope that you find a place that is right for you. Yvette also doesn't encourage students to apply only to top programs in their field. Instead, she asks that they consider applying to a range of programs: top tier, mid-tier, and programs that may not be top-ranked but can offer the right mentorship, training, and financial support.

Strategy #4

Consider, too, the location and/or distance of the institution from your current residence, as it is important not only for your professional but also your personal needs. Many nontraditional students have familial or other obligations that may keep them tied to one location or region and limit the number of programs for which they apply. If this is the case, it is critical to ensure that the programs you do apply for are a good fit. And again, it's more of a reason to ensure you tailor your application essays to prove that you have done your research and are a great candidate. For some, the location is essential since they want to ensure they can live in the area for two to eight years. We have femtored countless students in California who have moved to the East Coast for graduate school and, in each case, they considered how the stark differences in weather—from sunny and warm to overcast and cold—would impact their ability to thrive academically. Some of them chose to visit the schools in advance, while others sought advice from other Californians who had moved to similar locales. Sometimes students will avoid a region, state, or city altogether for feelings of insecurity or a lack of safety due to the demographics or political climate. Again, ensure a program is a good match for you but also know that you can live safely and happily in that location, at least during the time you need to be on campus. Better to know this now than later.

Strategy #5

A final and particularly necessary step to narrow down and finalize your graduate school list is to contact faculty and graduate students in programs of interest. We cannot stress this enough. As we know from experience, you won't always find the most recent information online, for many have not updated their website or websites in a year or more and you could be missing out on their latest research. You might learn, for instance, that they are on sabbatical or chairing the department, both of which impact the nature of their faculty-student relationships. You might also learn from a conversation with them about funding opportunities, job placements, and the culture of the department. Or, they might speak about the larger relationship between the campus and local community, aka "town and gown" relations. Finally, you can ask them about where they see themselves as well as the program and/or department in the near and distant future so that you have an idea of what's in store once you advance in your education. Certainly, they will want to make a good impression, but some might be more candid than you might think.

Another reason to get in touch with the faculty is to determine, to the best of your ability, what kind of rapport you have with the proposed advisor. Might they become a femtor or mentor as well as an advisor to you? They don't have to be both an advisor and a trusted guide, but it does help. It is important for you to determine if this is the kind of person with whom you can envision yourself having a long term happy and productive professional relationship. If you're applying to a master's program, you're going to engage this person for the next two to three years. If it's a doctoral program, you will be working with them for four to eight years. And it is likely going to be longer, assuming this person is going to continue to write letters of recommendation for you as you move on in your career. That same person might also continue to serve as a reference for you as you go on to apply for jobs in industry, government, or education outside of academia. Think about that. It is key that you can picture yourself working with this person for a while, that you enjoy their mentoring or advising style, and that you get along with each other. You won't begin to know this unless you have a conversation with them and preferably with several of their students, which we discuss below.[1]

It is equally important to contact faculty because of the high probability that they will have a say in the admissions process and impact whether you are admitted or not. This is very different from applying to college, where a centralized admissions office makes nearly all decisions. For graduate school, especially for a research degree like the PhD, most decisions come from the department or program. Miroslava, working in a department that admits graduate students, has seen that almost all faculty play some role in the admissions process, as they are ultimately responsible for admitted students they have agreed to advise or sponsor. As such, a positive impression of you will translate into a strong recommendation for your admission. Given the increased attention and use of holistic review, where each component of your application receives close attention and consideration, a faculty member's vote of confidence and willingness to take you on is more than half the battle for your application to move forward. If the match is not great or the timing is wrong, the meeting has still not gone to waste, as you can use it as an opportunity for a referral or referrals to faculty who are available to you and a great match for your interests and needs. If anything, learning that the program and/or faculty is not a good fit for you or your research is in your best interest, as you will avoid wasting time, money, and mental resources thinking about that application.

We understand, however, how intimidating it may feel to reach out to faculty, especially if it is someone you have never met, or if it is someone with a national or international reputation. You do not have to have a long list of programs to get started with contacting these individuals. Three to four programs is fine to start, although we recommend applying to anywhere from five to eight or maybe even up to twelve programs total so that you are in the position to have options. When you are considering reaching out to faculty, take a look at the program's website (or their personal site) for their publications and, if you can, try to read at least one of their recent articles so that you get a sense of their background and expertise before you meet and/or talk with them. At that point, you are ready to contact them.

To help you get started with drafting an email, here is a sample script. We recommend you modify it to ensure that you are using *your* words:

CONTACTING PROFESSORS: EMAIL TEMPLATE

SUBJECT LINE: Meeting with a Prospective **[name of university and program]** Applicant

Hi/Hello/Dear Dr./Professor **[last name]**,

My name is **[your first name]** and I am a **[describe where you are academically—for example, rising senior at X University; recent graduate of Y University]**. I have participated in **[describe research experience]** and plan to attend graduate school in **[name of field]**, with a focus on **[describe your research area(s)]**.

In **[the research I conducted for my undergraduate thesis, a class taught by Professor X, while I was working on Y topic]**, I read your work on **[describe their current research, article, book]** and I found it very useful for my own future research. For graduate school, I am interested in exploring **[name your topic/question]**.

I am emailing to inquire whether you are currently accepting graduate students. If you are, would you be willing to meet with me for a brief **[call, Zoom meeting, in-person meeting]**? I understand you may be very busy at this time. However, I would very much like to learn more about your work, your department, and any other insights you may offer. I am available on **[include days and times]**. Thank you for your time. Best,/Sincerely,/Warm regards,

[your full name]

If you reach out to professors and you do not hear back from them, do not worry. Professors are busy and often have full email inboxes or sometimes don't check email frequently. After a week or two, you can send them a reminder email and forward them your last message. If you still do not hear back, consider reaching out to another faculty member in that department. Please note that you want to be able to identify at least two professors you can work with for each program. This is to ensure that you are not "putting all your eggs in one basket" in case the one person you wanted to work with changes institutions, retires, is unable to take on new students, or turns out not to be as good of a match as you'd hoped.

Let's say you reach out to professors and they do respond but they are not currently accepting students. Now what? In this case, we recommend you ask them to refer you to someone else. They might direct you to another colleague in their department or they might mention other programs for you to consider that were not already on your list. Don't think that you are spinning your wheels. This is progress because it is getting you one step closer to meeting with the professors who are taking students and are in departments that are a good fit for your interests and needs. You don't want to apply only to have your application rejected automatically. Eventually, if you meet with enough people, you'll have a better sense of which programs to keep, which to remove, and which new ones to add so that you can finalize your list and apply to these programs.

Reaching out and setting up the meeting is only half the battle. Now comes the tough part—developing an engaging conversation where you communicate your interests, curiosity, and passion for the research. You do this by forming questions that are specific to the faculty member or individual with whom you're meeting. The queries should also be pertinent to the program as well as the institution and larger setting. To help you develop your own questions, we have provided a list for you to get started. Keep in mind that this is not an exhaustive list. When in doubt, consult a trusted femtor or mentor for guidance, as they are likely to understand your needs better than others.

Questions to Ask Faculty

- I was really interested by your take on [**X topic**] in [**journal article**]. How did you come to write about that?

- How does the program pair students with a faculty advisor? Do you select advisees? How does it usually work?

- What do you value most about the work you do and why?

- When you work with students as an advisor, what is your approach to advising? Is your approach to mentoring similar?

- What do you value in students? What characteristics do you look for in students?

- What is the department's culture like? What is the program's relationship to the wider department, university, and local community?

- What type of funding is available to graduate students in this program? How do some of your graduate students fund their education?

- How long does it typically take for students to graduate?

- What types of jobs are recent graduates getting? What are some career outcomes I might expect from this program?

- Are you accepting any students this year? If not, might you suggest I reach out to anyone?

Please keep in mind that the professors you meet will not have all the answers to your questions or may not have much time to offer. Assuming that your meeting will last about fifteen to thirty minutes, what are the most pressing questions for you? What is the outcome you want from this meeting? Do you want to get to know them more as a person or as a scholar? Do you want to get to know what they value and what they plan to do in the next five and ten years? Do you want to know what they're like as an advisor and what they look for in their students?

Do you want to learn more about the program, its culture, and the academic and financial support provided to students? Is it essential for you to learn from them about career outcomes from recent alumni or from their recent advisees? Or, is the purpose of your meeting to simply find out if they're accepting students? No matter the reason, determine your outcome and prioritize your questions accordingly. When in doubt, allow the conversation to naturally play its course and make sure to get your top two to three questions answered before your meeting ends.

We understand that it can be quite time-consuming and overwhelming to reach out to professors, review their work, prepare questions, and meet with them. But don't let this hold you back. Yvette has witnessed students go from being afraid to reaching out to feeling confident about their applications in a relatively brief span. I've seen them, too, become enthusiastic to have developed good rapport with the people they meet. Some students have shared with me how they panicked that they would get quizzed on their knowledge and be outed as a fraud. They feared, too, that the person would meet them and automatically reject them for making a poor impression. In most cases, this did not happen. Instead, the student was in the position to interview the professors to gauge whether they could see themselves working with them for the next two to eight years.

Another proven strategy to help you hone in on your graduate school list is to reach out and make time to meet with current graduate students in the programs. It can be useful to contact graduate students because it is more likely that they will give transparent and current advice on the process of applying, how they feel about the program, and what it's like working with their advisor. They may also share more about their research experience, insights on the local area and community, funding opportunities, the reasons for choosing their current program, and what they wish they had known before enrolling. While graduate students, like faculty, will have their own perspectives about the graduate program, don't dismiss their advice and/or words of warning. They may provide much-needed information you won't be able to obtain elsewhere. How do you find graduate students and reach out to them, you might ask? Unlike professors, who have faculty directory pages on departmental websites, graduate students do not always have their contact information publicly available. If this is the case, you can send an email to the graduate advisor and have them forward it to their graduate student email listserv or more specifically (for example, to students of your prospective advisor, or to students that share one or more aspects of your identity). Again, if you're nervous to reach out to graduate students or a graduate advisor and are struggling to find the words to draft an email, see a sample template below for you to modify and use.

CONTACTING GRADUATE STUDENTS EMAIL TEMPLATE

SUBJECT LINE: Meeting with a Prospective [**name of university and program**] Applicant

Hi/Hello/Dear [**first name**],

My name is [**your first name**] and I am a [**describe where you are academically: rising senior at X University; recent graduate of Y University; been employed in industry for the last five years**]. I am looking to apply to [**name of university and program**] and was hoping to be in touch with a graduate student like you to learn more about the program and your experience in it.

I received your contact information from [**name of professor, staff member, and grad student who referred you, or mention the departmental website**] and was hoping to meet you given your experience with/as [**name what you have in common: potential advisor, research interests, where you're from, identity markers, etc**]. I understand you may be very busy; however, I was hoping you might be able to make time for a brief meeting over [**the phone, Zoom, in-person**]? I am available on [**days and times**]. I look forward to hearing from you.

Thank you,/Sincerely,/Warm regards,

[**your full name**]

Once you start to hear back from graduate students who are willing to meet with you to share about their experience in a graduate program of interest, you may be wondering what questions to ask them and how they might differ from those you ask the professors. Here are some sample questions to help you get started.

Questions to Ask Graduate Students

RESEARCH

- What's it like to work with your advisor?
- Are first-year graduate students paired up with a faculty advisor right away? If not, when and how?
- What does a graduate seminar look like? What is the role of the students?
- What type of courses are offered in this program?
- What are the expectations for writing and reading?
- What is the expected and actual time-to-degree, or number of years it takes for a student to graduate?
- Is this program retaining their students (retention rates)? Is this program losing many students (attrition rates)?
- What types of relationships does the department have with alumni, if any?

PERSONAL AND FUNDING

- How does it feel like to be a graduate student here? Are you happy with your decision to come here?
- What is the campus climate (in terms of race, ethnicity, gender, sexuality, dis/ability, etc.)?
- Where do graduate students live? Is it affordable here?

- Is graduate student housing available? Is there family housing? Is it subsidized?

- Do students live close to campus? Do they commute? How long is the commute?

- How do you like your healthcare? What does your healthcare cover (vision, dental, mental health services)?

- Are you comfortable with your funding?

- When and how often do students TA in this department?

COMMUNITY

- What is the relationship between the department and the surrounding community?

- What is the surrounding community like? Demographics? Class? Politics?

- What do graduate students do for fun on this campus?

- What are the graduate organizations like?

- Do you have a graduate student union? Is it active?

- Where would I find affinity groups, that is, groups focused on, for instance, racial, ethnic, and gender identity or identities?

Let's take some time to unpack these questions a bit more. You want to ask about what it's like working with the advisor you're interested in, assuming this person works with the same person. This is important since you will be maintaining a professional relationship with this person for quite a while, at the very least for the full duration of your graduate program. Is their advisor hands-on or hands-off? And does that match the mentorship support you need? Is this advisor approachable and easy to talk to, or cold and curt? And does their demeanor work well for you based on your personality traits? More general questions include: what is the process for selecting an advisor? Do you go in with an advisor in mind or select them later on? Some students would prefer to enter a program where they get to work with a variety of professors or rotate labs before selecting an advisor, while others would prefer to know right away with whom they will work. Other queries to consider include, what do seminars look like and are students excited about the course offerings? In some programs the course offerings are large while in others they're small and you may be required to take courses outside of your department. Are students graduating "on time" or are they taking longer than expected due to lack of funding, too many teaching obligations, or too little guidance? Find out what the common reasons are for people taking longer than expected. Does the department bring back alumni and have a positive relationship with them? If they don't bring back alumni, why not?

You might also pose personal and community-based questions that help you envision your life as a graduate student at that location or place. What is it like living on a graduate student stipend? Some programs are in lower cost of living areas but have similar stipends as programs in high cost of living cities. What are the implications of this for your budget and lifestyle? Will you need to take on a part-time job to make ends meet? Where do students live? Do most students live close by or do most students commute? And are you willing to commute? What are the demographics of the area? Will you find a community based on your race, ethnicity, gender, sexuality, and other identities important to you? Is this a big city or a smaller college town? How will you get around? Will you be able to socialize or feel isolated in this area? Are you satisfied with the quality of healthcare you are receiving? Healthcare is not the same in all programs and the cost is different too. What about childcare? Does the department and/or campus provide support for graduate students with a child or children? If so, what does that look like? Are students expected to teach and if so, to what extent? Some programs may expect you to teach every year, some may require you to teach two or three years, while others may not provide you with any teaching opportunities.

As you can see, you could ask a graduate student many more questions about their experience in the program and they can provide you with valuable information that you would not otherwise find on a departmental website or by doing your own online research. An added benefit of reaching out to graduate students is that sometimes they might be generous enough to offer to share their own application materials with you or to offer to review your own application essays. Nevertheless, it is valuable to talk to as many people as you have the capacity for because each individual will have a different experience in a program and the more information you have, the better informed you will be. Ultimately, you want to make the decision that is best for you.

As you are finalizing your graduate school list, here are some other questions we recommend you consider asking yourself to help you feel more confident in your decision to apply to the programs that remain on your list.

QUESTIONS TO ASK YOURSELF BEFORE APPLYING

- What are my personal values and goals and is this program aligned with them?
- Can I imagine working with this individual as my advisor for the next four to eight or more years?
- What training is provided? Will I be trained for the career of my choice in this program?
- What professional skills do I want to learn and can I gain them in this program?
- Would I thrive in this program, campus, and city?
- What is the intellectual and campus climate like? Is it a collegial and supportive environment or cold and competitive?
- What is the weather like here year-round? Will the weather here have an impact on my ability to thrive?

- Will I feel comfortable, safe, and/or secure living in this area? Why or why not?
- What are my graduate school dealbreakers? What can I not compromise on?
- Are there any red flags or unsettling details? What are they and how do they impact my decision to enroll or not?

When Yvette applied to graduate school, no one ever asked about her values. If you are unsure of yours, do a quick online search of "personal values" or "core values" and you'll find a long list of them, including free assessments. See what resonates with you. What if you value teamwork? Does this program provide opportunities to collaborate and work in a group setting? What if you value diversity and equity? Does this program reflect the kind of diversity and equity you are seeking? Do you value recognition? And, if so, is this program recognized or are graduates in this program recognized in ways that will serve your needs?

Another thing neither of us had considered deeply when applying to graduate school was the importance of the advisor-advisee relationship. We had not realized that one could be working with an advisor—one person alone—for two to eight years, and even longer, depending on how long you maintain contact after graduating. Given the investment of your time and life, you need to talk and meet with prospective faculty advisors and ask yourself if you can imagine yourself working with them for this extended period of time. Yvette, for example, had not met her advisor prior to starting and instead had only read their published work, which is a poor indicator of a successful working relationship. Indeed, it is difficult to get a sense of what it would be like to work with someone solely from their research, writing, and presence online. Ultimately, Yvette's first advisor was not a good fit and she ended up switching advisors. Had she done more of this early research, she might have been able to avoid that situation altogether.

The last thing we want to cover are dealbreakers, that is, absolutely "must haves." Dealbreakers come in many shapes and forms and are not the same for everyone. Here are a few examples that some first-generation, low-income, and/or nontraditional Students of Color may have:

Potential Graduate School List Dealbreakers

- Little to no funding
- Little to no racial, ethnic, gender, etc., diversity among students and faculty
- The preferred advisor is too hands off and/or unavailable
- Poor job placement of recent graduates
- Bad relationships between faculty and/or public scandals
- Students taking longer than expected to graduate
- Students leaving the program or transferring departments

This is not an exhaustive list of dealbreakers and red flags. Again, identify your own. Some individuals might be applying to programs where it is expected that they will pay for the program out of pocket (such as professional master's programs). Some fields are well known for a lack of diversity when it comes to race, gender, sexuality, and so on. Some folks work well with hands-off advisors. And, most departments have some sort of internal politics that do not always directly impact a student's experience in their program. These may not scare you away, especially if your eyes are wide open.

Finally, you may have other dealbreakers that are specific to your identity and circumstances. Location might be what leads you to walk away, especially if the campus is known to be a commuter campus and you want to avoid driving or taking the train or bus. Or, perhaps the availability of full funding is non-negotiable, particularly if you're on your own, or are an undocumented or disabled student with limited monetary support and many financial responsibilities. Perhaps your dealbreaker is ensuring you have good quality healthcare and access to a wide range of specialists due to a medical condition or disability. Another may be ensuring that the program or institution is in close proximity to communities of color and to resources for parents, including schools, family housing, family healthcare plans, and childcare programs. Whatever it might be, figure it out and take it into consideration when making your decisions.

We know we've covered a lot in this chapter and know that it is overwhelming for prospective graduate students to think about what is needed to prepare before you even begin applying to graduate school. You can, however, make it manageable by focusing on the different components of the process and, more importantly as we've emphasized in this chapter, by getting organized. We therefore provided a number of tools and techniques as well as tips and tricks to make the process smoother and easier for you. Certainly, not all of them will work for everyone, nor have we covered all of them that are available to you. Rather, we have offered a sample of the kinds of approaches that have worked for us and our students. Find one that works for you.

Equally important to getting organized is creating your application timeline as well as graduate school list so that you stay on top of deadlines and requirements. As you have seen, the application process has many components and no one person can keep it all "in their head." Take time to tailor your graduate school list and to ensure that those schools are not only viable but also a good fit or match for your professional and personal needs. To demystify those lists, we have provided sample elements of what goes into them. Find ones that work best for you. A key component in forming that list that you don't want to miss is contacting prospective faculty advisors and current graduate students who can provide you with many more insights on the programs as well as the larger campus and community environments. To help you do that, we have provided sample emails and templates.

Our final piece of advice is, again, not to let the process overwhelm you. Break it down into bite-sized pieces, organize the tasks in a realistic timeline akin to what we've described here, and keep moving forward towards your goal. To help you see that the process is not insurmountable or beyond your reach, we provide detailed insights and more samples from the key components of the application process—the statement of purpose, personal statement, and diversity statements—in the next two chapters. With these on hand, you will be on your way to crafting a strong application that speaks to your strengths, abilities, and promise as a graduate student.

KEY TAKEAWAYS

- Time management tools, timeblocking, monotasking, and accountability methods: we have offered a number of different time-, task-, and project-management tools to help you get organized, reduce overwhelm, and set yourself up for success.

- We also provided you with a graduate school application timeline.

- And, we shared common and effective strategies for creating a graduate school list.

- With efficiency in mind, we presented sample email templates as well, and questions to ask when reaching out to prospective faculty and graduate students.

- To help you refine your graduate school list, we outlined a short list of dealbreakers and red flags to consider before making your decision.

5

THE STATEMENT OF
PURPOSE

||||||||||||||||||||||||||||||||||||||||||||||||||||||||||||||||||||||||||||||||||||||||||||||||||||||||||||||||||||||||||||||||||||||||||||||||||||||||||||||||||||||||||||||||||||||||||||||||||

WHEN APPLYING TO GRADUATE SCHOOL, you must remember that graduate admissions committees have little wiggle room in terms of how many students they can and will admit. Shrinking budgets, especially in the humanities, demands for "highly competitive" students, and *implicit bias,* that is, preconceived notions of an individual's ability based on group stereotypes, often results in low admissions rates, especially for first-generation, low-income, and/or nontraditional Students of Color. Fortunately, graduate admissions committees are beginning to practice *holistic review,* taking into account all aspects of the applicant's lived experiences and how that contributes to their preparedness and overall fit for the program. This is where the statement of purpose, personal statement, and diversity statement allow you to convey your strengths, experience, and commitment to higher education and beyond. Generally speaking, the *statement of purpose*—the focus of this chapter—conveys your academic, research, and career interests and goals and how they align with the program, while the *personal statement* centers on how your background and experiences have shaped or influenced those interests and goals. The *diversity statement,* in contrast, demonstrates how your personal background as well as your academic, research, career interests have come together to contribute to diversifying higher education and academia more generally. Given the significance of this portion of the graduate application, let's dive deeply into the statement of purpose to demystify its goals and content. At the end of the chapter, you'll have the opportunity to see some real-world examples. We will then say much more about personal and diversity statements in chapter 6.

PARTS OF THE STATEMENT OF PURPOSE

The statement of purpose is typically given the most attention and weight in evaluating your application, as it demonstrates your potential as a graduate student and your fit with the program. As such, we recommend you spend the most time on this portion. Plan to use all the space that the programs allow or have provided, for they will expect you to take full advantage of the opportunity to communicate your strengths and assets and how they shape your interests and align with the program. The statement normally consists of five components: introduction, previous research experience, proposed research, match with the program, and conclusion.

Introduction

The statement of purpose opens with a one-paragraph introduction where you lay out your academic trajectory, talking specifically about your research interests and reasons for choosing to pursue the specific field and program and/or campus. In this section, work to provide an understanding of the academic qualities that make you stand out as a candidate for graduate study. As such, you will want to focus on your intellectual curiosity and ambitions as well as your professional and personal goals, which are often interconnected. Schools especially want to see, hear, and feel the passion you bring. To catch their attention from the beginning, open the essay with a "hook" or bold statement about what you or your research brings to the field or what attracts you to the work. Is it the methodology or data you'll use? Is it the time spent in the lab, field, or archive? Or is it the pursuit of finding answers to life-long questions you've had but have been unable to answer on your own? If you've decided to switch fields, from what you studied as an undergraduate to what you plan to pursue in graduate school, explain why you did so. Did you make the move because, after ten years of being out of school, you decided to return to study your secret passion for French literature, which you gave up for a practical career in data management? Or, is it due to your need to improve your ethnographic research skills in order to enhance your resume as a writer? Be honest, creative, and engaging. Readers will see through disingenuous writing. If the application calls for only a statement of purpose and no personal or diversity statement, you will need to include more of your lived experiences in the essay and may choose to highlight something related in the introduction to the statement of purpose. Don't fret, too, if you struggle to come up with a compelling opening. It normally takes time to land on one that works well. Most people will tell you that it takes multiple revisions—and another set of eyes—to develop an engaging as well as polished statement.

Research Experience

The next section of the statement of purpose focuses on your research experience and generally is one or two paragraphs in length. This part of the essay tells the reader that you are prepared, qualified, and ready to take on graduate-level work at their institution. It speaks specifically to the training and tools you have acquired and demonstrates not that you have already perfected the skills necessary to succeed, but that you have the ability and desire to learn, adapt, and innovate as a student researcher, making you an exciting and desired prospect. Specifically, you want to discuss two to three research projects that, taken together, say something about the evolution or growth of your training and preparedness for graduate-level research in a specific field. If your training is in the same area of proposed graduate study, even better, as you can demonstrate preliminary knowledge or familiarity with relevant methodologies and/or approaches. If you've participated in formal programs such as the McNair Scholars Program, Mellon Mays Undergraduate Fellowship, or a summer program or honors course you completed as an undergraduate, be sure to talk about what you learned, produced, and/or discovered through your research. Don't just name drop or rattle off a list of studies, however. Rather, spend quality time discussing the project by providing the title as well as describing the nature of the problem or question you sought to answer, the methods and sources of information you chose to include and why, and, finally, your conclusions. If applicable, you should also state if you had the opportunity to present or publish your work in a formal setting, such as in a journal, or via an oral and/or a poster presentation at a conference, on your campus, or elsewhere. Be sure to include any experiences with showcasing your work in public-facing venues, such as in an online news site or a community news media outlet.

If you have been out of school for a while and did not participate in any formal research program or training, consider the work that you've been doing in the last five to ten years. Have you had roles and responsibilities that require you to investigate and find solutions to problems or issues? If so, what kinds of resources (websites, software, libraries, experts, community members, and so on) have you turned to and what have you been able to deduce from your work? While you don't want to stretch the truth or claim expertise with a methodology usually found in academic settings, you can say and show that you have an inquisitive mind and are responsive and resourceful. Importantly, you want to demonstrate that you have the capacity and willingness to be advised by faculty that may be younger than you, but also that you have real-world skills and insights to contribute. Lastly, don't forget to point out any personal and professional strengths you've developed over the course of your lifetime. While you may not have had formal training in leadership development, for instance, you may be resilient, that is, able to bounce back from setbacks, resourceful, and skilled at following through on significant projects. Dig deep into your family and community history experiences to draw out those organic skills you've perfected over the years. To help you identify those skills or strengths that resonate, we've provided a list:

- Analytical skills (interprets/perceives patterns, trends, and/or main ideas)
- Writing skills (writes clearly, persuasively, and engagingly)
- Communication skills (speaks clearly, persuasively, and engagingly)
- Interpersonal and "people skills" (listener, patient, empathetic, discreet)
- Conflict resolution skills (helps resolve issues and brings people together)
- Works well under pressure (self-motivated, takes initiative)
- Problem solving skills (knows how to find answers to issues or questions)
- Leadership (organizes, facilitates, and leads teams)
- Team player (works well in groups, keeps collective efforts and goals in mind)
- Overcoming adversity (such as financial, family, health, and/or mental health issues)

- Language skills (bilingual, trilingual, native speaker)
- Cultural broker (ability to translate and/or mediate between and among cultures)
- Resilient (weathers difficulties and bounces back from challenges)
- Project management (execute assignments or tasks from beginning to end)

Future or Proposed Research

Once you have communicated your previous experience, you will want to transition into a discussion of the kind of research you hope to pursue in graduate school. This part of the essay, which should consist of one to two paragraphs, should flow naturally, particularly if you're moving smoothly from undergraduate or work experience into a similar field of graduate study. We know, however, this is not often the case for first-generation, low-income, and/or nontraditional Students of Color. If you're shifting from one area of research to another that is quite different, you need to speak with some knowledge about the field you wish to study and where you see yourself in that specialty. This portion of the essay is for you to demonstrate your familiarity and fluency in your chosen discipline. You do that by mentioning key texts, theories, or arguments you wish to engage or significant contributions or innovations you hope to make or produce. You also do that by talking about your proposed research project in as much detail as possible without communicating that you've already completed the work or have all the answers. You will want to describe the topic of interest, the questions or issues you hope to address, the arguments and/or literature you wish to engage, and, importantly, the sources or data you plan to investigate. You might also want to add any kind of hypothesis or working notion of what you expect to find and what you plan to do with the results. Finally, don't think that because you have committed your research interests to paper, you will be obligated to stick with the proposed research. Rather, admissions committees use the statement to evaluate a candidate's preparedness and ability to articulate a proposed area of study. We believe graduate school is a time for discovery and exploration. Communicate that you plan to use that opportunity wisely.

"Fit"

Next, you will want to discuss how and why you are a good fit or an ideal match for the program and how and why the program is a good place for you. Using your research interests and experiences as a point of departure, you want to make a case for why the program, department, campus, and/or local community or region is the perfect home for your work. For that, you'll need to know the research specialty of two or three key faculty with whom you wish to work and with whom, presumably, you have already been in contact. (See chapter 4 for whys and hows on this point.) Discuss their work briefly and connect it to your own interests, highlighting the rationale for the working relationships. In preparing for this portion of the essay, you will also want to read an article or two or read a book review or two related to the faculty members in question and, if it's appropriate, refer to them. Consider, too, pointing out what your research interests will bring to the program. If your work aligns with a particular niche or specialty, highlight how your work will enrich the research of a newly established center, for instance. Don't go overboard in trying to convince them they need you. Rather, simply point out the contributions your work brings to the program.

Mention, too, other reasons for choosing the program. It might be its interdisciplinary nature, which makes sense for your research and career aspirations. Or it might be the library holdings, special collections, or media labs that serve your research needs as well. To discuss these topics with some confidence, be sure to investigate the profile and strengths of the program and campus as well as the community and region in which it is situated. Remember, whatever you choose to highlight, make an argument for why it connects to and enhances your research and how it, in turns, complements the institution.

Conclusion

Finally, you will want to conclude by describing your long-term academic and professional goals. This might include a tenure-track assistant professor position or it might not. The state of the academic job market has grown so unpredictable and weak that most admissions committees will not reject you for your honesty in saying that you want to be a researcher but not necessarily within academia. You might mention your interests in the public or private nonprofit sector, including government, health care, or other similar areas. If you know where your interests lie, talk about the state of your chosen field and suggest where you think it might be by the time you hope to graduate. You may also want to conclude by returning to a point you raised in the introduction—perhaps about your time away from academia and what it means to be able to return—as a way of bringing your statement full circle. Remember, you want to keep the tone upbeat and remind them of your strengths and skills, your research interests, why you and your work are a great fit for the program, and why the program is right for you.

PRE-WRITING TIPS FOR THE STATEMENT OF PURPOSE

As much as we know that you want to get started—because we've been telling you to get started—you need to accomplish a few key tasks before writing the statement of purpose. First, pull up the prompts for the statement of purpose for each of the programs of interest, as some may have different requirements or ask different questions. You want to make sure that your response addresses directly the entirety of the prompt and speaks specifically to that program. And do not assume you will write a single statement of purpose for all your applications. You need to tailor them to the specifics of the program: changing the names of faculty and institutions, fields of study if relevant, points about "fit," and perhaps shortening or lengthening them. In special cases, you might need to write new ones altogether. Again, follow the instructions and pay attention to details. If you're unsure or it is not clear, have someone else you trust read the prompt and explain it to you in their own terms. Next, pay attention to technical requirements, such as word or page count limit, font type or size, and single or double spacing. If no word or page count is indicated, we generally recommend contacting the graduate staff advisor or sticking to a two-page single- or double-spaced essay using a twelve point font, preferably Times New Roman. As standard practice, use a one-inch margin as well.

If you have been out of school for a while and don't know where to begin, we suggest you start by brainstorming, as we often do, by listing the reasons why you wish to pursue graduate work. Consider what motivates you to want to attend graduate school generally and the specific programs you have identified specifically. Are you interested in meeting and collaborating with a racially and ethnically diverse group of faculty and graduate students? Do you want a program that not only encourages interdisciplinarity but also provides the tools and training for that kind of work? Does the program prepare students for the kind of career that you desire? Look up the job placement of recent alumni and make sure your goals align with theirs. You can also go on LinkedIn, the professional networking website, and look up your program of choice to see what jobs its graduates currently have. In explaining how and why you became interested in the field, you might also discuss a formative event or influence that inspired you. Was it a school field trip or a teacher that introduced you to a subject? Or was it a beloved grandmother or cousin who shaped your knowledge? If you have an understanding of the arguments and approaches in the field you wish to pursue, you might also point to the specific quality that motivates you. Is it the methodology, that is, the nature of the field work, lab work, or investigations? Is it the sources, that is, the study of ancient texts or artifacts? Or, is it your desire to make a contribution to a larger argument or to revise and update a longstanding theory or belief about a particular social movement or phenomenon? Whatever your motivations, write them down to figure them out. We believe that seeing them written down—on paper or a digital screen—is the first step in identifying your passions and professional and personal goals.

To assist you with writing about your research experience, we suggest that you develop a list of the skills you have acquired that have prepared you for graduate school (see above for suggestions). Consider your training in educational, professional, and community settings and the tools you have gained and refined in those spaces. They may include writing, reading, speaking, and/or performing. They may also include the ability to analyze, quantify, synthesize, and/or organize information. Think about the interpersonal skills you have mastered, too. Identify the moments when you worked collaboratively and/or took leadership on a project and the process you developed as well as what you accomplished as a team and as an individual. Other experiences to note: Did you work as a research assistant or did you perform a job that required heavy research skills? Did you participate in any summer research programs? Did you take relevant courses or learn specific software? Did you present at a professional conference or meeting? Equally effective is putting down on paper the challenges and adversity you have faced and overcome throughout your life. We don't suggest revealing anything that makes you uncomfortable or shines a light on an aspect of your life you would rather keep private. But what you do want to mention is what you have learned from those experiences and how they have transformed you and your perspectives, particularly as they apply in academia.

Using the list of attributes and experiences you have created, select three or four you want to highlight for the essay and develop the most significant ones into a narrative that explains the reasoning for your proposed area of study and speaks to your skills. Remember, you want your statement to set you apart from other applicants, which is no easy task. To do that, use specific language, using examples whenever possible, that illustrate your strengths and perspectives. Avoid terms that can apply to any applicant. You want the admissions committee to remember you as much as possible. You want to convey that you are prepared, are an excellent fit, and bring a fresh perspective to the program and academia more broadly. If you have all those elements, you are on the right path.

The reality is that, like many of us, you probably will struggle with writing the statement of purpose. Some will face the impostor phenomenon, "feeling like a fake," while others will confront writer's block, the inability to put words down on paper. For some, the attempt to achieve a goal that has seemed too lofty or ambitious might become too emotional and draining. But don't worry. These feelings or thoughts are common. We had similar experiences with writing our essays yet, over time and with support from trusted femtors and mentors, we succeeded in doing so. It is not a perfect or easy process but we advise starting early, drafting, writing, rewriting, and refining the statement as you move along the application process. Consider, too, another piece of advice we've heard: don't keep tinkering with the essay; let it "stew," preferably overnight or for a day or two. When you come back to it with fresh eyes, it will read differently. Trust us. You might even ask, "who wrote that?" Try reading it aloud, as well, to catch any errors. Miroslava practiced that approach when she prepared for giving job talks; there's nothing worse than mispronouncing or reading aloud an incomprehensible sentence you have written. Remember, don't be afraid to ask for feedback. No one does this alone. If someone tells you they did it by themselves, they're being untruthful.

If writing is too daunting at this stage, we suggest using a voice recorder to record yourself talking about your research experiences, future research interests, and rationale for why you are a good fit for the program. If you can articulate those ideas in a conversational setting, you can then transcribe and craft them into prose. Before you know it, you will have the ideas to build an outline and finally a fleshed-out draft. Again, think of it as a continuously evolving document, parts of which will continue to live with you well into your first and even perhaps your second and third years in graduate school. As former UCSB McNair writing specialist Christopher Morales has stated, "good writing is usually not about good writing, but about good revising."

Finally, we want to reiterate that, as we advise for all essays, after you revise and refine it as much as possible on your own, share it with a femtor or mentor or other trusted individual to provide you with feedback. Tell them you need help with making the statement of purpose into a well-written and relevant essay that speaks to the admissions committee and establishes your voice and vision. We guarantee that a second set of eyes will make the difference in taking your essay to the next level.

To get you started on your statement of purpose, we provide you with a prewriting exercise in which you answer a series of questions to assist you with articulating your interests and journey to graduate school. We have broken out each component of the statement to help you address the essay in manageable pieces rather than tackling the whole task in one sitting. Don't feel, too, that you need to answer every query. You don't. But the more you can articulate, the stronger your statement. As you will see, we have also included real-world tips to help you develop each portion of your essay to the best of your ability. Remember, give yourself time and space to carry out this work.

STATEMENT OF PURPOSE—A PREWRITING EXERCISE

Introduction

- What program are you applying to and why?

- How did you get interested in your field? What inspires you to pursue this field? Do you have a formative event or individual that shaped your interests? Did you take a college course that inspired you?

- What is it about your field of study that motivates you to pursue research?

Tip: Consider including a brief anecdote, quote, or hook to set you apart from other applicants.

Research Experience and Relevant Experience

- How have you prepared for graduate school? What skills have you gained and how did you gain them? Have you been a research assistant, participated in a summer program, taken relevant courses, mastered software, or presented at a conference? If so, describe what you learned and how you did so.

- What is your major research project? If multiple, describe the most relevant. If published, cite the project. If unpublished, give a working title. Describe the hypothesis or main argument, methodology, and/or findings. You might also talk about any collaborations.

- What have been your most significant and/or challenging academic experiences and why? What have been the tangible outcomes, skills gained, and lessons learned from such experiences?

Tip: Start by listing all your research experiences (perhaps using your CV or resume as a guide), then draft a detailed narrative about those experiences. While you don't want to repeat the content of your CV in the statement of purpose, this exercise will help you articulate the full range of your experiences and expertise.

Research Interests and Research Aspirations

- What do you plan to study in graduate school?
- How is this similar to or different from your undergraduate work?
- What do you intend to accomplish with your research project while in graduate school?

Tip: Envision how you would expand your current research project. If you are switching projects or disciplines, describe your new project or how you would expand your previous project with a new approach and/or disciplinary lens.

Fit with the Program

- What attracts you to the program and why?
- What professors interest you as advisors and/or femtors or mentors? Include a sentence or two about their research, mentioning a relevant article and/or book.
- What is it about that particular institution or location that makes it an ideal place? What resources, labs, or centers make sense for your professional and personal goals?

Tip: Look up the professors' most recent publications to ensure they are a good match for you. Inquire, too, about what the program is best known for (interdisciplinary research, critical theory, applied research, other?) and pay attention to whether this also matches your interests.

Conclusion

- What are your long-term academic and/or professional goals?
- How will this program help you meet your long-term goals?

Tip: Look up the job placement of recent alumni. What jobs are they landing? Are they professorships? Are they careers in research, industry, or entrepreneurship? Make sure your career goals align with the types of jobs for which they prepare their students.

SAMPLE STATEMENTS OF PURPOSE

To demystify the process of writing the statements of purpose and to ease stress or negative self-talk related to that process, below we showcase sample essays. Please keep in mind that these are highly polished statements, which required many hours of revising and editing to get to this stage. We, too, have done some light editing, as needed. They represent successful statements for students who applied to master's and doctoral programs nationwide. You will notice that we have withheld certain identifying information, including the names of schools, programs, and professors mentioned in the essays. This is to protect the privacy and identities of the individuals who graciously and generously agreed to share their statements. We hope that by reviewing these statements, you will get a sense of how to structure your own and what type of information you might want to include. We recommend that you read all of them, including those outside of your discipline, as the purpose of sharing samples with you is not for you to replicate them, which would be unethical. Rather, it is to inspire and motivate you to write your own essays based on your knowledge, experience, and career goals. Do not hesitate to reach out to your own trusted femtors and mentors to assist you with feedback and edits that will help you develop essays that you are comfortable with and confident about submitting.

We hope the variety of samples shared in this chapter below demonstrate both the flexibility and formulaic nature inherent in statements of purpose. Certainly, you must bring creativity, passion, and flair for communicating your research interests and personal determination. At the same time, you must demonstrate the training, preparedness, and strengths you bring and show how those align with those of the program. Your purpose is to show that you and the intended program are a good match. As we noted, the statement of purpose is often given the most weight in evaluating your application. To that end, we encourage you to make sure you cover the five essential components: introduction, previous research experience, proposed research, match with the program, and conclusion. With that winning combination, we're sure you'll be off to a great start with developing a solid foundation for your application.

SAMPLE STATEMENT OF PURPOSE #1: HUMANITIES

It is a Saturday morning, and my big brother is launching socks at me from across the hallway, as we scramble to finish our chores before Mom walks through the door. "Hurry up," he shouts, and I move as fast as my 6-year-old legs will carry me. Our tasks were simple when Mom was running errands: pick up around the house, fold the laundry, and put the clothes away before she came home. Once these tasks were completed, only then could we turn on the Xbox, but as my brother saw it, playing games first and doing our chores quickly before Mom set foot inside would maximize our game time. As the youngest, it was my duty to blindly follow my brother—no matter my sister's warnings—because I wanted to be his shadow. Every Saturday was practically the same routine, and my time spent with my brother was filled with arguments over whose turn it was to play, his brotherly criticism of my gaming skills, his annoyance that I wanted our shared avatar to be female, and my asking him to beat the boss levels that would crush me but were no match for him. I never thought much of these weekly occurrences, especially as they became less frequent as we grew older; games are still a common interest between us, despite our playing separately. I never considered it to be something that would inspire my academic interests in new media, environmental humanities, and Pacific studies, until my first undergraduate research project. As such, I am deeply interested in pursuing environmental humanities, and race and gender studies in video games, a new means of cultural preservation.

As a scholar in [Program Withheld] and an English Honors student, I conducted research on cultural preservation and authenticity, exploring how traditions and practices are translated in new media. Using the lens of the Oceanic consciousness, a term coined to explain the connectivity between Pacific peoples, I studied three unique sites of preservation: the Polynesian Cultural Center, We are Mauna Kea, and TikTok. Although these sites have the same goal of preserving culture for future generations, their approaches are drastically different. This project, entitled "The Oceanic Consciousness: From Tourist Attractions to Trending on TikTok," also considered the notion of plasticity, where some Pacific Islanders were viewed or viewed themselves as inauthentic. From this experience, I gained insight into the type of research I would like to continue and a foundation for working with mixed media to examine the transoceanic experiences between Pacific Islanders. Additionally, I became deeply invested in the politics of archiving and how that impacts levels of authenticity in preservation.

In graduate school, I would like to extend this research, centralizing and celebrating Pacific work through a multitude of media in order to facilitate meaningful discussion that does not shut out the Pacific bodies, voices, and art it profits from. Video games are a viable avenue to pursue, as they use a variety of elements to engage players in storytelling, and storytelling is such a large component of Pacific cultures and their longevity. There is no work yet in this section of Pacific studies. Gaming studies provide a unique opportunity to explore fundamentals of storytelling and how culturally infused storytelling impacts its users, especially since the representation of Pacific characters is predominantly one-sided, when they exist at all. Essentially, Pacific Islanders are limited in this medium as the only games in Oceania are centered on war in America. In adventure games and first-person shooter games like *Shadow of the Tomb Raider* and *Call of Duty: Modern Warfare,* there are Polynesian men, but they are strictly supporting characters. Both of these games center on imperialist ideals and introduce indigenous peoples in a formulaic manner. Of course, there are several other games to consider such as *Cyberpunk,* which was released earlier this year, and even sports games such as *Madden*. I plan to explore the representation of Pacific peoples and the overall depiction of Oceania in video games.

I find the digital humanities incredibly fascinating for its ability to transform the past into stunning visuals and captivating stories, and I would be delighted to continue my studies at the [School Withheld] under the mentorship of Professor [Name Withheld], given his work with indigenous masculinity in the Pacific. Gaming studies is a unique path in academia, but I am confident that my research would fit in well with this program, examining new types of preservation and the politics of archiving. Additionally, I am able to provide some of my own funding, underneath the Veterans Administration Chapter 35 Benefits through the Dependents Education Assistance (DEA). I am committed to a long career in academia, pursuing cultural preservation studies through storytelling. I aspire to become a professor and hope to become a cultural consultant for Ubisoft and the *Assassin's Creed* franchise, which entails historical science fiction. I hope that the [School Withheld] is part of my academic voyage.

SAMPLE STATEMENT OF PURPOSE #2: HUMANITIES

Three generations of immigrant women have continuously carved the path for me to self-identify as a scholarly, fat, first-generation, Chicana lesbian student. My educational trajectory allows me to realize that my identities serve as spaces where I experience physical, social, and spiritual violence. Though this violence has impacted the way I navigate the world, my identities are, more importantly, spaces in which I actively resist overt and subtle antagonism in academia and social spaces. This refusal to succumb to "body terrorism" (Taylor, 2018) has shown itself through my research interests and scholar-activist projects. There is nothing more fulfilling as a blossoming Ph.D. scholar than to take the opportunity to share my testimonio, identity, and academic goals in the firm belief that they are interwoven into the Department of Women's Gender, and Sexuality Studies at [School Withheld].

I arrived at my goal of a Ph.D. in Women's, Gender, and Sexuality Studies as a scholar of Chicanx Studies and Women's Studies. Feminist scholarship, like that of Cherríe Moraga and Gloria Anzaldúa, encourages me to consciously center the first-generation, lesbian Chicana students I am writing for and about. The connections I made between my *teoría* (theory) in the flesh experiences of sexual assault, disordered eating, and homophobia would not have been possible without the *mucho amor* (plenty of love) that I encounter in the work of Chicana lesbian theory and praxis. These *feminista* connections have only been strengthened in my independent study, where I analyze the resistance to violence that Chicanas/Latina bodies experience in minimum wage environments. This is a research topic I intend to explore in depth as a doctoral student at [School Withheld].

My research as a [Program Withheld] fellow provides me the space to cultivate a queer, fat, and Brown epistemological framework against the fatphobia so rarely acknowledged in academia. Using Dolores Delgado Bernal's Chicana Feminist Epistemology, I document community resistance to fatphobic violence within higher education through qualitative research methods. I have presented my research at conferences such as the [Program Withheld] Western Regional Conference, the American Association of Hispanics in Higher Education (AAHHE) National Conference, the *Mujeres Activas En Letras y Cambio Social* (MALCS) National Summer Institute, and the National Conference for Chicana and Chicano Studies (NACCS). Additionally, my research internship at [School Withheld] Graduate School of Education strengthens my feminist work with the analysis of state archival collections on the history of sex education in California. My work in coding and analyzing national archives from the League of United Latin American Citizens (LULAC) as they relate to citizenship for service emphasize the displacement of Chicanx/Latinx bodies. This continued displacement has prompted my research lens to fully encompass the intersection of gender, sexuality, race, bodies, and immigration as a future doctoral student.

The opportunity to explore the link between personal and collective experiences with gender, sexuality, and Brown bodies was further enhanced through my body-positive events at the Women's Resource Center as a student programmer. Alongside this programming work, my experience in leading the initiative with another queer Chicana for Dominguez Hill's first ever [Name Withheld] Conference has been instrumental in shaping the way I advocate for queer student programming in academia. By centering active participant involvement in the creation of my research, I am creating ruptures in the traditional model of objectivity that is detrimental to our humanity as scholars. Thus, I strongly believe we must intentionally cultivate both theory and praxis in order to honor the testimonios shared with us as researchers. This is a scholarly goal I effectively see myself honing as a doctoral student at [School Withheld].

I aspire to continue my academic journey at the Department of Women's, Gender, and Sexuality Studies to center fatness, diverse bodies, and queerness as sites of resistance to colonial violence. The mentorship I received as an undergraduate scholar has been radical in its feminista centering of love; this is where I feel that [School Withheld]'s influence in my doctoral journey will flourish as a future member of the professoriate. Specifically, I view Professor [Name Withheld]'s scholarly work around disability studies, feminist theory, health activism, and Professor [Name Withheld]'s work on queer studies, mass culture, and feminist cultural studies align with my interdisciplinary research aspirations. I propose that [School Withheld]'s commitment to cultivating diverse research-activism in higher education, alongside my own commitment to deconstructing power structures that damage queer, diverse bodies are both complementary and inextricably tied to a greater, joint liberation.

SAMPLE STATEMENT OF PURPOSE #3: SOCIAL SCIENCE

My goal is to study the conditions that lead to school failure and victimization, and to develop evidence-based alternatives, specifically programs designed to bolster school performance, encourage emotional support from teachers/counselors, and provide navigational assistance for college applications and financial aid. I am interested in pursuing the following research questions: 1) What are some of the environmental factors that deter students living in the farm working communities of California's Central Valley from accessing postsecondary institutions? 2) How are institutions of higher education preparing underrepresented students for careers after graduation? 3) Do the efforts to increase diversity and inclusion align with actual enrollment rates at universities?

In high school I had mixed experiences with teachers and counselors. For example, my AP English literature teacher advised me to attend the local community college because attending [School Withheld] as an undeclared major would be a waste of money. Her remarks and criticism made me dread attending her class. I was fearful that she would call on me and make me feel stupid, something she did regularly. Fortunately, I received assistance in applying to college from a career counselor at South High. With her support I was able to complete the applications for college admission and financial aid. As a first-generation college student I was unable to seek assistance from my parents because their limited knowledge of higher education prevented them from providing me with navigational support to maneuver through the college application process.

My experiences in high school have influenced my aspiration to pursue a graduate degree and continue my research on strategies to provide underrepresented students with access to college experiences and increase their success rates after graduation. The following question has derived from my research interests: What resources are needed to better support underserved students in postsecondary institutions to maximize their college experience and academic and vocational success? My research interests further developed through my involvement on campus and my employment with the [Program Withheld]. I have held multiple positions with this program that have provided me with opportunities to be a mentor and leader and to assist underserved students in their transition to college. My personal involvement with underrepresented students and my own background prompted me to seek more research experience.

My specific research has examined pre-college characteristics that affect high school student college decisions. Professor [Name Withheld], my colleagues, and I reviewed thirty interview transcripts and coded messages about parent, counselor, and teacher support. Our project corroborates the literature on the importance of emotional support in fostering students' college-driven goals and sense of competence. We found that teachers and counselors are the gatekeepers, preventing and/or propelling these students to seek higher education. We presented our work at the American Educational Research Association annual conference in April 2016.

My independent research project as part of the [Program Withheld] involved examining the relationship between types of Latino parental support and their high school students' aspirations to seek higher education. I was particularly interested in understanding the informal messages that Latina/o parents deliver to their children and the ramifications for their educational aspirations. This involved carefully reviewing and coding thirty interviews with Latina/o high school students and identified emerging themes. Findings show that Latina/o parents value education and instill a college-going image to their children through direct messages about the importance of continuing their education. Parents entrust teachers and counselors to provide navigational support to their students in the college application process. Limited encouragement from teachers and staff deter students from believing in their intellectual competence and pursuing their educational aspirations. This research project culminated in a paper, *"Latina/o Parent Communication Influencing Students' College Aspiration."*

Specifically, my areas of interest focus on the college going identity of underserved pre-college students and how they remain resilient as they continue their path to higher education. I am interested in the pre-college, college, and graduate school timeframe because many students fall out of the educational pipeline. I want to study the political and institutional deterrents that inhibit these students from achieving academic success.

This past summer I had the privilege to conduct research and be a Research Technician intern at the Inter-University consortium for Political and Social Research at the [School Withheld] under the guidance of Professor [Name Withheld]. My research project, "Lifting the Financial Burden: The Impact of the Gates Millennium Scholars Program (GMS) on Student Aspirations for Higher Education," was composed of secondary data from the GMS program freshman cohort longitudinal survey. My study aimed to deduce the effects of financial aid availability for first-generation students on their expectations to continue education beyond their undergraduate work. Specifically, I wanted to identify the differences between first-generation GMS recipients and first-generation non-recipients. Furthermore, students who felt supported academically and emotionally were more likely to have higher graduate school expectations. I found that GMS did not have significantly higher graduate school expectations, however students who were not GMS had lower expectations for graduate school.

I would be honored to conduct research under the guidance of faculty at [School Withheld] in the Higher Education and Organizational Change doctoral program. I would welcome the opportunity to work with Professor [Name Withheld] whose qualitative approach to access to Higher Education opportunities closely aligns with my interests in examining the impact of creating a college-going identity for underserved students. I am also interested in examining the role of parents, teachers, and counselors on student expectations to enroll in college and continue their education past a baccalaureate degree. Professor [Name Withheld]'s mixed method approach and research on educational and occupational trajectories of underrepresented students match my interest in studying the social, emotional, and cognitive processes students encounter during the pre-college, college, and post college timeline. Professor [Name Withheld]'s applied quantitative methodology and research in college and university enrollment behaviors appeal to my interest in investigating the underlying procedural policies that impact underrepresented student enrollment rates. Their support will allow me to expand my research on accessibility and equity in Higher Education.

My interest in pursuing a Ph.D. in Education stems from my lived experiences with and commitment to empowering students to challenge the norm and pursue careers and degrees that have historically been occupied by white men. I want to become a professor at a leading research institution and bring my knowledge from my research into the classroom. My personal experiences coupled with my determination and eagerness to continue to challenge myself and grow attest to my ability to be a viable doctoral student.

SAMPLE STATEMENT OF PURPOSE #4: SOCIAL SCIENCE

My desire to pursue a Ph.D. in psychology initially arose after completing a sixty-hour Crisis Intervention Training at the [Program Withheld] when I began working with sexual assault survivors and their significant others on the crisis hotline. Our training had consisted of learning about the prevalence of sexual assault among the general population, while also highlighting the elevated rates among minority populations. It was in those sessions that I learned the importance of being a bicultural, bilingual counselor and the positive contributions I could make to the underrepresented communities of Santa Barbara, especially the Latino/a community. However, I was disheartened when I noticed that Latino/a survivors were utilizing our services at much lower rates than their white counterparts. This realization led me to focus my undergraduate research on the disparities of mental health service utilization among vulnerable and/or understudied populations, with a particular focus on Latino/as.

I think it is crucial to have research that is well informed by clinical practice, and clinical practice well grounded in research. Furthermore, I sought resources that could aid in my development as a practitioner well trained in evidence-based practices and the research behind them. I applied and was admitted into the competitive [Program Withheld] at the [School Withheld]. I also contacted Professor [Name Withheld] in the Department of Counseling, Clinical and School Psychology to pursue a research mentorship with her in order to further enhance my research skills and collaborate on projects that aligned closely with my research interest on mental health service utilization. Shortly thereafter, I began working as an undergraduate research assistant in Professor [Name Withheld]'s Proyecto HEROES lab, a program dedicated to understanding the impact of various forms of violence on the Latino community in Santa Barbara using community-based participatory research (CBPR). As a research assistant I conducted extensive literature reviews on Latino/a youth's exposure to community violence, sought and evaluated measures to include in our study's IRB proposal, transcribed and translated interviews, and coded transcripts to analyze themes in relationship to Latino/a families' exposure to school and community violence. Drawing from these research skills, I soon developed my own independent research projects that were supported and guided by my McNair faculty advisor, Professor [Name Withheld].

The findings of my research studies have further ignited my passion to continue to pursue the systemic and personal barriers that impact help seeking and thus, the impact on the academic and psychosocial success of underrepresented minorities. Across my various studies, the resounding barrier to help seeking has continuously been lack of knowledge about services available, thus indicating a need for greater dissemination of information. To investigate the impact of disseminating information on students' academic success and psychosocial well-being, I am currently conducting an independent mixed-methods study under the supervision of Professor [Name Withheld] in the Department of Psychological Brain and Sciences at [School Withheld]. I recently submitted an [Program Withheld] grant proposal to cover the costs of our study and the presentation of our findings at [School Withheld]'s annual undergraduate research colloquium.

Our study will examine the effects of participation in a transfer student mentorship program on first-year transfer students' academic success, knowledge of and utilization of campus services. Specifically, we will be administering a survey to first-year transfer students to examine the differences in academic GPA, knowledge of and utilization of campus services among transfer students participating in the mentoring program and transfers not participating in the program. The survey will be followed up with a semi-structured interview of short answer questions aimed at exploring transfer students' academic experiences and allow for a more in-depth analysis of the outcomes of mentorship on transfer students' success. In graduate school, I want to expand on these studies by also examining contextual factors that contribute to help seeking and examining more closely how service utilization affects Latino/as' academic success, career development and psychosocial well-being. I believe that a Ph.D. in social work is the best choice to conduct this type of research. Specifically, a Ph.D. in social work will prepare me to be able to apply my research to help communities understand and solve some of the problems minority populations face.

My research has inspired me to pursue a challenging issue facing society today: the underutilization of mental health services among Latino/as, one of our fastest growing populations in the United States, yet most under-represented and most vulnerable minority groups. It is important to me that I address both the mental health needs of under-represented groups, as well as the systemic and societal barriers to accessing needed care. Given my research interests I am convinced that the [School Withheld]'s Joint Program in Social Work and Developmental Psychology is the ideal place for me to pursue my doctorate. I would not only receive rigorous interdisciplinary training to increase my critical skills as a scholar and researcher, but also have the opportunity to work with faculty whose interests align so strongly with my own. I was delighted to find a department with many academics with whom I can see myself working. For example, combining the framework of justice and equity of social work and the qualitative methods of CBPR of the field of psychology, I can see myself following up one of my studies on Latino/a parents and their access to mental health services for their children. Specifically, I am drawn to the work of Professor [Name Withheld] who similarly investigates Latino health inequalities through CBPR efforts in collaboration with Professor [Name Withheld] who employs community-based research and practice through a social justice lens to empower and educate oppressed groups. Likewise, I see myself employing CBPR and mixed methodologies with Professor [Name Withheld] to investigate ethnic and geographic disparities in health and health services by contributing the knowledge I have gained here in California. I also see myself collaborating with many academics specialized in developmental psychology. For example, I am drawn to the work of Professor [Name Withheld], Professor [Name Withheld] and Professor [Name Withheld] who similarly investigate how contextual factors influence children and adolescents academic and psychological functioning. By investigating both the contextual factors and the individual developmental trajectories of Latino/as, I can better understand the mechanism of help seeking and the impact on academic success and psychosocial well-being.

I see it necessary to ensure that research is properly disseminated, and that under-served populations gain increased attention as targets of study and clinical practice assistance. I intend to continue to work on breaking down the barriers that Latino/as face when accessing mental health services and academic support programs. My greatest reason to pursue a doctoral study is because I want to pursue research and academia at a leading research institution, where I can apply the knowledge from my research to the classroom. I believe my personal record of persistence and success in the unfamiliar territory of research as a first-generation college student of color shows my resilience as an individual and as a scholar.

One of my proudest accomplishments to date has been my ability to excel academically and conduct research, despite being a mother of twin boys and simultaneously working several part time jobs. My success thus far can be attributed not only to my love for the research I conduct, but also to my willingness to actively pursue valuable resources that can assist me in accomplishing my goals. My persistence in balancing school, work and research demonstrates that I have the personal motivation and capability to excel in a demanding yet invigorating course of study. My academic history and work experience have proven that I am committed and wholeheartedly passionate about this area of study and furthermore, am a highly driven student that can pursue and successfully complete a doctoral degree. I look forward to the challenges ahead and the opportunity to continue to grow and develop as a researcher. For these reasons, it gives me great honor to apply to the Joint Doctoral Program in Social Work and Psychology at the [School Withheld]. Thank you for your consideration.

SAMPLE STATEMENT OF PURPOSE #5: SOCIAL SCIENCE

"You are a product of all who came before you. The legacy of your family. The light and the dark. The good and the bad. It is all a part of who you are" (*Shang-Chi and the Legend of the Ten Rings*). Watching this movie, I did not realize how impactful it would be to see my culture being represented on the big screen. As an Asian American, family is central to my identity. Because family is highly valued, the choices I make are not only what is best for me, but also to make my family proud. As a first-generation college student, there were expectations that I would succeed, but no clear guidance.

Because of cultural expectations and lack of empathy, I felt unable to confide in my parents and struggled with mental health. Throughout high school and my undergraduate education, I've observed first-generation students, including myself, dealing with impostor syndrome and feeling a lack of support due to cultural mismatches among mental health services and resources. Because of my own identity and familial background, my research focuses on the barriers that Asian Americans face when accessing mental health services, and how these are complicated by intersections of race, class, culture, and education.

As a research assistant in the Emotions, Motivation, Behavior, and Relationships (EMBeR) lab, I examined interpersonal relationships, particularly involving secrets. I coded video data, assisted with literature reviews, and ran experimental sessions over Zoom. Our results indicated that gaining useful, new information may mitigate negative judgment about the secret-sharer. I observed this firsthand when participants reported feeling closer to the secret-sharer after being told a secret rather than upset about the gossip. In this research experience, I not only expanded my research skills in survey construction, data analysis, and scientific writing, I became more intrigued by the importance of trust and communication. This understanding increased my interest in the therapist-client relationships. I hope to strengthen these skills further in my future practicum experiences where I will work to establish trust and maintain open communication with clients.

Under the mentorship of Professor [Name Withheld] at the [School Withheld], I conducted qualitative research on the Asian American experiences of discrimination and coping post-COVID-19. From semi-structured interviews with Asian American participants, we gathered recommendations for methods and sources to support the Asian

American community. Results suggested that incorporating a community-based approach and developing multiple interventions for the different generations would be particularly beneficial. Through this experience, I reviewed literature on generational differences among Asian Americans and events that resulted in racial trauma. I also co-authored the final article that was accepted into a special issue of *International Perspectives in Psychology* entitled *Psychology and the COVID-19 Pandemic: A Global Perspective*, which is in-press to be published Spring 2022. We found that Asian Americans feel more distressed over their external environments and desired more safe spaces. This research inspired me to continue advocating for underrepresented populations and contribute knowledge to the field by taking an ethnographic approach to create culturally-sensitive strategies that support access to mental health.

My senior thesis examines whether first-generation students create goals aimed at gaining rewards or avoiding punishment, and how these goals may impact resource utilization. For example, I explore whether academic success for first-generation students was driven by intrinsic motivation or fear of disappointing the family. I explain the needs and types of support appropriate for this community. In graduate school, I will integrate my previous research into clinical practice for other vulnerable populations.

I am applying to the Ph.D. program in Counseling Psychology at the [School Withheld]. I want to expand my undergraduate research to different cultures. By learning about other groups, biases can be better recognized, and resources can be further developed for groups of different backgrounds.

A professor whose research interests align most with mine is Professor [Name Withheld], whose research on cross-cultural well-being and development of multicultural counseling connects with my prior research experience on Asian Americans and their mental health needs. His current research on the Social Cognitive Career Theory mirrors my own research on first-generation college students, and how their challenges may often be due to their identities, lack of familial support, and mismatch of resources. I hope to incorporate more culturally appropriate resources for underserved groups to increase success and translate the research into clinical practice, using both my undergraduate and graduate knowledge of multicultural counseling and vocational guidance. Another professor that aligns with my interest is Professor [Name Withheld]. My previous work on the Asian American racial identity and its impacts during the COVID-19 pandemic can be expanded to examine challenges that other minority racial groups encounter. Particularly, I am interested in the Historical Experience of Racism Questionnaire project and Clinical Self-Awareness project as this will allow me to grow my research with another group, African Americans, and increase my clinical knowledge.

As an underrepresented minority myself, I look forward to expanding my research identity by developing culturally appropriate interventions with current clinical researchers and learning from experts in the field. I expect to join academia as a clinical researcher and faculty member soon, hoping to address inequities in diverse and underserved communities.

SAMPLE STATEMENT OF PURPOSE #6: SOCIAL SCIENCE

As a Latina first-generation college graduate working in higher education public policy, I conduct research to understand how policy can advance equitable outcomes for students with similar experiences as mine. I want to develop my research skills further by pursuing a Ph.D. in the Education Policy and Program Evaluation Concentration at the [School Withheld] Graduate School of Education. Through my graduate work, I plan to explore how policies focused on costs beyond tuition can impact student success. Ultimately, with a Ph.D. in Education, I plan to pursue a career as a researcher at a think tank to support education leaders in adopting equitable college affordability policies.

I grew up in Brownsville, Texas, a city with one of the lowest attainment rates in the country. Only 65 percent of individuals 25 or older in Brownsville hold a high school diploma; less than 20 percent hold a bachelor's degree. My high school did not invest in developing a college-going culture, and my immigrant parents lacked the language and tools to help me navigate educational systems. However, my parents understood that college graduates are more likely to experience socioeconomic mobility than individuals without a college degree. They emphasized the importance of education, which influenced my determination to go to college.

Although I gained admission to [School Withheld], I was ill-prepared to succeed there. I struggled academically, had difficulty navigating campus life, and questioned whether I belonged there. The challenges persisted even when I was away from campus. I could not afford to pursue summer internships because many were unpaid and required students to secure their own housing. I could not afford to rent a storage unit like many of my peers did, as we could not store our items in the dorm over the summer. I learned that if higher education works only for some individuals while creating barriers for others, it cannot be the great equalizer my parents proclaimed it to be.

The idea that higher education levels the playing field is nuanced, and I don't have to look beyond my experiences to see that nuance play out. During my first year working at HCM Strategists, a public policy and advocacy consulting firm, I compiled a catalog of state efforts to improve students' access to basic needs, including food and housing. While I was working on this project, my brother, who was attending college, became homeless. I was disappointed that my professional expertise in higher education and my degrees were not enough to help my family build the safety net that would have helped my brother secure housing. I realized that the challenges my brother and I faced would continue to be barriers for others unless systemic policy changes are made. Therefore, the research I do on behalf of our clients, including state agencies and large foundations, has a deep personal meaning to me.

Last year, for example, on behalf of the Bill and Melinda Gates Foundation and Lumina Foundation, I co-led a research project to understand the conditions that create equitable postsecondary ecosystems. Using data from the Integrated Postsecondary Education Data System (IPEDS) and the U.S. Census Bureau, my colleagues and I ranked states' performance on increasing degree completions and closing equity gaps. We sought to understand whether the states that performed well or poorly share any key traits. We analyzed the states across myriad factors, such as postsecondary finance policies and student success initiatives. While our analysis eliminated far more factors than it confirmed as being meaningful, we found that states can create strong postsecondary ecosystems by prioritizing strong affordability policies. In addition to being a challenging and gratifying project, this work reaffirmed my commitment to understanding the impacts of college affordability policies on student success, which I plan to explore in graduate school.

I often leverage existing research in my work to help state leaders understand how financial aid policies can help them meet their state goals. However, while the impacts of financial aid on enrollment, persistence, and completion are well-documented, financial aid is only one component of college affordability. For example, we have just begun to understand the prevalence of food and housing insecurity among college students. We need more empirical research to help us understand the impacts these challenges have on student success and, more importantly, the effectiveness of policies that seek to address these issues. For my graduate work, I plan to research how policies focused on costs beyond tuition, including basic needs, can improve student persistence and completion, particularly for students from low-income households. I will leverage data from state agencies to conduct difference-in-differences analyses to investigate the effects of specific policies, such as emergency financial aid or the coordination of public benefits, on student outcomes. This research is critical to the field and timely; as the pandemic has underscored, students' access to basic needs can be fragile and disrupted by unforeseen emergencies.

I am convinced that the Education Policy and Program Evaluation Ph.D. Concentration at the [School Withheld] School of Education is perhaps the only program that will provide the ideal setting to pursue my research goals. Moreover, the researchers with whom I may collaborate render this program a unique opportunity. I plan to work with Professor [Name Withheld] and Professor [Name Withheld]. Their work to understand the effects of financial aid aligns closely with my interests in evaluating policies that address costs beyond tuition. Additionally, the work Professor [Name Withheld] leads at the Center for Education Policy Research excites me. I value the practical applicability of my research findings, including the development of policy briefs and toolkits to support state policymakers and decision-makers.

I hope to leverage my personal and professional experiences to develop new research at the [School Withheld] School of Education with support from the institution's faculty and unique initiatives. Ultimately, a Ph.D. in the Education Policy and Program Evaluation Concentration will help me contribute to the field and advance student success in collaboration with education leaders and through robust affordability policies.

"A picture is worth a thousand words," the saying goes. However, that picture also holds information which can be interpreted using computational methods. When constructing these algorithms there are two desires that are difficult to achieve simultaneously: minimized computational time and optimal computational accuracy. Seeing the potential of these methods in various fields such as particle physics, medical imaging, and data analysis, I plan to study machine learning during graduate school. Working towards my ideals in academic research and service, I am applying to the Applied Mathematics PhD program at [School Withheld] as a step to become a research professor.

I am intrigued by problems that lie in the middle of the pure-versus-applied spectrum, such as the throttling problem I researched during the 2020 SMALL Math REU at [College Withheld] under Professor [Name Withheld]. Our group aimed to classify the throttling interval for all orientations of various graph families. In application, these graph families could be electrical networks or quantum systems, in which the throttling problem could provide insight in how to best monitor them. We discussed what was known and unknown about throttling numbers for directed graphs, attempted to find examples and counterexamples for our conjectures using SAGE programming language, until we finally constructed a proof. Our work was submitted to the *Australasian Journal of Combinatorics* and became a presentation at the 2021 Joint Mathematics Meeting, earning the Outstanding Poster Presentation Award. Because of the SMALL Math REU, I experienced the mathematical research process—project design, proof techniques, and science communication—and enjoyed every aspect of it, realizing I wanted to pursue a research career in graduate school.

Since August 2020, I have been studying image processing methods for my [Program Withheld] research project. Working under Professor [Name Withheld], I investigate the relationship between linearized optimal transport (LOT) and the 2-Wasserstein (W_2) distance by proving inequalities relating to the metrics and numerically investigating their sharpness. Currently, I am constructing two classes of measures, one in which the LOT and W_2 distances agree and another when the error bounds proposed by Delalande and Mérigot can be improved. I learned that mathematics research requires resilience and dedication, as I had to master measure theory, statistics, and partial differential equations before completing an optimal transport reading course. This allowed me to spearhead my project by coding numerical simulations that became the foundation of my NSF GRFP proposal. In graduate school, I hope to continue this line of research by investigating each methods' suitability for varying data sets to add to optimal transport's applications in medical imaging, among others.

The Mathematics PhD program at [School Withheld] would provide me with the intellectual environment and support in becoming an expert in machine learning and a research professor. I am drawn to the department for its faculty who specialize in this area of research and would be ideal advisors. I would value Professor [Name Withheld]'s mentorship to continue my research in optimal transport and its implications in machine learning. I hope to study other image processing methods such as image segmentation, in which Professor [Name Withheld]'s expertise in spectral clustering would be essential in pursuing this research avenue. I am also interested in creating fair and transparent machine learning algorithms, especially in the lens of social justice. Professor [Name Withheld] would be an insightful collaborator for his work in deep fair discriminative clustering. The training and support offered at [School Withheld] will ensure that I become the mathematician I aspire to be--knowledgeable of machine learning's applications in both the academic and non-academic realms and dedicated to fostering inclusivity in the discipline.

SAMPLE STATEMENT OF PURPOSE #8: STEM

My passion for public health and infectious diseases was solidified when I enrolled in an upper division parasitology course during my sophomore year. Throughout the course, I learned about neglected tropical parasitic diseases through an ecological lens, as well as how these diseases are exacerbated due to systemic issues in public health. I discovered that ecological solutions could mitigate transmission and complement inaccessible medical treatments. Since parasitic diseases are influenced by ecological factors, I am interested in studying life cycle dynamics to evaluate transmission strategies and discover methods to disrupt transmission.

I took special interest in parasitic diseases through an international context, such as malaria, schistosomiasis, and leishmaniasis. Parasitic diseases, especially those impacting international countries, are often overlooked. For example, Chagas Disease, a significant contributor to mortality in Latin America, is usually glossed over by the general public and scientific community in the US. As a result, diagnosis, prevention, and treatment of Chagas has not been as developed in the United States. This is alarming because Chagas has been found in reservoir hosts (such as dogs) in the Southern US. Cases have increased throughout the last few years, mostly impacting underserved communities.

Growing up, I witnessed family members struggle with access to preventative care. Though some parasitic diseases are preventable, the US is not prepared to do so effectively. My greatest concern is for people in underserved communities—such as the one I was raised in—who already struggle with access to healthcare. My goal became to tackle parasitic diseases affecting international communities who already experience them. Parasitic diseases such as Chagas, malaria, leishmaniasis, etc. are expected to expand into the United States in the future. My intention became to 1) relieve disease burden in international communities and 2) apply my international work to the United States and prevent disease burden among underserved communities.

My newfound curiosity in parasitology, ecology, and public health led me to pursuing research opportunities relating to these subjects. To learn more about parasites in an ecological context, I joined the Parasite Ecology Group. I first learned to dissect tree frogs from Yosemite National Park to quantify larval trematode metacercariae in their organs. Every day after my three-hour Zoology lab, I would go to the Parasite Ecology lab for fun. My love for parasitology developed as I enjoyed analyzing the parasites I found under the microscope, often losing myself in the task so that I was in the lab for hours. Taking the parasitology course equipped me with the knowledge to pursue my own research inquiries as well. I soon switched to a project focusing on *Prosthenorchis* sp., an acanthocephalan (thorny-headed worm) suspected of contributing to population declines of the endemic San Miguel Island fox. To analyze the parasite load in the foxes, I assisted my graduate student mentor by recording the number of *Prosthenorchis* and nematode eggs found in fox scat samples. I joined this project because I wanted to learn more about life cycle dynamics. I was interested in dissecting potential intermediate and paratenic hosts (e.g., mice, reptiles, roaches) to elucidate *Prothernorchis'* life cycle, as well as to expand our knowledge of the mammalian and reptilian parasite communities on San Miguel. My participation in projects with the Parasite Ecology Group showed me how laborious science can be. The sense of excitement and accomplishment I felt when I learned something new (such as when I mastered the fecal flotation/sedimentation techniques), contributed in some positive way, or completed my tasks after hours in the lab fostered my desire to pursue a career in research. Most importantly, the Parasite Ecology Group equipped me with foundational knowledge required to think about how ecology can be used to address infectious diseases.

Having extensive knowledge in ecological parasitology, I chose to find a project that incorporated human parasitology, ecology, and epidemiology. In summer 2021, I participated in the Basic Science Institute Summer Internship Program (BSI-SIP) at the [School Withheld]. Alongside my mentor Professor [Name Withheld], I investigated the benefits and limitations of a rapid diagnostic test (RDT), and its use in malaria reduction efforts in different ecological zones in Zambia. From my mentor I learned that I am able to apply several fields into my future research. For example, I learned how much ecology and epidemiology are intertwined. Concepts from both fields can be used to analyze transmission patterns, such as when we used information from the RDT to explain that more villages near bodies of water experienced more cases of malaria compared to villages near a drier climate. I also learned how to apply epidemiological concepts when evaluating the sensitivity and specificity of the RDT, and how changes in the test's sensitivity can improve diagnosis of malaria. I was introduced to issues in medical parasitology as well, including how detection of asymptomatic people is an issue in diagnostics and difficulties in accessibility of diagnostic tests, like blood film tests, for people in rural communities. Additionally, this research was in an international context, which gave me a glimpse of the kind of research I can conduct in my career. This experience heightened my desire to further investigate medical parasitology as well to understand more of the biology behind symptoms, diagnosis, and treatment. Ultimately, I plan to bridge that new knowledge with my experience in ecological and epidemiological research to become a well-rounded researcher.

I am interested in the MPH in Infectious Diseases and Vaccinology program at [School Withheld] because I am ready to focus more on infectious diseases, especially neglected tropical diseases caused by parasites. The broad curriculum will provide me with the opportunity to dabble in several fields like my mentor at [School Withheld]. For example, the courses in statistics and epidemiology will provide me with the quantitative background I need to understand disease trends. The molecular parasitology, molecular epidemiology of infectious diseases, and infectious disease research in developing countries courses will prepare me for the future research I will be pursuing in graduate school and in my future career. I am also interested in conducting research on an international parasitic disease during my time at [School Withheld]. I am interested in working with a few professors or with the Placer Mosquito and Vector Control District, CDPH Vector-Borne Disease Section, CDPH Office of Binational Border Health. Overall, I believe that a public health degree from [School Withheld] will provide me with the skills and knowledge I need to accomplish my goals of reducing parasitic disease burden affecting underserved communities here in the US and internationally.

SAMPLE STATEMENT OF PURPOSE #9: STEM

My undergraduate thesis, teaching assistantships and four years of industry experience solidified my passion for research and awakened my profound desire to become a professor of plant biology. Research wise, my goal is to explore the influence of stress on root development to engineer agriculturally important crops that combat climate change. I am especially interested in working with Professor [Name Withheld] on engineering SPACE tomatoes, Professor [Name Withheld] studying plant stress tolerance via nanotechnology and Professor [Name Withheld] on root immunity against M. phaseolina. I believe the [School Withheld] has distinguished mentorship opportunities for me to pursue my passion for plant biology and fully realize my dream of becoming a professor.

My decision to study plant biology is the culmination of my experiences beginning as an undergraduate student at the [School Withheld]. I trained in the lab of Professor [Name Withheld] where I studied orchid seedling development and independently performed aseptic technique, RNA extraction, SDS page and qPCR. My senior thesis found previously discovered genes in our lab, NID2A and NID4A, were auxin-mediated during first leaf emergence and opened the door for more studies regarding this stage of orchid seedling development. I was admitted into the Honors Program which allowed me to take advanced interdisciplinary courses alongside my biology coursework. I became a teaching assistant for Biology 101, Animal Biology and Plant Biology where I enjoyed setting up and leading experiments, proctoring and grading practical examinations and being challenged by motivated students; all while balancing extracurriculars and schoolwork. Instructing my peers in biology cemented my love for teaching and put me on the path to becoming a professor.

My first industry job at [Company Redacted], under the supervision of [Name Withheld], further taught me how to independently structure my lab work, design and implement experiments and communicate my research to business and scientific professionals. I designed novel lateral flow assay strips by analyzing current immunology research. I performed antibody-antigen conjugations, ran ELISAs and gels, prepared reagents and designed serial dilution schemes for buffers to mimic patient samples. I was a Research Assistant on the Research and Development team for a year when I was promoted to the Research Associate II role. After my title change, I trained Research Assistants and gave talks and weekly slide deck presentations to our international clientele. I wrote the final reports for two reproductive health products targeted at patients undergoing IVF treatments and personally transferred our technology to our manufacturing team. Though I enjoyed my time at [Company Redacted], I wanted to study problems relevant to plant systems and began working at [Company Redacted], a plant bioengineering company.

At [Company Redacted], my fascination with root systems took hold. As a member of the Cell Biology team, I eagerly dove back into plant biological sciences. Alongside our Technology Development team, I investigated direct root meristem (RM) to shoot meristem (SM) conversion in canola plants based on primary research in A. thaliana. I tailored the experimental design based on canola propagation requirements, subcultured protoplasts and root explants onto various cytokinin and auxin treatments and prepared media. I reduced RM to SM conversion times from four to two months, dramatically improving process timelines. Another experiment was inspired by my curiosity and love of rummaging through primary research. I noticed our root induction media lacked a reagent shown to increase root growth and ROS homeostasis. I proposed an experiment to titer this reagent into our current media preparation to enhance root growth and further decrease RM to SM conversion times. These projects sparked my interest in studying root biology and pursuing a PhD.

In preparation for graduate school I have identified my undergraduate transcript as a potential weakness from the perspective of the graduate admission committee. Over the past year, I have been resolved to show my current academic prowess compared to when I received my BSc five years prior. I retook Biochemistry at [School Withheld] with Professor [Name Withheld] where I received an "A" and executed two independent projects at

[Company Redacted] with high praise from my supervisor. Being in a classroom environment by day and working in a professional lab setting by night showed me how motivated and dedicated I am to the study of plant biology. I am confident I will excel in my future graduate program because I have the ability to balance challenging coursework and independent research.

I am now conducting primary research at [Company Redacted]. Here, I uncover physiological mechanisms that contribute to mitochondrial dysfunction in Mus musculus and ribosomal assembly intermediates in E.coli using cryo-electron tomography (cryo-ET). I image cells for the collaborative studies of Professor [Name Withheld] and Professor [Name Withheld], independently perform cryo-ET on samples, maintain cell cultures and perform transfections. I present my findings to postdocs and help write and edit manuscripts for publication. In this short time, I have learned what it means to produce cutting-edge research and how valuable a PhD is in the pursuit of my passion to become a professor.

I expect I will thrive at the [School Withheld]. My contributions to [Company Redacted], [Company Redacted] and [Company Redacted] have taught me experimental design and execution, research presentation and academic writing. My research has analyzed auxin-mediated gene expression during first leaf emergence in orchid seedlings, investigated the direct conversion of RM to SM in canola and explored cryo-ET imaging. My four years of industry experience would be a valuable asset in my pursuit of a PhD due to the breadth and depth of my research experience and knowledge of advanced lab techniques.

My interest in attending [School Withheld] was strengthened when I recognized the faculty's outstanding contributions to combating climate change and fostering human life in outer space. I not only learned about Professor [Name Withheld]'s collaborations with NASA, but was excited by the vision of the Plant Transformation Research Center. Interacting with Professor [Name Withheld]'s studies on plant stress tolerance using nanotechnology fascinates me for it sparks the same curiosity I had at [Company Redacted], making colloidal gold and performing antibody-detector particle conjugations. I also had the pleasure of learning about Professor [Name Withheld]'s research on root immunity against M. phaseolina which delves deep into rhizosphere interactions I am eager to learn. Overall, the Plant Biology PhD Program excites me because it would uniquely prepare me for a career as a professor for it emphasizes preparing students for plant biology teaching positions. For those reasons, I would like to spend my next six years at [School Withheld].

KEY TAKEAWAYS

- We distinguished between and defined the three most common graduate school application essays—the statement of purpose, personal statement, and diversity statement.

- We broke down the statement of purpose into sections and shared strategies for how to approach writing each of these sections.

- We also offered tips and exercises for how to start writing this essay if you are feeling stuck, including sharing a pre-writing exercise with a series of questions to answer as you develop a first draft.

- The chapter ended with sample statements of purpose for the humanities, social sciences, and STEM fields.

6

THE PERSONAL AND DIVER-
SITY STATEMENTS

||||||||||||||||||||||||||||||||||||||||||||||||||||||||||||||||||||||||||||||||||||||||||||||||||||||||||||||||||||||||||||||||||||||||||||||||||||||||||||||||

UPON FIRST GLANCE, the personal and diversity statements appear to be quite similar, as they ask you to convey your personal motivations and goals for pursuing graduate study. We argue that they are not the same and serve quite different purposes. The personal statement asks you to speak about the personal experiences—both challenges and rewards—that have shaped you as an aspiring scholar in your chosen field, while the diversity statement requires you to speak to how your research, teaching, and/or service interests contribute (or have contributed) to the diversity of higher education, that is, making it a more inclusive and equitable space for first-generation, low-income, and/or non-traditional Students of Color. Programs will require the personal statement more often than the diversity statement. Nevertheless, we urge you not to discount the significance of your diversity work, as it often supports and reinforces your larger mission in pursuing a graduate degree. To clarify the uniqueness of each statement, let's look deeper into each separately.

THE PERSONAL STATEMENT

The personal statement focuses on how your background has shaped your academic, research, and/or career goals. Unlike the statement of purpose, the personal statement does not have a specific structure you must follow. Rather, it's a collection of two or three episodes in your life illustrating how your experiences have influenced your past, present, and future aspirations. Importantly, the personal statement also tells committees what you've learned from your experiences, particularly the challenging moments you have faced and overcome. Keep in mind that, ultimately, you have the power to relate or frame a narrative in the way you want it reflected. Be mindful of what you choose to reveal and how you do so. Christopher Morales, a former writing specialist for the UCSB McNair Scholars Program, reminds us that, through the personal statement, you are curating an image of yourself as an academic.

A personal statement generally opens with an introduction that sets out the attributes and pivotal experiences that have influenced your academic, research, and career goals. Remember, you choose the portions of your life you wish to highlight. The point is not to list your traumas or triumphs from childhood to date. Rather, it is to show how these specific episodes or moments have shaped or influenced your professional and personal goals. The introduction can include, for instance, details of your home life, community, and culture, including religious beliefs and language use. It can also contain descriptions of your childhood, adolescence, or early adulthood if—and only if—these examples lead to the "how" and "why" of your research interests. They should follow and flow naturally.

The next few paragraphs provide the personal vignettes that speak to your motivations. These brief narratives usually reflect what has motivated you to improve your educational or professional training. Typically, applicants will write about events in a chronological order, recalling moments from their formative years in K-12 and college, regardless of where or how you grew up. If you're a nontraditional student, it makes sense to include what you've done since you have been away from school for the last five to ten or more years and describe what or who has inspired you to return. To get started, we recommend making a list of those challenging moments or uplifting episodes in your life that impacted you deeply. Don't dwell too much on what happened. Instead, focus on how you transformed that experience into something useful and meaningful for your intended life's work.[1]

PRE-WRITING TIPS FOR THE PERSONAL STATEMENT

In our experience, writing an effective personal statement can be challenging. Many times applicants don't know where to begin or what to write, believing they have nothing to contribute or that they have too much to say and are overwhelmed by the task. To get started, we recommend paying attention to the prompt, as we recommend doing so for writing the statement of purpose. Pay attention to the elements the prompt wants you to discuss. You will often see elements of a diversity statement intertwined with the personal statement. Diversity statements, as explained below in further detail, reflect how you have contributed or will contribute to diversifying higher education and academia more broadly. But, again, it's not unusual to see personal statements asking you to talk about how you have worked to build inclusive, equitable, and accessible spaces for students from diverse backgrounds. In such a case, you would write about how your personal experience, including your accomplishments and achievement, have furthered the possibility for students like you to access higher education and succeed in their educational pursuits.

THE PERSONAL STATEMENT—A PRE-WRITING EXERCISE

To lay the groundwork for the personal essay, we suggest brainstorming about the experiences or moments in your life that shaped your decision to apply to graduate school. Here are some general prompts to get you started.

- What three to five things about you make you stand out?
- Who have been your favorite teachers, professors, or public educators and why? How did they influence you? What did they say or do or teach you that inspired you?
- What is the best paper, exam, or project you've completed in your major or field, and what makes it so great?
- What are three most memorable things you've done since starting college? How did each experience change you? What did each moment mean to you?
- What were you doing when you decided to pursue graduate school?
- What work, volunteer, or travel opportunities or experiences in your family life or history have you had that have contributed to your desire to pursue graduate school?
- How have you overcome hardships or obstacles in your life?
- What personal attributes make you likely to succeed in your chosen field?
- If you've taken a gap year or been away from school for a while, how has taking this time influenced or further motivated your desire to pursue graduate study? What skills, insights, or experiences have you gained?

THE DIVERSITY STATEMENT

The diversity statement showcases how your personal background as well as your academic, research, and career interests contribute (or have contributed) to diversifying higher education. Many people get stuck on this statement because they don't understand what is meant by "diversity" or "diversifying" academia. Let's rule out what it's not. It is not an opportunity for you to talk about your personal identity—your racial, ethnic, gender, sexual, class, undocumented, and/or disabled identity—and call it a day. It is also not about making an argument about how your presence in graduate school will suffice to diversify academia. Rather, the diversity statement is meant for you to communicate your values around diversity and to demonstrate, with specific examples, what you have done or plan to do to create opportunities for those, like us, who have been marginalized through structural inequality and the "isms" found throughout society.

As with the personal statement, begin with a brief introduction, laying out your commitment to diversifying higher education. Next, choose two or three personal examples and talk specifically about the kind of effort, time, and work—and sacrifice, if relevant—you have made to unlock educational doors for underprivileged and underrepresented students. Discuss any teaching, tutoring, or mentoring you have done, in or outside of the classroom, and the students who participated in the program. What lessons did you impart and what influence did you have? If possible, discuss how you know your approach created a meaningful impact for the students or participants. Beyond pedagogy, how have you been involved in efforts to create effective change in K-12 or higher education? Did you or do you volunteer or participate in political battles to diversify curriculum and classrooms? Did you or do you serve on any educational boards, discipline-specific organizations, or special interest groups dedicated to issues related to diversity, equity, and inclusion?

You should also talk specifically about your plans for continuing this work in graduate school and beyond. Perhaps you're interested, as Miroslava was and is, in pursuing a field with little representation of first-generation, low-income People of Color as professors. Don't just mention that obtaining the PhD will assist in the battle for diversity, equity, and inclusion. Instead, mention the kind of research you intend to pursue and how that will contribute to new knowledge about under-represented populations. Talk, too, about the kinds of programs for underserved communities you hope to build, and the kinds of nontra-ditional students you expect to support. Again, articulate the specific ways that your work will make a difference in providing opportunities in higher education and academia to those generally excluded.

Pre-Writing Tips for the Diversity Statement

The diversity statement, much like a teaching statement, is difficult to write because of the challenge in pinpointing what we mean when we say we are committed to diversifying higher education. In writing about your values and commitment to diversity, take time to reflect on what you think is gained by cultivating racial, ethnic, gender, sexual, and disability diversity in academia and beyond. What do you think is learned by teaching in a diverse classroom and with a curriculum that reflects the diversity of the students? How do the teacher and students—including white, middle-class, and those non-disabled—benefit from such environments? In demonstrating how you have worked or plan to work to diversify higher education, give examples of how you helped foster an inclusive and welcoming environment where all voices and perspectives were or are heard. What activities did you carry out? You might also consider ways that your research interests support or connect with understandings of diverse populations. What-ever you choose to highlight as your aims, be specific and connect it to your academic, research, and career goals.

The Diversity Statement—A Pre-Writing Exercise

To help you get started, we provide queries for you to think about and reflect. If you get stuck or develop writer's block, reach out to femtors, mentors, or trusted peers for support. Look, too, at the sample statements we provide at the end of this chapter.

- How do you self-identify? What are your various identities? In what ways are those identities diverse? Remember, diversity is based on your race, gender, sexuality, age, class, ability, legal status, and so on.

- How has your research helped to diversify or expand the pipeline to higher education? How has your research contributed to diversity? How have you collaborated with diverse individuals on research in a way that has shaped the outcome of your work?

- What service, leadership, or work experience have you had that have involved diverse perspectives and communities? Are you or were you involved in any student organizations, professional memberships, committees, jobs, or internships that focused on diversity?

- In what capacity have you worked or collaborated with diverse individuals? If you have not, do you plan to work with diverse individuals and, if so, how?

SAMPLE PERSONAL AND DIVERSITY STATEMENTS

Like chapter 5, this section is dedicated to providing you with sample personal and diversity statements so that you can get a sense of what these documents look like. We want you to keep in mind that we have not included essay prompts for any of these sample statements. Personal and diversity statements can look very different depending on the prompts you receive for your programs. Some prompts may be very specific and include several questions to answer, as you will see below. Others may be short and/or broad. As always, make sure that you answer your specific prompts in your own words and look to these for ideas and inspiration as to how you may structure your information or the parts of your story you may feel comfortable sharing in these types of statements.

We hope that this chapter, along with the statements shared below, has given you a solid grounding in understanding the specific elements of the personal and diversity statements. While they may contain similar kinds of information, they seek to convey your personal and professional commitments to graduate study and beyond. Look at them as an opportunity to convey the talents, perspectives, and experiences you bring that will enhance your intended field of study as well as the program you attend. Do not be afraid to share the unique parts of yourself that specifically showcase your motivations and inspiration behind pursuing your program of interest and career choice(s). After all, they are called "personal" and "diversity" statements for a reason.

SAMPLE PERSONAL STATEMENT #1: HUMANITIES

Before my parents and I immigrated to the United States, my relatives gave their wishes for our journey. I think many of them asked me to study hard and bring honor to the family. But I have long forgotten about their exact words. The only words that stayed with me, and affirmed my passion to study Chinese history and culture were those of my great-grandfather.

The night before we left China, we visited him for the last time. In our ancestral house, my great-grandfather gave me an anthology entitled, Yüe Ou. As I flipped through the worn pages of the anthology rather aimlessly, my great-grandfather smiled and said, "These are songs written by a poet of our city two centuries ago. Take care of the book and remember our roots." When I heard him, I looked up from the anthology. At that moment, I saw the history of our family and city all embedded into the thousand wrinkles on his face. I thought to myself: this is a promise I need to keep. Holding my hands, my great-grandfather sang to me a verse from the anthology, "Erstwhile as I faced the east wind, I vied in singing the songs of Guangzhou. The most unforgettable is the sound of my dear home." These were the last words I heard from my great-grandfather.

I am a twenty-fifth-generation native of Guangzhou, China. But unlike my great- grandfather, who spent his entire life living in Guangzhou, my parents decided we would join our relatives in Los Angeles. Without a choice, I became a first-generation immigrant at twelve. In L.A., I tried to familiarize myself with the new environment and an extended family previously unknown to me. Although learning a new language was initially difficult, I left the English as a Second Language Program quickly and entered the advanced curriculum along with local students. Yet, I never sought to become fully integrated into American culture. Unlike my Americanized relatives, I didn't want to lose my connection with China and its culture. But Los Angeles, despite its large immigrant population, shows no trace of my home; my relatives, despite our common roots, have no attachment to Guangzhou. For those in the immigrant community built upon the illusory aspiration of an English-only immigrant, I was always considered the other.

My life is defined by constant movements. For a long time, I thought I was shackled by an immigrant's burden, lost in a liminal space between cultures and histories. I was forced to move to L.A. by my parents' pursuit for better opportunities and an ideal of family reunion. Yet, in spite of having no choice over my movements between China and the U.S., I was able to make the choice about my own identity. Like my great-grandfather, I chose to identify with Guangzhou. In the U.S., whenever I feel lost or frustrated, I would pick up my great grandfather's Yüe Ou anthology. Just like how his farewell aroused an imagination in my heart for the history of my family and city, Yüe Ou showed me a vivid image of nineteenth century Guangzhou. Along with my great-grandfather's words, these songs made me believe that I could find a linkage between the past and present of my life.

At the [School Withheld], I became a member of various organizations. My participation in the Chinese American Student Association reestablished a connection between myself and my home and introduced me to a newer and far more diverse China than I remembered. I am employed under the university writing center as its only English writing tutor capable of communicating with Chinese students in Mandarin and

Cantonese. Fully conscious of their difficulties, I didn't want immigrant and international students to experience discrimination like me. As a [Program Withheld] student, I also forged bonds with other low-income, first-generation, and underrepresented students. Together, these experiences made me realize that not only do I wish to preserve and understand my roots and culture, but I also wish to contribute to the efforts of creating mutual recognition and bridging the spaces between Chinese, American, and other cultures and individuals.

During my last night in Guangzhou, my great-grandfather asked me to remember our roots. In the U.S., I thought I was shackled by an immigrant's burden. But during my time in this country, I grew strong enough to carry my burden and pursue my freedom. I realized I have a choice of who I become and what I do. I am an immigrant. But I am also a native of Guangzhou. My experiences with diverse students reinforced my belief in the freedom of immigrants to become anyone they want. I kept my promise and maintained my roots, but I can do more. I know now that I want to become a professor of Chinese history and mentor students who are interested in history and culture. Ultimately, I wish to provide guidance for immigrants who experienced cultural alienation in higher education and ferry those who think they are lost in a liminal space between different boundaries to the destinations they choose and deserve.

SAMPLE PERSONAL STATEMENT #2: SOCIAL SCIENCE

Growing up as a Black/White biracial female in a mostly White town, I struggled with experiences that are unique to multiracial people, like facing multiple types of stigma and struggling to understand my racial identity. My White friends described my dancing style as "straight from the ghetto" and said my Black dad dressed like a "gangbanger." Yet when I would visit the Black side of my family, they saw me as the light skinned girl who sounded White and did not know how to do her hair. I have always had a close relationship with my mother, so in high school when I started having confused feelings about my racial identity I talked about my multiracial identity with my White mother. While she could not personally relate to my multiracial experiences, she encouraged me to embrace my multiracial identity and be proud of my blended cultural experiences. However, I also experienced identity denial (when someone tells a multiracial person that they cannot claim a specific racial identity) from extended family members. It seemed like I would never truly be accepted by all of my family or friends, and since I did not have any other multiracial peers, I thought I was the only person experiencing these feelings. It was not until I became involved in a research lab and started reading the social psychological literature on multiracial identity that I learned that the experiences I had are common among multiracial people.

Attending [School Withheld] also allowed me to explore the Black side of my racial identity more because [School Withheld] has a Black Student Union and Black studies department. My experiences of not fitting in with my Black family and not fitting in with my White classmates made me apprehensive about taking Black studies classes because I was not sure if the history I would learn was really mine to claim. However, after my first Black studies class I started to see that Black history is still my history. While half of my family did not live through the experiences of being Black in America the other half of my family did, and their experiences and stories that were passed down to me have impacted me in a similar way that it impacted my fully Black cousins. As I was learning more about my Black history I was also feeling more pride toward my multiracial identity. Attending college provided the social and academic space to learn more about myself and my perceptions of my racial identity. Ultimately, my experiences at [School Withheld] helped me form pride in my multiracial identity. As I envision my next steps in my career, I plan on earning a Ph.D. in social psychology and researching questions to help others have pride in their racial identities too.

As a multiracial, low-income, and first-generation freshman at [School Withheld], I felt unprepared for balancing the rigor of college classes while working to support myself financially, as I am a fully self-supporting student. I was lucky enough to find resources catered to low income, underrepresented students very quickly at [School Withheld], including an organization called [Program Withheld] Committee. This organization identifies different resources (e.g., scholarship opportunities or tutoring services) and provides a sense of community for low income, first generation or underrepresented students at [School Withheld]. The organization also focuses on recruitment by encouraging low income, first generation and/or underrepresented high school students to attend and complete their college degree. As part of the recruitment team, I tutored at a local high school and helped prepare a college trip and multiple workshops throughout the year. Most of the students were Latinx, low income individuals who were striving to attend the local community college. Some students wanted to continue their education beyond the community college, while others needed convincing to attend the community college at all.

I have always enjoyed tutoring, mentoring, and encouraging underrepresented students to continue their education. I plan to continue this broadening of participation in higher education in graduate school by engaging in organizations that teach undergraduate students about graduate school, and by mentoring undergraduate students who want to pursue research or graduate school. I also intend to introduce undergraduate students to resources such as fellowships for graduate school, faculty members with similar research interests, or summer research program opportunities. During graduate school and later as a professor, I will focus my research on underrepresented populations, such as multiracial and minority racial groups, women in STEM fields, and low-income students in higher education. Studying how we can foster pride in underrepresented identities is one pathway to helping learn how to create opportunities for success for underrepresented populations.

By attending a social psychology Ph.D. program and focusing my research on understanding how to foster pride in underrepresented identities, I can help educate society on ways to uplift people with many different identities. I strive to fulfill these goals because I believe that having more diversity in academia will allow these institutions to better answer questions that affect the whole world. Having a diverse group of students, faculty, and staff at a university brings new ideas and new questions that may not have been a priority for a university with less diversity. I think attending graduate school and studying underrepresented groups in my research will enable me to further examine ways to increase diversity in higher education institutions. This will advance scientific knowledge by increasing the groups of people we study, and it will benefit society by providing solutions to problems affecting different populations in our world.

SAMPLE PERSONAL STATEMENT #3: SOCIAL SCIENCE

From a young age, my parents emphasized the importance of education, and taking it seriously. They wanted me to understand that without generational wealth, education would allow me power and control over my own future, and opportunities I would not have otherwise. While I had the full support and encouragement of my family as the youngest, but the first in my family to graduate from a 4-year university, I was left with a lack of guidance on how to prepare for the years ahead.

Being a queer Black woman at a predominantly white institution, I was quickly made aware of how the academic spaces I inhabit were not created with people like me in mind. Impostor syndrome is a term I became very familiar with upon entering [School Withheld] as a Physiology major. In my lower-division courses of nearly 400 students, I would often scan the room, desperate to find a face that resembled mine, only to come up short. This feeling of not belonging was only exacerbated when peers would often pose micro-aggressive questions like, "what sport do you play?" Or, professors would express surprise with how "well spoken" I am.

I remember speaking with my grandpa over my first Winter break about how lost and undeserving I felt. I hoped that my Papa, being the only college grad in my family and the person I looked up to the most, would know just the encouragement to offer. To my surprise, he began to tell me about his years as a young college student in Detroit in the 60's and the immense pride he had for being one of the few Black pre-med students. Following the '67 riots that forever changed the city, he began to reevaluate his priorities. Like me, he was not sure if he was following a path that served him and his passions or if his presence at [School Withheld] was worth anything. While he did not exactly offer me direct advice or tell me what I should do, our conversation sparked a major turning point in my journey at [School Withheld]. It was a reminder that, in reality, my feelings were not unique. My confusion and fear were something he, and countless other Black students, had and were currently experiencing.

Upon returning to college in the Spring, I changed my major to Global Studies, and began exploring future graduate studies. It was through my Papa's story that I recognized my worth and the necessity of harnessing my passions. And more importantly, if we had such similar experiences, half a century apart, there is far more work to be done in bettering higher education to serve students of color. As one of my other greatest role models, bell hooks, discusses in *Teaching to Transgress* I realized that professors, and the academic environment they choose to create, has the potential to transform the academic experiences of Black and Brown students. It is the professors who went out of their way to encourage me and create a more equitable university environment that have given me the extra push to thrive and succeed. It is through academia that I have found how to bring my experiences into an academic setting, take control of my future, find my voice, and demand it be heard. The struggles I experienced as a Black woman in higher education have led me to find that not only is there space for me in academia, but there is a *need* for me in academia.

In finding a community of peers in the [Program Withheld] who, like me, aim to transform higher education for the better, I have hope that my grandchild will not have to share my same experience or question her value.

SAMPLE PERSONAL STATEMENT #4: SOCIAL SCIENCE

What sparked your passion for research and graduate study?

I wish I could state that my passion for research started as a result of my niche undergraduate experience. While that is a significant component— it simply began with my tendency to never stop talking. From the moment I could formulate words coherently I asked questions about everything. I was passionate about finding the answers to obscure questions, and even continually questioning the outcomes I found in hopes of finding a better solution. My most extroverted characteristics led me to a passion for research that I hope to pursue at the [School Withheld]. My research interests include communities and crime, and the effect of incarceration on individuals and communities. I have developed and formulated these interests through participating in various research labs and my own lived experience being a child of an incarcerated familial member. I had the privilege of being a research intern at Evident Change, an organization seeking to make equitable research tools and systems. Through this experience, I have been able to develop literature reviews and coding that have aided in developing their Juvenile Assessment and Intervention System (JAIS) — a tool that seeks to develop an understanding of juvenile needs when incarcerated or at risk of incarceration and use this gender-specific information to aid workers in supervision. This experience has equipped me with the tools to be a successful researcher and candidate for this field — the ability to look at situations from an unbiased perspective, and use a multitude of resources to make an informed decision about the information at hand.

What personal characteristics or skills do you have that make you a strong candidate for this field?
My characteristics and skills as an undergraduate student and research assistant make me an ideal candidate for this master's program. My adaptability, resilience, curiosity, and overall unwavering passion for incarceration and criminology I believe are significant characteristics and tools I have used to succeed in undergraduate and will take with me into graduate school. I have demonstrated adaptability and resilience by persevering in personal circumstances as a formerly homeless independent student that continually sought to take and make space for other foster youth and formerly homeless students that aspire to defy their odds. My passion for criminology was formulated from the personal experience of being a child of an incarcerated individual. However, I did not know the implications of this background until I stepped foot in my first criminology course at [School Withheld]. I was briefed on what it meant to be first-generation and low-income, and heard a professor give a lesson on my own lived experience and childhood and the seemingly grave statistics that lay ahead of me. I aspire to be able to take space in the field of criminology with the unique insight and knowledge of someone who has been impacted by these systems.

What exactly are your career goals, and how does graduate school play into them?
My career goal is to become a researcher that develops tools to benefit communities and families that are directly affected by incarceration and create equitable circumstances and life outcomes for those affected by high recidivism rates and community policing. The opportunity to become a beacon and pursue my passion for criminology is an integral part of my career plans. Professor [Name Withheld]'s work at [School Withheld] particularly resonates with research interests—intersecting with my passion regarding communities and crime, the impact of incarceration on individuals and communities. Being able to pursue a more specialized approach to my interests plays an important role in my postgraduate education and career aspirations.

What have you learned about this field already? When did you first choose to follow this path, and what do you enjoy about it?

Being able to partake in multiple research projects and archival work in my undergraduate has inspired me to pursue my master's in sociology. I currently am a research assistant for two labs on campus—Wayne Laboratories and Trada Lab. As a research assistant for Wayne Laboratories under Professor [Name Withheld], I have been able to look at my interest in criminology through a social psychophysiological perspective. My work focused on studying the impacts of heart rate variability (HRV) of those incarcerated, and how that aided their emotional regulation. I studied incarceration through the lens of marginalized communities and social stressors they face, such as incarceration, and how that can overall affect their physical and mental health. The complexities of incarceration continually challenge my idea of what equity within communities and in correctional facilities looks like. Furthermore, the onset of the COVID-19 pandemic has allowed me to further develop my passion for advocating for incarcerated individuals and the injustices they face while incarcerated. I currently work on the archive called Prison Pandemic at [School Withheld], an archival project aiming to collect stories from California correctional facilities and those who are serving time. My time served on these hotlines allow me a first-hand witness to the stories and horrors within correctional facilities. The awareness of the dire conditions those incarcerated are facing are severely lacking—the desperation in their voice to be heard and them thanking us as a team re-enforces the passion I have for pursuing my career path and higher education endeavors. I enjoy the never-ending opportunities to learn new material or research methods or ideas that are an integral part of criminology. It is such a multi-faceted field that continually challenges me to be better and further develop my perception of concepts and findings.

Are there any discrepancies or causes for concern in your application you need to address? For example, is there a career and schooling gap, or a low GPA at one point? This is the time to discuss whether a personal hardship may have affected your academics or career.

The discrepancies in my GPA reflect circumstances I faced but not my potential to be a successful graduate student in the [School Withheld] sociology program. My transition to college was a tumultuous one— transitioning from an unstable, chaotic senior year of high school where I was homeless and continually re-evaluating where I would spend the night coupled with taking on the difficulties of my brother's abrupt transition into foster care left me emotionally strained and exhausted when I reached the stability that [School Withheld] provided me. Additionally, I went undiagnosed with Attention Deficit Hyperactivity Disorder until my third year of undergraduate where I was faced with the dilemma of understanding and processing the material, but unable to sit down and focus. However, despite the circumstances, and in conjunction with accessing resources that allow me to be a successful student, I have been able to navigate my undergraduate education while making meaningful progress in my career and establishing a lifelong passion for criminology and incarceration.

What factors in your life have brought you to where you are today?
My sheer curiosity coupled with my life experience and passion for community has brought me to where I am today. I love to ask questions. I love being able to pick apart analysis and foster a deeper understanding of the material presented to me. The most beautiful thing about academia to me is that it is continually progressing, no matter the field of study. Partaking in research labs has fostered an environment where I can continually ask questions and have them contribute to my project at hand rather than plaguing my professor at office hours with my never-ending questions. Additionally, truly I would not be in the position I am today, a first-generation college student who has overcome every circumstance thrown at me, if it was not for the community I came from and the ability to find community wherever I go, including [School Withheld]. Being able to make sense of and process the experience of living through the effects of incarceration in a logical and academic sense has changed the trajectory of my career, and how I view my obstacles.

What skills (for example, leadership, communication, analytical) do you possess?
My skills and diverse professional and life experiences I believe make me an exemplary graduate school candidate. I have worked with different communities on and off-campus which has aided me in developing personal and professional skills such as a pristine work ethic, being community-oriented, dependability, being team-oriented, punctuality, and a continuous pursuit of passion. My work ethic can be attributed to the self-sufficiency that is required of someone who is financially independent of their parents and a formerly homeless student. I understood that

my future was entirely in my hands, and I ensured that my involvement and dedication to my work reflected that and will continue to do so in my graduate school studies. Furthermore, throughout my undergraduate career, I have been able to balance working multiple jobs while simultaneously being involved on campus within various organizations—including the President of my organization Foster Student Ambassadors, and progressing and investing in my studies. Being a research assistant for multiple labs has allowed me to not only grow in my passion for criminology but also learn how to be dependable and self-sufficient in my work and studies—while learning how to ask for help when needed. Lastly, being able to invest in my community through service has reinforced my graduate school aspirations. Serving as a discussion leader for [School Withheld]'s Summer Bridge program allowed me to teach a discussion section three times a week regarding navigating college life as a first-generation college student. The roots I have been able to lay within my community through mentoring thirty first-generation incoming freshmen on the complexities of undergraduate life has been one of the most rewarding experiences of my undergraduate career so far. The ability to be a leader in my community is something I cherish and has allowed me to lean into growth that is often disguised as discomfort.

SAMPLE PERSONAL STATEMENT #5: SOCIAL SCIENCE

Growing up with diabetes helped me develop positive mental health strategies. This link between physical and mental health led me to advocate for and conduct research on Asian American mental health. For most of my life, I have felt inadequate and different from others. During breaks in elementary school, my friends went to the playground while I went to the nurse's office to monitor my blood sugar. My mother came on field trips to administer injections, leaving me embarrassed because I could not eat a simple meal without her. I was not comfortable telling classmates. How do you explain to other children that you gave yourself shots without it sounding terrifying?

When I entered college, I was surprised to hear discussion on mental health. I realized I was my harshest critic and that this originated from my family's expectations of being perfect. I attended a workshop where first-generation students discussed homesickness and being at the university. Hearing others inspired me to share. Disclosing feelings and hearing myself speak, I received validation from peers and *myself*. I shared more with friends, advisors, and even led discussions on mental health at my workplace. I still struggle in embracing myself, but with a support system and willingness to share, I can accept myself and advocate for others. At the Disabled Students Program, I've helped students while acknowledging that it's okay to ask for help. I support discussions about health as I share my experience while listening to others. This has led to positive mental health practices including journaling and meditation.

I found a home with Asian American organizations, especially [Name Withheld]'s high school outreach program. As a housing chair and co-mentor, I was one of the first college faces these low-income, underrepresented students encountered. I created a safe space and taught them about resources to assist in navigating higher education. I bonded with students of similar background, creating a space to discuss mental health. Though students were unfamiliar with these issues, they soon realized the importance of mental health for academic success and happiness.

As a lead peer mentor at [School Withheld]'s first-generation student center, I build community and develop resources for underrepresented populations. I created a workshop on being a STEM undergraduate and introduced resources to enhance study and time management skills. My research on Asian American mental health reflected my struggles with my intersectional identity. I lacked a safe space and was attending an institution unwelcoming for individuals like me. Repeatedly, I have seen that resilience matters more than one's roots and that one should not be ashamed of one's identities.

I bring a perspective to my research that encourages diversity and recognizes the demands of minoritized populations. I understand how each part of one's identity impacts decisions, and how decisions may be made due to lack of appropriate resources. As an Asian American first-generation female, I am motivated to highlight diverse voices in the literature and broach difficult topics such as disabilities and mental health. My research aims to destigmatize mental health and support the academic success and wellbeing of marginalized communities.

SAMPLE PERSONAL STATEMENT #6: STEM

"You don't look like a math person," I was told by a classmate. To an extent, he was not wrong. I was one of seven female-identifying students and of even fewer people of color in our cohort of 22 students. Rarely did the men invite the women to work on problem sets with them, so we would get together and collaborate. As the year progressed, the number of women dwindled to four as more discovered the environment was not for them.

There were additional challenges that came with being a first-generation college student, as I did not grow up with the same preparation or role models as many of my peers who already knew proof-based mathematics. This made it difficult for some classmates and professors to understand why I struggled with simple concepts like induction, and I would often receive discouraging comments. While the thrill of discovering connections between math and reality and the unconditional support from mentors kept me motivated in my studies, I do not want others to face the isolation and microaggressions I went through. In my mathematics career, I am dedicated to creating inviting spaces where everyone can be their authentic self and reach their highest potential.

I became involved in the Society for Advancement of Chicanos/Hispanics and Native Americans in Science's (SACNAS) work to uplift the voices of Black, indigenous, and people of color in STEM as the 2019–2020 vice president of the [School Withheld] undergraduate chapter. As the vice president, I helped organize a luncheon where 43 students connected with faculty from diverse disciplines in a casual setting. For our general body meetings, we had socials and invited industry recruiters from Google, professors, and a former NASA astronaut José Hernández, all of whom gave insight into different science careers. By bringing alumni, faculty, and students together, we created a support system for our members during their undergraduate studies.

I dreamt to create an undergraduate research program that welcomed underrepresented students to STEM. This dream came to fruition in 2021 when I became the student coordinator for the 2021 [Program Withheld], the research program where my research career began in 2018. Knowing the importance for everyone to feel seen and valued, my team and I completed training in equitable teaching practices in mathematics, queer and transgender identity, and effective mentoring strategies. I strived to create a positive first research experience for our scholars, so I organized a workshop session for our graduate mentors planning the research projects to become aware of concepts novice scientists may struggle with. Sometimes our scholars would come to my office hours to discuss their challenges managing our intensive program and personal matters during the global pandemic. I saw our scholars as people first and was a mentor who would listen and provide support to ensure their completion of the program. The summer institute coordinator position helped me realize that my influence in mathematics is not just through the research I produce, but also by my initiatives to make STEM more inclusive.

Through my mathematics career, I hope to create intellectual spaces where everyone feels safe to be themselves and grow, allowing us to learn the most from each other. I will begin to create these spaces in my graduate studies at [School Withheld], when I am a teaching assistant leading discussion sections. I also plan to lead a reading course on optimal transport through the [School Withheld] Mathematics Directed Reading Program for undergraduates, to serve as a graduate mentor for mathematics students in the [Program Withheld], and to contribute to the STEM outreach led by the [School Withheld] SACNAS chapter. With the intellectual and social environment at [School Withheld], I will become a researcher, a mentor, and a proponent for change within the academic community.

SAMPLE PERSONAL STATEMENT #7: STEM

In August 2007, Martin Luther King Jr. Community Hospital (MLK), the hospital dedicated to the Black and Latinx communities of South Los Angeles, closed due to malpractice issues. Growing up four minutes from MLK, I witnessed its fall, which sparked my interest in public health. Many succumbed to preventable causes of death. I wanted to know how these "preventable" deaths occurred in the first place, and which actions could be taken to ensure they would never happen again. The hospital's closure meant my family members were now left without a local hospital. Watching my family members, who are undocumented, struggle with access to healthcare and quality medical care instilled a desire in me to advocate for underserved communities and improve medical accessibility.

My interest in public health led me into the biology program at [School Withheld]. My first year at [School Withheld] was challenging. As a first-generation and low-income student, I was used to being within the South

Central Los Angeles area. My newfound freedom gave me the time to recognize and accept my sexual orientation and gender identity, which I struggled with given that I did not have the freedom to do so at home. During my first year in college, I also faced discrimination from a supervisor who mocked my accent, claimed "all Mexicans are lazy" while referring to me, and threw gang signs at me when I mentioned I am from South LA. For a while, I internalized this experience and reevaluated my pursuit of science and public health. The common challenges a college student faces, such as anxiety, homesickness, and impostor syndrome, were enhanced in my experience due to the several identities I hold. For some time, my timidness prevented me from reaching out for academic tutoring and professional help, which led to losing my sense of direction. I realized that I was seeing my identities, and what people thought about them, as detrimental to my personal and academic goals. Over time, I learned that my identities allow me to see the world through multiple perspectives, which will help me connect with more people throughout my career as a public health official. Though these experiences hindered me throughout my freshman year, I recognized that I had the power to control and craft my experience this time around.

Growing up, it was rare to see someone like myself involved in the sciences. My negative experiences from my first year inspired me to show students from similar backgrounds that they are also capable of attending college and becoming a scientist. Therefore, I decided to join the [Program Withheld] during my sophomore year, which helped me rediscover my sense of direction. I was an instructor for this program and helped design lesson plans to teach minority students at [School Withheld] and [School Withheld]. I taught redwood ecology at the local Botanical Garden and wetland plant adaptations at North Campus Open Space and quickly realized the importance of communicating science effectively. To engage the students, I would incorporate interactive exercises such as allowing them to explore the landscape with magnifying lenses. I would also converse in Spanish to strengthen their understanding of the lesson. Participating in [Program Withheld] showed me why I want to promote diversity in academia and public health. Seeing how much the students enjoyed my lessons made me realize that I must remain in academia to empower minorities to pursue science.

My college experience was finally looking up until the pandemic struck. I immediately moved back to Los Angeles, and as the oldest sibling, watched over my younger siblings through the pandemic while my parents worked. Despite becoming a caregiver for my siblings, I was able to continue my intensive upper-division schedule while remaining involved with research. However, during the pandemic, more than half of my family (I live with extended family) became sick with Covid; we unfortunately lost our grand-uncle at our home. Luckily, my family was able to obtain some resources to help us fight COVID-19. However, I know of some neighbors who were not as fortunate to have these resources, and of my family in Mexico who have less than we do. This situation pushed me to my limit; therefore, I decided to take a break during Winter 2021 to focus on myself and my family. Throughout my break, I strengthened my relationship with my family and recentered myself in order to return to school in Spring 2021. Even with a missing quarter, I was able to raise my GPA from a 3.09 to a 3.54 in three quarters and two summer sessions. Experiencing the pandemic firsthand reminded me of the extent to which infectious diseases impact underserved communities. Though the pandemic has brought many challenges, I returned as a stronger individual and became more motivated to accomplish my goal of becoming a public health professional.

My extensive background in science, skills in communicating science, and involvement studying transmission patterns and control strategies has prepared me as a strong candidate to pursue graduate studies in ecology, epidemiology, and infectious diseases. Additionally, my encounters with discrimination, and experiences with inequalities in public health have given me a focused perspective—I seek to help because I understand what it is like to feel helpless due to things that are out of my control. I am pursuing a master's degree next in order to advance my knowledge of infectious diseases. This way, I can have more perspectives with me when working on the reduction of disease burden affecting underserved communities.

SAMPLE DIVERSITY STATEMENT #1: HUMANITIES

My research, teaching, and service reflect my commitment to transforming the academy from an elite institution to a site of diversity, inclusion, equity, and social justice. Through my scholarship, I seek to recover the voices, experiences, and histories of some of the most marginalized peoples in the United States. They include Mexican women caught up in the U.S.-Mexico war in the nineteenth century and youths of color sentenced to correctional facilities in the early twentieth century. My purpose is not only to bring these specific stories to bear on contemporary audiences but also to highlight the racial, ethnic, class, and gender diversity of peoples and communities in the United States. I view my research as part of a larger project that works to develop a more accurate and relevant understanding of our past and contemporary society.

My teaching, like my research, focuses on cultivating diverse and inclusive spaces in which first-generation, low-income, and/or nontraditional students of color, like myself, see themselves reflected in the curriculum. As I have learned throughout the years, we need models and "mirrors" in the classroom where we can see our profiles, cultures, and communities in the subjects we explore and themes we investigate. When we fail to see ourselves in the curriculum, the message is stark: you are invisible and irrelevant to the larger society. I seek to overturn these perspectives and am purposeful in the readings, assignments, and activities I assign, always working to allow for diverse points of view, safe spaces, and alternative voices to emerge. This approach enables students like myself to learn about how we and our communities have contributed to and remain central to the building of our larger world.

My service, too, is dedicated to strengthening diverse communities in and outside of the academy. For the last two years, I have worked purposefully to mentor high school and first-year undergraduates of color for successful educational experiences. To that end, I have participated in workshops and hosted campus visits—organized by the Black Student Union and Latinx Student Union—to enhance the skills, build networks, and expose the students to the many opportunities in higher education. I continue, too, to volunteer to guide high school students prepare their college and scholarship applications.

As my profile demonstrates, I am dedicated to fostering diversity, inclusivity, and equity in higher education. I believe it is important to continue to follow through with this critical, unfinished work, as the representation of nontraditional students of color in graduate school and with graduate degrees remains painfully low. I look forward to the opportunity to continue to serve my constituency proudly.

SAMPLE DIVERSITY STATEMENT #2: HUMANITIES

I come from a working-class family and grew up in a farmworker town. I am a high-achieving, first-generation student, and I come from what many would consider a tough background. In the past year alone, I have dealt with my mother having stage three breast cancer, my brother and father being admitted to the hospital, and my own unexplained hearing loss. My father was gone for over half of my childhood, deployed overseas, and when he was home, he was an intoxicated stranger struggling to cope with his own trauma. On one occasion, an intervention turned into a violent evening, as my brother stepped in to defend my mom and me. I once found him on the floor, reeking of booze, when I was twelve. My mom had just departed to Samoa to attend her sister's funeral, leaving my older brother and me under my father's care. My brother arrived home shortly after I found my father. I cannot recall my brother's exact steps to help my father recuperate. The only images that remain in my memory are what my father looked like unresponsive and my brother dumping his alcohol down the sink, topping it off with water. I still hear my brother's instructions to not say a word to my mom so that she could focus on grieving her sister. In the same year, I witnessed my neighbor shoot his pregnant girlfriend before he tried to break into my house while I was home alone. These are a few of the unique obstacles I have overcome, and I have worked so hard to heal.

These challenges nearly deterred me from pursuing higher education at all. I was already discouraged as a young Samoan who did not know anyone outside of my educators, or with a similar cultural background, who attended a university. Thankfully, my counselor reminded me of my strength and resilience and encouraged me to see myself in a new light. Since then, I learned to not let any hardship deter me from bringing my goals to fruition, and I have not since. It is because of my experiences that I know I can rise to the occasion and thrive in graduate school. I am driven to earn a master's and eventually a doctoral degree because I am passionate about my work and would like to set an example for others who can relate to my experiences in any way. Of course, I know that throughout my schooling, I am likely to encounter others who in no way relate to me, so I hope to shed light on such unique, important issues. I try to channel the characteristics of my name, which is one of the smallest songbirds yet it has one of the loudest voices, demanding to be heard. I always strive to have my voice be heard, and at the [School Withheld], it would be no different.

KEY TAKEAWAYS

- We unpacked the different components of a personal statement, offering general recommendations about the type of information to include, such as personal attributes and pivotal experiences that speak to your graduate school motivations.

- As in chapter 5, we offered writing tips and a pre-writing exercise that includes a series of questions to answer that will help you draft your personal statement.

- We then transitioned to discussing the diversity statement and how, while it may have overlapping information, it also differs from a personal statement.

- Once again, we offered writing tips and a pre-writing exercise for the diversity statement.

- The chapter ended with sample personal and diversity statements from a wide range of disciplines.

7

LETTERS OF RECOMMENDA-
TIONS, HIDDEN COSTS,
OTHER COMPONENTS, AND
THE ADMISSIONS TIMELINE

REQUESTING LETTERS OF RECOMMENDATION is a daunting prospect, especially if you've been away from academia or if you're a first-generation, low income, and/or nontraditional Student of Color. We often don't know who to ask or how to do so—or know why we need to do so.

Let's review some groundwork. A *letter of recommendation* is an endorsement on behalf of the writer that you have the necessary strengths, attributes, and potential to be successful in your chosen field. Within the context of the graduate school application process, a letter of recommendation is a trusted verification from a professor, ideally a tenure-track professor with a PhD, who can speak specifically to your qualifications as a potential graduate student and to your qualities as a colleague. We say "ideally a tenure-track professor with a PhD" because, as we have seen from our experiences, admissions committees tend to regard their letters as having more institutional credibility than those of *adjunct professors* and *lecturers* who are contingent and non-permanent instructors at the university, especially if they do not hold a PhD (though many do). Your letter writers form an integral part of the application as they provide insight about you from a vantage point that is not readily available in grade point averages or first-person essays. In theory, they are evaluations of you in which you have little influence or say, particularly if you agree to "waive your right"—that is, opt not to have the opportunity to read the letter after it has been submitted. As such, they are thought or meant to be impartial. As you might have guessed from what we have communicated in this book, little in admissions is impartial or objective.

Waiving your right to review the letter is almost always an expectation, but this might seem opaque for those unfamiliar with the hidden curriculum of graduate school (see chapter 1). Contrary to what most people believe, it is not an insignificant step. The application portal will ask if you agree to have your recommender submit a letter on your behalf without your reading it first. Again, most, if not all, institutions will expect you to sign the waiver, as they are interested in receiving recommendations from letter writers who have near complete confidentiality to express their professional views about your candidacy. If you fail to sign the waiver for whatever reason, some professors may refuse to write you a letter, for they might be unwilling to provide a candid assessment if they know or think you might read it. The idea is for your letters to serve as an independent assessment, even though they are always influenced by the recommender's own biases. The letter is meant to let the program and/or institution know that their investment in you will not go to waste. You shouldn't feel uncomfortable waiving your right to review the letter, fearing that the professor might say something that will hurt your chances for admission. If you have any misgivings, have a conversation with the recommender, or find someone else you trust completely and you know has your back.

Another thing to keep in mind when requesting a letter of recommendation is that while this may be your first time asking for a letter, it is likely not the first time that your recommender has been asked and has written letters for students. Writing recommendation letters is a part of a professor's job and likely something that they do often. Some have written hundreds over the course of their careers. It is not uncommon for students to reach out to professors to ask them to write letters for a dozen schools. This may seem like a lot to you but, in actuality, professors come up with their own system of writing letters and may reuse and update old letters they've written for you in the past—they use templates just like you will use for your emails and admissions essays to cut down on the amount of time it takes. Most professors do treat letter writing as part of their jobs but that does not ensure that they will always say "yes." They have the right to assess a student who reaches out to them and then determine if they will accept or deny the request. However, if they work closely with a student, particularly if they serve as a faculty mentor to a student working on an undergraduate capstone or thesis project, they almost expect to write a letter or letters for graduate school and other opportunities now and in the future (such as scholarships, fellowships, research positions). You will have an even better chance for the letter if you did well in their course, were an active participant in class or office hours, or developed an informal mentoring relationship with them.

We know that asking for letters of recommendation for graduate school can be a dreaded process, as students don't always have the skills or confidence necessary to make such requests. And, as you might know, most schools or programs request three letters of recommendation minimum. Ideally, you want three professors within your field. This often creates a challenge. Many applicants are able to come up with at least one trusted source, a former professor with whom they completed a senior thesis or capstone project or with whom they met talk about their work within office hours. Many students, especially those less familiar with the hidden curriculum, including first-generation, low-income, and/or nontraditional Students of Color, however, are unable to think of others they can approach for a similar positive endorsement. It is not unusual to have infrequent interactions with professors. Professors' weekly office hours sometimes conflict with students' schedules and are inflexible. And, quite honestly, many professors are unapproachable or seem aloof or insensitive to students' needs. If you're stuck, think about professors with whom you took more than one course. Did you perform well—with an A or B+—in those classes? If so, then it is likely you can ask that professor for a recommendation. Be sure, too, to ask if they are willing or able to write you a strong letter, with an emphasis on "strong." If they hesitate, move along—or as Yvette says, "no means next." We believe it is much better to know what you're getting than to be surprised or disappointed.

If you have managed to identify at least two potential professors, in all likelihood femtors and mentors, to write for you, you may still need to be creative for a third letter of recommendation, especially if you have no other professors to ask. Believe it or not, this is a common scenario among applicants, especially with increased online classes, where you have few chances of talking or meeting with professors or even speaking up in class. If you have no other options, think about whether you formed strong relationships with teaching assistants (that is, current graduate students). If so, you might ask that graduate student to write the letter and have the professor who taught the course co-sign the letter, if they are willing. Another option, particularly for transfer students who spent their formative years in the community college system, is to ask a former community college professor who has known you for a while. As a last resort for academic programs, especially if you have been employed outside of academia, you can ask a current employer, such as a supervisor or manager, a senior colleague, or trusted community leader to write on your behalf. While it might not reflect on your potential in academia, it will go a long way in talking about the personal qualities—that is, the drive and passion—you will bring to the classroom. Plus, some professional programs will ask for letters from former supervisors and/or managers, as they want to know about your real-world experience, expertise, and passion for the work.

With a potential list of recommenders in hand, the next step is to reach out to them and request the letter, which you should do no less than a month, ideally two months, before they are due. In a perfect world, you would meet with them in person and talk to them about your next move and need for a recommendation. As we have seen, it is much more difficult for professors to turn you down in person than to do so over email. An in-person meeting will also help the professor recall your interactions with them in and outside the classroom. If it's not possible to meet, set up a virtual visit or phone call. Another option is to communicate with them over email. However, you want to get as much attention from your recommenders as possible so that they are able to write you a detailed letter with specific examples. If they fail to respond to your request for support, find other ways to get in contact. Look for their office hours, find a graduate student who works or sees them regularly, or, as a last resort, contact the graduate advisor to see if the professor is available or away on *sabbatical*—which is when a professor takes a paid leave of absence, typically to dedicate more time towards their research and writing. Given the infrequency of sabbatical, professors who are on leave guard their time and are unlikely to respond. But it never hurts to try, especially if they are someone with whom you've built a strong relationship over the years. If possible, alert them before they go on leave to ensure you have your bases covered.

Along with the request for the letter of recommendation, plan to provide the recommender with a packet of detailed information that will allow them to write the strongest endorsement possible that speaks to your specific qualifications, qualities, and fit with the program. Be sure to emphasize what you need from your letter writers (that is, topics to address or focus on). Include your *curriculum vitae*

(CV), which is a current list of your academic accomplishments, as well as your graduate school list, as discussed in chapter 4, which includes the names, contacts, and deadlines of each of the schools for which you are applying. Fortunately, nearly all institutions now request letters electronically and will ask for their submissions through an online portal). Give your letter-writers drafts of your statement of purpose, personal statement, and, if necessary, diversity statement. Even though you may feel nervous about sharing unpolished or incomplete statements, know that it is necessary for the letter writer to have as many talking points about you as possible. Don't fret about the state of your essays one month away from the deadline. If it makes you feel reassured, you can let your recommenders know that these are early drafts and you will send them updated statements as soon as you have them ready. Finally, be sure to attach copies of your transcripts and any Graduate Record Examination scores, if your recommenders request them. Keep in mind that the professor or individual may ask for any additional materials that they feel would be helpful in writing a strong letter. They will often, for example, request a writing sample of a previous essay or access to the files of a digital project you completed in their course. The more details they have about you and your career, the better and stronger letter they can write.

Here is a list of essential items that go into your letter of recommendation packet:

- CV
- Graduate school list with deadlines
- Statement of Purpose
- Personal Statement, if required
- Diversity Statement, if required
- Transcripts, if requested by recommender
- GRE scores, if requested by recommender

- Writing sample or previous project, if requested by recommender

In some instances, you might also have a professor who asks you to draft a significant portion of the letter. If you still want or need to use this recommender, you will need to craft that endorsement to the best of your ability. This is not always easy, especially as this might be the first time you are writing this type of document. This may also be the first time you are writing about yourself in the third person. And, it is especially difficult for first-generation, low-income, and/or nontraditional Students of Color to write their own letters, as many of us come from cultural backgrounds where it is frowned upon to "brag" about our accomplishments, which ends up in us downplaying or underselling ourselves in applications. If possible, ask the professor or another trusted mentor for a sample recommendation letter to give you a sense of what they look like and what type of information they like to include. Last but not least, be sure, too, to explain any glaring gaps or dips in your educational history or record. If you decide not to disclose any of that information in your statements, we suggest letting your recommenders know about why you had to leave school for a year or two or why you failed your courses in the second semester of your first year in college. The letter writer can often explain difficult situations much better than you can, and programs will listen to what they have to say.

Now that you've accomplished the big "ask" and given the recommenders everything they need, the work is not yet done. What's left? First, you need to submit their names and contact information to the online portal and let them know to expect an email with the request. This can get confusing as some application portals will send the email with a link to upload their letter only after you have submitted your application. Others will send the link as soon as you input their contact information, without you needing to submit your full application. Please make sure to review all of your schools' application portals to determine which schools require that you submit the completed application before sending a link to recommenders. We recommend working on those applications first, or at least ensuring that you submit those applications a few weeks in advance. We would not want you rushing to meet a deadline only to give your recommenders a day or two to submit their letter.

Don't forget, too, to follow up with the professor or recommender to make sure they have submitted the letter in a timely fashion. Before you check in with your letter writer, try to check the application portal and/or contact the program to verify if the letter has been submitted. If they have not and you're less than a week away, we suggest sending a "gentle reminder." Professors appreciate such messages, but only if they have not yet completed their task. Do not inquire with the professor unless you know for certain that the program has not yet received the letter. Many professors don't appreciate emails that appear like "check-ins" when they have kept their word. If you're unable to know for certain they have submitted the reference, email the recommender and let them know you lack access to the status of your application, so want to confirm that everything is set. After all is said and done, follow up with a thank you card or an email to show your appreciation; they will be welcome. Even though writing letters of recommendation are recognized as "service," and often given little attention at the time of promotion and review, many professors keep these notes as evidence of their impact in and outside the classroom. If possible, provide them with periodic updates, perhaps monthly or as you hear from institutions, about your application status. More often than not, your letter-writers will be invested in your application process—they're part of it, after all—and will want to know or will appreciate hearing the outcome of the effort. We can attest that nothing is more fulfilling than hearing about the accomplishments of former students.

We know that identifying recommenders, requesting, and following up with letters of recommendation is not an easy or quick process.

From our experience, we know that it can be one of the most stressful components, for it seems that it is out of your control and is a method of gatekeeping or excluding underrepresented groups of people from academia. The reality is that, if you do not get strong letters of recommendation, you cannot apply to graduate school. Nevertheless, know that you do have people who will support you and that you have the wherewithal to achieve your goals if you put your mind to it.

To assist you with the process, we have provided you with three templates of emails for requesting letters of recommendation that you might send out. The first is an email to a professor who may not know you well. In it, you'll see that you have an opportunity to refresh their memory of you and your work and update them with what you're currently doing. The second template is an email to a professor who knows you well. Here, you remind them of your working relationship with them and your future plans. The last template includes the list of schools requiring letters along with their respective due dates to share with them after they've agreed to write the letter. This approach helps the letter writer keep track of when they need to send it out and/or when to expect to receive the request to submit the letter. Again, all of this is done electronically so be sure to remind your letter writer that they will need to upload their letters.

REQUESTING A LETTER OF RECOMMENDATION
EMAIL TEMPLATE #1

Subject Line: Letter of Recommendation Request

Hello/Dear Dr./Professor [**last name**],

My name is [**your first name**] and I am a former student of yours seeking your support. I completed [**name course areas**] courses with you throughout my four years ([**list years**]) at [**name your university**] as an [**list major**]; those courses were [**course title** 1] and [**course title** 2].

I found that your course [list **what you liked, gained from, or learned about the course**].

Since [list **brief update—for example, graduating from X, taking your course**], I have been [list **research experience or internships**] and am now preparing to apply to graduate school. Specifically, I will be applying to [list **programs**] and was hoping you could support me by writing me a letter of recommendation. The deadlines for these programs are in [list **general deadline**].

I realize that you may not remember me since [list **reason why— for example, I am a few years removed from my undergrad studies, I took your course via Zoom and have had limited in-person classroom interactions**] and therefore, I'm more than happy to meet with you via [a **phone call, Zoom, an in-person meeting**] and provide you with a packet of materials to help you draft the letter. I can send you a copy of my graduate school list, statement of purpose draft, personal statement draft, and my CV, no later than [list **a date that's 2–4 weeks before the first deadline**], unless you'd prefer to receive them earlier.

Thank you for your consideration. I look forward to hearing back from you.

Sincerely,/Best,/Respectfully,
[your full name]

REQUESTING A LETTER OF RECOMMENDATION
EMAIL TEMPLATE #2

Subject Line: Letter of Recommendation Request

Hello/Dear Dr./Professor [**last name**],

I hope all is well. I want to send you an update regarding my plan to apply to graduate programs this fall. As you know, I have been working on preparing for graduate school by [describe **what you've been working on**]. During this time, I have benefited greatly from your mentorship and have decided to apply to [describe **program types**]. I was hoping you could support me and would like to ask if you could write me a letter of recommendation for these programs?

I ask because I believe you are someone who knows me well. The deadlines for these programs are all in [**list general deadline**]. Perhaps we can schedule a time to meet so that I can share more about my plans as I would benefit greatly from your advice. I can send you a copy of a letter of recommendation packet with a graduate school list, application essays, my CV, and any other materials you may need in [**list a date that's** 2–4 **weeks before the first deadline**], unless you'd prefer to receive them earlier.

Thank you again for your continued support.

Best,/Sincerely,/Warm regards,

[**your full name**]

REQUESTING A LETTER OF RECOMMENDATION
EMAIL TEMPLATE #3

Subject Line: Deadlines and Information for My Recommendation Letters for Grad School

Hello/Dear Dr./Professor [**last name**],

As promised, here is the letter of recommendation process for the graduate programs that I am applying to this fall. Listed here are the universities to which I am applying and the deadlines for each letter.

1. [University 1], Program 1 (Deadline: [Month, Date, Year])
2. [University 2], Program 2 (Deadline: [Month, Date, Year])
3. [University 3], Program 3 (Deadline: [Month, Date, Year])
4. [University 4], Program 4 (Deadline: [Month, Date, Year])
5. [University 5], Program 5 (Deadline: [Month, Date, Year])
6. [University 6], Program 6 (Deadline: [Month, Date, Year])
7. [University 7], Program 7 (Deadline: [Month, Date, Year])
8. [University 8], Program 8 (Deadline: [Month, Date, Year])

You will receive an email from each institution listed above with specific instructions on what to include in the letter, the deadline, and how to submit the letter. I hope you don't mind, but I will also send you a reminder email a week before the deadlines.

To assist you with the process, I am providing you with a packet of detailed materials. The packet includes a copy of my:

- graduate school list
- statement of purpose
- personal statement
- CV

Please let me know if you need anything else or if you have additional questions. Thank you for your support.
Best,/Sincerely,/Warm Regards,

[your full name]

HIDDEN COSTS OF GRADUATE SCHOOL APPLICATIONS

While letters of recommendation do not cause financial hardship, the process of applying to graduate school can drain resources quickly, especially if you are unaware of the hidden costs. Paying GRE scores, transcripts, and application fees, among other things, can make a dent in your budget. Consider, too, that, during the application season in early to late fall, you will need time away from your regular activities, such as work, school, or childcare, to focus on your packets with minimal distractions. Time away from those responsibilities and commitments, particularly the hidden emotional labor, will not go unnoticed and you will need to pay for someone or something to cover them during your absence.

GRE Scores

If you need to submit GRE scores as part of your application, expect to pay for sending those to each program that requires them. Along with sending scores to three or four or up to ten schools, depending on how many you plan to submit, you may also need to consider the costs for any prep courses or materials to perform competitively. Training classes can range from a couple hundred to over two thousand dollars, depending on how you want or prefer the instruction and where you go to receive it (synchronous or asynchronous course, online or in-person support, group or one-on-one tutoring). Fortunately, more and more these days, GRE scores are no longer required or requested, especially in the humanities and social sciences. Many science and math related fields do continue to ask for them but this too can vary across programs and institutions. Be sure to inquire or look into the possibility of having to submit GRE scores when you're taking note of application requirements.

Transcripts

An expense you are likely to incur are the costs of sending your *transcripts*—a record of your courses and grades spread across the years you spent at that institution—to the programs for which you are applying. Pay close attention to whether they want official or unofficial transcripts. If no specific details or instructions are provided, it is safe to say that unofficial transcripts—ones that you can access or download from your student account at no cost—will suffice. If "official transcripts" are requested, however, you will need to order them from the registrar's or bursar's office of all the colleges and universities you have attended. The difference in costs between official and unofficial transcripts is significant, especially if you have spent time at a community college or two before transferring to a four-year institution. If they want official transcripts, you will have to pay each school to send your transcripts and you will need to order them early to ensure they arrive on time. These expenses will add up swiftly, even more so for transfer students. Fortunately, you are able to solicit the transcripts from the institution's website relatively quickly and easily. Gone are the days of running to campus during business hours—as Miroslava recalls—and waiting in line for that service.

Application Fees and Fee Waivers

As you may know, you will need to pay for every application you submit. These fees can range from $60 to $150, depending on the program and institution. Again, if you are applying to eight or ten schools, this expense can add up to nearly or over a thousand dollars. And it will accumulate along with your transcripts and GRE scores, if required. Fortunately, many programs provide fee waivers to applicants who qualify as low income and who may struggle to pay for graduate school applications. In many ways waivers function like vouchers, allowing the applicant to bypass the cost for submitting the application. Every program and/or institution has a different policy for handling fee waivers. Some are generous and provide you with a code for the waiver as long as you provide proof that you're low income or part of a program like the Ronald E. McNair Scholars Program or the Mellon Mays Undergraduate Research Fellowship. Sometimes fee waivers take anywhere from five to ten business days and have separate deadlines from the graduate program's application deadline that can be tricky to navigate. Pay attention to what the program asks or requires. Follow instructions closely or you'll risk losing the waiver and having to pay full price. Don't forget, too, to process your waiver on time or early, if possible. The same goes with ordering the transcripts and with submitting GRE scores. Give yourself at least two weeks in advance of the deadline. A lot of offices close during major holidays, especially over the winter break, and that will result in shuttered doors and/or empty desks, leaving you without recourse if you have a question or technical glitches. Ideally, you want to be able to talk to someone to have them guide you through the process, if necessary.

Emotional Labor

A final hidden cost we want to highlight is the time you will need to spend on your applications and away from your roles and responsibilities in your home and family. You may end up spending more time than your peers on applications if you are applying for fee waivers or need extra time studying for exams if you are not a great test taker or have been away from school for a while. As parents, we understand the time it will take away from your everyday activities as a parent, sibling, adult child, or other significant member of a household. In most cases, this labor is the invisible or emotional care that we provide to those who depend on us for their basic needs. If we must spend evenings or late night hours, after work, or on weekends, attending to the details of the application process, we may not be present to provide meals, attend softball or basketball games, or help an elderly parent with their nighttime ritual. In such a case, you will need to find help, paid or unpaid, to ensure the emotional labor is minimally disrupted until you are able to rejoin the activities. Remember, however, that the application process is only the warm-up for thinking about how you will find ways to manage the demands of graduate school with your family and personal time. It is not impossible or overly burdensome, but we do want to alert you to the potential challenges it might bring. Then again, we know the joy and purpose a family or extended household can bring in pursuing a dream or life-long goal. As many student-parents have told us, their families help them stay focused and grounded in the pursuit of a graduate degree.

OTHER APPLICATION COMPONENTS
Curriculum Vitae

Often compared to the resume, the *curriculum vitae (CV)* is a document that showcases your academic experience, accomplishments, and skills. Whereas the resume tends to be one to two pages long, CVs do not have a page limit. In fact, many senior professors may have CVs that are upwards of fifty pages long. No need to worry, however, because the typical CV of a graduate school applicant will be anywhere from one to three pages long. While you can structure your CV in different ways, be aware of the standard sections or parts that are included, beginning with your name at the top, front and center. Below your name you should include your contact information, such as your institutional or home address, your phone number, and your email address.

Following your name and contact information comes your first main header, which is the "Education" section. Here you include a list of your degrees, the institutions and departments you received your degrees from, and the year of completion. If you are a transfer student, make sure to include all colleges you attended, whether 4-year or 2-year. The headers that come after your "Education" section can be rearranged depending on what you want to highlight, but we recommend you focus on your "Research Experience." The discussion of your research experience typically includes your title or role, the name of the opportunity or program, and a brief description in bullet form of what you studied and your tangible outcome. For instance, if you completed a summer research program, you would include that you were a summer research fellow, the name of the summer program, the topic, methods, and if the program resulted in you writing a paper or giving a presentation. Following the research experience, many CVs will have a "Research Presentation" section that lists all of the opportunities where you presented your research, which can include a local or national symposium or conference. A *symposium* tends to be smaller in scope and size than a conference but it is still a great opportunity to gain valuable public speaking skills and something to add to your CV.

Next, many will include "Publications," if you have any, followed by a section of "Awards and Honors" or "Grants and Fellowships" depending on which of those you have received. If you have a publication typically you will include the full citation; you can even include papers that are "under review" so long as you genuinely have submitted it to a journal. You may also indicate "in preparation" or "in progress" to demonstrate you are working on current projects. The "Awards" and "Fellowships" sections each should list the title and dates of the opportunity, and you also have the option to include the amount you were awarded. Sometimes applicants who have these kinds of experience will include sections on "Teaching Experience," "Leadership Experience," and "Service." Applicants who have taught as a teaching assistant, instructor, or tutor may include the first of these sections. Similar to the research experience section, you'll want to indicate—in bullet form—your role, the name of the department, program, or organization, and what duties you carried out. "Leadership Experience" and "Service" are similar, although it is ultimately up to you to decide if your experiences align more with leadership or service. If you had an officer title in an undergraduate organization, that could fall under both, but if you are applying to a graduate program that values leadership, you might want to include that as a section. Similarly, if you are applying to a department that prioritizes community-based work, you may want to include a "Service Work," "Community Involvement," or "Related Service Work" section. As you can see, the section titles are not set in stone. While you have many common titles to choose from, some section titles can be modified to better match and group your experiences.

Lastly, it is typical to see a few sections come near the end of your CV. These include "Skills," "Languages," "Professional Memberships," and "References." The "Skills" section should include a list of relevant academic and research skills that would be valuable to the program you're applying to, which often includes technical skills or familiarity with certain software and is much more common in STEM and the quantitative social sciences. The "Languages" section should include a list of all languages you know and your proficiency level in reading, writing, and speaking, such as "Spanish: native fluency in reading, writing, and speaking" or "French: excellent in reading, good in writing and speaking." If you are a member of one or more national associations in your discipline, you can also include that information in your CV by listing them alphabetically and including the year that you joined. Lastly, a "References" section is another optional section to include in the CV. We recommend asking your recommenders if you can include them as a reference in your CV. If so, you can list two to four. Sometimes students opt to not include specific names and instead type "Available upon request." Either option is acceptable.

Rules for formatting CVs may vary but it is often acceptable to follow similar fonts, font sizes, and margins as your application essays. This means using one-inch margins, twelve-point font size, and Times New Roman font. Any other serif-type font, such as Garamond and Georgia, also work. The CV should be single-spaced throughout. Headings should be the only bolded text in your CV. Be sure to "left justify" your information. Some applicants choose to include years of experiences on the right side, similar to a resume, while others choose to include it on the left with a tab separating the year from the text entry. We recommend including years on the left-hand side of all entries because it makes it easier to find as we read from left to right, and also to distinguish it from a resume. If you find it difficult to get started on your CV, consider identifying sample CVs from graduate students and faculty in your fields of interest. You can often find links to CVs in departmental websites and personal websites belonging to academics, and you can also ask your TAs or other graduate students you know to see theirs.

Writing Sample

If you are applying to PhD programs in the arts, humanities, or social sciences, you are most likely going to be asked to submit a *writing sample,* or a manuscript that provides evidence of your written work, academic potential, and research experience. This can be especially stressful for someone who has been removed from schooling for several years and has not written anything academic in a while. Before getting concerned, take a look at the programs on your graduate school list to find out exactly what it is that they want or need. Questions to consider include: What constitutes a writing sample? Are they asking for a copy of the senior thesis or master's thesis? Will they accept any polished seminar paper, literature review, or research report? Do they prefer a sample that reflects your future area of research or will any topic do? Will they accept published work and do they expect it to be sole-authored work or can it include a piece you co-authored with a faculty or graduate mentor or with a peer? What is the minimum and maximum page length requirement? Many writing samples do not go over twenty-five or thirty pages; however, few graduate programs will clearly state page limits. And, if that's the case, it is acceptable to reach out to a graduate advisor or staff member in that department to ask for an average page length. Before deciding what to send in, take a look at what kind of writing materials you have in your academic repository and see if you have anything that closely meets the requirements, even if it needs revising or editing. We recommend working with a femtor, mentor, recommender, or even an academic coach to help you get your writing sample in top shape, particularly if you are uneasy about this component of your graduate school application. Writing samples carry weight in the application process, especially as GRE scores are no longer required or reviewed and letters of recommendations can sometimes promise too much. Many faculty believe that the written work speaks for itself.

Grade Point Average

The *grade point average (GPA)*, or the average of your accumulated grades over time, is—unfortunately—not something you may be able to change about your application. Many first-generation, low-income, and/or nontraditional Students of Color find that their GPA deters them from applying to graduate school. Yvette has had many students tell her that they're afraid that their GPA "is not high enough." You should know that the question of "high enough" is relative to the department and program of interest. While we cannot deny that college grades have historically been a strong indicator about who can access graduate education, it is increasingly common for there to be a more holistic admissions process that includes, but is not limited to, reviewing your transcripts and GPA. If you are concerned that your GPA is not high enough to apply to graduate programs, consider reaching out to a trusted femtor or mentor and asking them. Perhaps your GPA is not competitive for doctoral programs but you may be an excellent candidate for a post-baccalaureate or master's program. Or, perhaps your low GPA is balanced out by a competitive GRE score. In some cases, a concerned student's GPA is actually fine. Just because you do not have a 3.9 or 4.0 does not mean that your score is not competitive for admission into graduate school. If you have genuinely have a fairly weak GPA and choose to take the leap of applying anyway, we strongly recommend addressing this concern in a recommendation letter, your personal statement, or a section of the application portal where you may be asked if you have anything else you want them to know about you. Take every opportunity for the admissions committee to know who you are and what you bring to the table.

Graduate Record Exam

Much like the GPA, the *Graduate Record Exam (GRE)* is an average reflecting the scores from a series of tests, general and subject-based, that measure your skills in verbal reasoning, quantitative reasoning, critical thinking, analytical skills, and subject-specific topics. Historically, the GRE has been a strong indicator of an applicant's access to graduate school. Research has shown, however, that the GRE often fails to predict student success and leaves out underrepresented populations that traditionally tend to score lower on standardized tests, which have many biases (too many to list here). Fortunately, in recent years an increasing number of programs have removed their GRE score requirement altogether. We hope that the dropping or discarding of the GRE requirement in all fields—not just the arts, humanities, and social sciences, but in STEM as well—will continue to be a trend nationwide. The removal of the GRE as an admissions requirement is not a centralized decision at most institutions, which is why we still recommend that you take a close look at your graduate school list to identify if any of your programs require the GRE, both general and/or subject tests. If they do not, you are in luck and can move on to another component of your application. If they do, we recommend that you study as best as you can and sign up to take the exam several weeks in advance of your first graduate school deadline. We say this because it can take a few weeks for scores to get sent to your programs. Some students may opt to enroll in a GRE preparation course in the form of an online (synchronous or asynchronous) or in-person class or even hire a personal tutor. We know that not all students can afford this option. Yvette bought a GRE preparation book and did what she could to study the material, as that was all she could afford at the time. How much you study and what score to aim for depends on your discipline. If your program has a required minimum score, they will state it. When in doubt, ask. For those that do have to meet a certain score or percentage, we recommend studying well in advance, ideally six months or more, so that you have time to take it twice, if need be. If you are interested in a program where the GRE score is required but no such minimum score is required, it is more than likely that the department pays little attention to the exam. If so, study and do the best you can and then move on to other components of your application.

Portfolios, Demos, and Auditions

Other components of graduate applications that are common in praxis-oriented fields and certain professional master's programs include portfolios, demos, and auditions. A *portfolio* is a carefully curated collection of work that can include your work of art, advertising, animation, or architecture, among others. A *demo* refers to a demonstration of your abilities related to that discipline. For instance, for a master's in a teaching program do not be surprised if they ask you to submit a prerecorded teaching demo. Similarly, an *audition* is a sample performance that you may give to be granted admission into a music, theater, or other performance-based program. In all three cases, the admissions committee uses these added components to assess your skills and experience in that particular field. If you are asked to submit a portfolio, demo, or participate in an audition and are less experienced with these practices, we highly recommend reaching out to others who have successfully completed this step and ask for their input. If they're comfortable, ask them to review your materials.

PHD ADMISSIONS TIMELINE

Now that we've reviewed a process that might appear beyond your control, the admissions process, let's cover what you can and should do to put you in the driver's seat. As you turn your attention to the fall and early winter application season, depending on your programs of interest, prepare by giving yourself some space and breathing room. You might do this by reducing your load either at school, if you're in an academic program, or at work, especially if you have intensive or high-level stress responsibilities. Remember, treat your application process like a job by setting firm working hours, deadlines, and, if possible, dedicating a space in your home for the task. To do that, you will need to cut back on your regular activities as much as you can. Make it work for you. If you're in school, choose wisely any elective courses or student leadership positions you might consider taking on. If you're at a job and/or a caretaker of children or elderly parents, find, or, if possible, hire help to assist you with your daily responsibilities as you prepare your applications. You don't need someone for eight hours of the day, every day. Rather, organize your calendar so that you have four to five hours per week to focus on all aspects of the process. Creating structure will give you the freedom to know when to work and when to have time off and be with your family or tend to other responsibilities. It is also important to give yourself some time off, a day or two during the week, when you are not fixated on the applications. If questions come up, and they certainly will come up, ask your femtors and mentors as well as peers and current graduate students for assistance.

In preparing to apply, we encourage you again to reach out to the program or faculty for clarity. In most instances, they will respond to your query, as they too are interested in receiving not only well-prepared applications but also as many as possible, which increases, as noted earlier, selectivity and prestige. Remember, applications for doctoral programs are usually due in the fall, while those for a master's are submitted in the winter and early spring. Above all, pay attention to the precise deadline, as some programs run off season or year round, and these will likely have an alternative timeline.

Timeline Overview

We provide the following monthly highlights as a bird's eye view of the application season. This list will not conform precisely with your own needs but generally it follows what to expect. Use it to develop your own and include your specific due dates and deadlines.

August–September	Online applications open
Mid to end of October	Early deadlines for external fellowships such as the National Science Foundation (NSF) Graduate Research Fellowship Program (GRFP)
December 1–15	Department deadlines for doctoral programs

Mid to late December	Continuing deadlines for external fellowships
January	Departmental nominations for internal central fellowships begin
January–February	Interviews and admissions notifications begin to be processed
February–March	Open houses, campus visits, and admissions notifications continue
April 15	Statement of Intent to Register (SIR) deadline
May 1	Final application deadline for many master's programs
May 15	Registrar contacts students who SIR-ed confirming registration
June 1	Graduate division requests final decisions for remaining SIRs

AUGUST–SEPTEMBER

By the time fall rolls around in August and September and the online applications have opened, the goal is to have nearly completed or, at minimum, drafted the major components of your application. Ideally, you should have finalized your graduate school list, statement of purpose, personal statement and diversity statement, if needed, and curriculum vitae. You should have secured, too, the faculty or individuals who will write your letter of recommendations, ordered or accessed your transcripts, and polished your writing sample, if required. At this point, as well, you should have contacted and followed up with prospective faculty about the possibility of establishing a working relationship with them in their program. You won't get responses from everyone, but cast your net widely for as many bites as possible. Don't forget, too, that you will likely need to spend time filling out the online application for each institution. Minimize any surprises by previewing the instructions and requirements as soon as possible. Some may ask for short responses to their queries rather than one or two long essays.

The fall, or at least one to two months in advance, is also the point at which you will want to give your recommenders the application packet with everything they need to write your letters. If you qualify as low income, you will want to secure fee waivers by contacting the graduate division or graduate school at each institution in plenty of time. The process of accessing waivers varies significantly and you may be out of luck if you think you'll be able to get one when you go to submit your application, which is not the case with private universities and colleges. They require you to obtain it in advance of the application submission. Finally, you will want to identify and apply for any external funding you might qualify for from federal and private agencies such as the National Science Foundation, the Paul and Daisy Soros Fellowship, and the Hispanic Scholarship Fund, among others.

OCTOBER–NOVEMBER

For these months, we advise completing final drafts of your statement of purpose, personal statement, and, if required, diversity statement. Continue, too, to apply for external funding and revise and edit writing samples, if required. You might even contact femtors or mentors or writing specialists for last minute feedback. If possible, stay focused on any short- or long-term research projects, which will enable you to enhance your research skills and experiences. At this point, you should also order official transcripts, request the waivers if you haven't done so already, and send GRE scores, if applicable. It would also be beneficial to plan on submitting your applications in early to mid-November—before the national "Thanksgiving" holiday—for any early December deadlines.

By December, you will need to complete your graduate school applications, especially for doctoral programs, and prepare to hit "submit." Generally, submissions to master's programs take place in the winter and early spring months. As such, you are likely to hear back from master's programs a few months after doctoral programs, which start contacting applicants in mid-February until April 15, the last day to submit your Statement of Intent to Register (SIR). In rare instances, we also see PhD programs reach out in January or a few weeks after applications have been submitted. We have seen this when institutions are particularly interested in recruiting underrepresented students in STEM fields, which remain dominated by white men.

JANUARY–FEBRUARY

In January, most applicants will need to fill out the Free Application for Federal Student Aid (FAFSA). We highly recommend doing so, as most institutions will require you to provide your income information not only for possible loans, grants, and fellowship but also for their records of the student population's financial profile. Even if you decline all loans, you are still required, in most places, to fill out the FAFSA. In January, too, it is common to continue to apply for graduate programs, particularly master's programs. By mid-to-late February, you will begin receiving notifications about admissions, although do not be surprised if you receive admissions decisions in January; this is becoming more common and varies widely across disciplines and specific departments. Usually, the acceptances go out first, then waitlisted notifications, which are contingent on how many—and how quickly or not— applicants accept their offers for admission. (Any rejections usually come last, right around or after April 15, after all the accepted and waitlisted persons have made their decisions. This is not a hard and fast rule, however.) Depending on the outcome of your applications, you will likely prepare for preview days or open houses, which will be in-person campus visits or possibly online. Before you meet or talk with anyone, especially faculty, do your homework and closely study their research, teaching, and service interests. While it's not always easy to find, with some creative searching at the institution's website or contacting the graduate admissions officer, you are sure to find faculty involved with different activities on and off campus. Find out, too, more about the graduate students, including any field-specific and campus-wide graduate student organizations.

Ask graduate admissions staff to put you in touch with active members of the department. And make every effort to attend prospective graduate student days that are put on by the graduate staff. In many cases, the departments or programs will provide some kind of funding or support to cover some of your costs related to the visit. In the interest of diversifying the graduate student population, many graduate divisions or graduate schools will provide small stipends or will cover travel and lodging expenses for first-generation, low-income, and/or nontraditional Students of Color. If it is not mentioned explicitly, ask about any such opportunities. Costs for visiting campuses add up quickly, especially if you're traveling across the country, staying for at least two nights, and having three meals a day. Most units are aware of the constraints and do what they can to have you visit their campus and get to know you better.

MARCH

Acceptance notices, often sent out in February and March, don't always come with details about your financial support. In many cases, funding packages—in the form of fellowships, teaching assistantships, or other plans—are announced a week or sometimes weeks after admissions. We have also seen many students get additional boosts to their offers as other forms of institutional support become available. While you may start off with a package that includes a small stipend and your full tuition and fees, that package might increase with a heftier award, enabling you to pay for your housing with less worry. Before you begin to celebrate or fret about your offers, create a graduate school budget that reflects all your monthly and weekly expenses along with your sources of income. Include everything: housing, transportation, meals, books, technology, supplies. Be sure, too, to include entertainment as well as your everyday expenses, as you will need time away for yourself.

APRIL

As much as we've been waiting for April to roll around, now that it is here, you are fairly certain what you will be doing in the fall. If you are accepted to your top school on your list, April 15 is the final date to submit the SIR and time to think about the transition to graduate school. If you have been waitlisted and have yet to hear back on the status of your application, we encourage you to contact the program. If it is a dream school, reach out often, biweekly or even weekly, as April 15 approaches, letting them know your interest. If you do not receive an acceptance to a school of your choice, it is time to think about your next options, which we discuss below. We caution you, however, to not make a final decision until you see the funding package. If it is insufficient, you will need to negotiate more support, especially if you have several acceptance notices from other campuses. You might relay, in a professional manner, that you have funding opportunities available elsewhere but that you are committed to attending their school. Let them know that you would like to come but are in need of more support.

MAY–JUNE

By May 1, the application deadline has arrived for any remaining applicants. If you've accepted an admissions offer, by the end of that month you will be in the process of obtaining a new student account and email as well as completing any online registration. Within a few weeks, in June, you will receive a final admissions decision. The university might request final transcripts, too, especially if they didn't receive your grades for the spring semester or for winter/spring quarters.

You will also need to look into your options for transitioning to your new residence, if you're moving away to another city or state. Spend time conducting research into your location. Does the university provide graduate student housing and other opportunities for incoming students like you (first-gen, low-income, and/or nontraditional Students of Color). You might also want to ask your department about when you should expect to receive your first funding payment and the total amount you will receive. In some institutions, graduate students may be working a full month or two before they receive their first payment. Plan accordingly. Financial troubles are stressful and you don't want to start your program feeling under pressure. We also advise, when possible, that you secure a summer job to save for the move or pay off as much significant debt as possible, including credit cards. (The exception is student loans, as they will typically be deferred until after graduate school. If your undergraduate loans are structured so that they will accumulate interest while you are in graduate school, you should consider making interest-only payments so that the loans do not grow. Generally, be sure to contact an advisor before making any significant decisions about your finances.) Lastly, practice self care and find time to recognize your accomplishments.

KEY TAKEAWAYS

- · The chapter began with a discussion on how to request a letter of recommendation, who to ask, and what they are used for.

- · We then shared tips and strategies for creating a letter of recommendation packet to ensure that your recommenders can write strong letters. As noted, those items include the CV, graduate school list with deadlines, statement of purpose, personal and diversity statement, if required, transcripts, GRE scores, and/or writing sample or previous project, if requested by the recommender.

· We shared a few sample email templates to request recommendation letters.

· And since there are many hidden costs related to applying to graduate school, we shared a few of them, including paying for GRE test prep courses, taking the test, sending the scores, sending transcripts, application fees, and the time and emotional labor which can also translate into monetary costs (such as for childcare).

· We then transitioned into discussing other common components of a graduate school application such as writing a CV, submitting a writing sample, and expectations for the GPA, among others.

· The chapter ends with detailed information on the graduate school admissions timeline so that you know what to anticipate throughout your application process.

PART THREE

AFTER APPLYING

8

THE APPLICATION REVIEW PROCESS AND PLAN BS

||||||||||||||||||||||||||||||||||||||||||||||||||||||||||||||||||||||||||||||||||||||||||||||||||||||||||||||||||||||||||||||||||||||||||||||||||||||||||||||||||||||||||||||||||||||||||||||||

REMOVING THE VEIL OF THE APPLICATION PROCESS

At this point, after months of writing and revising essays, reaching out to professors and others to write you letters of recommendation, and communicating with femtors and mentors as well as potential faculty advisors, you're likely breathing a tremendous sigh of relief. You might wonder, what's next? Now comes the waiting game. We call it a game because it is often a period of time in which you try to come up with a variety of strategies to reduce the feelings of tension and anxiety surrounding the graduate admissions process. Some of us try to put it out of our minds by distracting ourselves with our routines and responsibilities. Others ruminate about different parts of the applications, including the essays, wondering if we have communicated the proper strengths and abilities as well as the leadership skills and diverse perspectives we bring to the table. And yet another group checks email constantly or peruses online boards or pages to learn about the latest news in the graduate school hunt. But what really happens to your application once you hit "submit" and the deliberations begin behind closed doors?

The reality is that few people have an understanding of what goes on behind the curtain of graduate admissions and how decisions are made. What we do know is that graduate as well as undergraduate admissions have become highly competitive in recent years, making access to higher education increasingly elusive, especially for first-generation, low-income, and/or nontraditional Students of Color. We've seen and heard the illicit lengths to which the wealthy and powerful will go to gain admission for their children to highly prestigious four-year undergraduate universities and colleges. While we have yet to see similar criminal activity at the graduate level, the competition for access to master's and especially doctoral programs can be cut-throat. As Julie Posselt has argued, increased demand for graduate degrees as well as the need to limit the size of departments and increase prestige and ranking, encourages institutions "to remain highly selective and competitive."[1]

In previous years, grades, GRE scores, and the reputation of the undergraduate institution were the primary criteria used to evaluate applicants. Researchers found, however, that neither GRE nor reputations predict the student's ability or likelihood to complete the PhD. You might be surprised to learn that few programs, especially those in highly selective institutions, use rubrics to evaluate applicants. Instead, as Posselt finds, most programs use a set of complex and dynamic criteria to admit, waitlist, and reject applicants. The difference among those three outcomes is small, often difficult to pinpoint, and can change from year to year, depending on the profile of applicants and faculty reviewers. Moreover, faculty judge applicants not based on an absolute set of criteria but in relation to others in the applicant pool of that year as well as on beliefs and values that resonate with their own—part and parcel of implicit bias—and with institutional needs in mind. The process, Posselt reminds us, is "cloaked in secrecy."[2]

At this point you might be thinking, as we have been told throughout our lives in the US, that admissions are—or should be—based on merit or academic achievement. Merit, however, is not an absolute assessment, and not based solely on grades, scores, or awards. It is deeply complex and dynamic as well as hotly contested, especially since networking and nepotism, across all types of institutions and industries, continues to play a large role in who gets afforded opportunities over others. Merit, then, is conditional and dependent on what the faculty, committee, or department deem "quality." You are identified as meritorious for admission because you are judged to have the attributes as well as the values and interests that the faculty have deemed legitimate grounds for drawing the line between the many who would like admission and the few who are granted that opportunity. Sometimes you are admitted to help balance out another field, while at other times you are selected to help pursue or build a specific interest in the department.[3] Admissions also usually reflect the collective cultural priorities of the program or institution. Merit, thus, isn't the "sum total of an applicant's 'deservingness'" to be admitted based on what they have done or how they will do in graduate school. Rather, "merit and quality are subjectively assessed and socially constructed."[4] In short, credentials, connections, and effort can propel you to the short list, but the outcome is impossible to predict and may be subject to a variety of factors outside of your control.[5]

Our discussion is not meant to make you feel powerless or make you lose hope of being admitted to graduate school. Instead, it is to help you understand that admissions decisions behind closed doors are complex and reflect the culture of the department. Certainly, not all faculty think alike or vote in the same way. Miroslava, as a professor in a department that admits graduate students, has seen heated disagreements about the candidacy of particular applicants, with faculty arguing over the focused or unfocused nature of the proposed research. Fortunately, she has not seen these struggles regularly, but likely some of her colleagues have been in institutions where they have many disagreements about who should be admitted and why. What she has seen is that admitted candidates are those who have the support of faculty who have agreed to take on the responsibility of advising, femtoring, and/or mentoring them. Without this vote of confidence, a sponsor of sorts, applicants are almost never accepted. Institutions also usually don't accept doctoral students that they cannot support financially with funding from internal or external sources, which usually comes along with the acceptance. They are, however, willing to take unfunded master's students, as they often will charge them full tuition for the two or three years of the program, unless the student can find a teaching or research assistantship. Departments will often refuse to take students who have proposed an area of study that has not been developed or that is not of interest to the faculty in the department. To avoid unnecessary disappointments, study the department's website and reach out to faculty in the field to make sure they are taking students, as we advise in part 2, and that they have interest in you. As long as you have found communicative and supportive faculty, crafted your best essays possible, gathered strong letters of recommendation, and submitted all required materials on time, you have done your due diligence. All you can do now is wait.

Despite all the sacrifices to craft the strongest application necessary, we know you will receive denials. Almost everyone does. Rejections are, nevertheless, hard to take, as many of us interpret or view them as personal reflections of our self-worth. Similar to the term "failure," the word "rejection" induces or triggers a lot of feelings of shame, inadequacy, and envy and may reinforce feelings of impostor phenomenon.[6] In a culture that prizes "winners," it is normal to have these feelings. What's more important is how you handle the outcome, that is, the thoughts and actions that come from the experience. If you find yourself worrying about why you were denied admission, contact the graduate officer or the proposed faculty advisor and ask for feedback on your application, specifically for ways you can strengthen your candidacy. Be willing, too, to meet in person, talk on the phone, or meet online or virtually. The graduate officer and/or the faculty advisor are more likely to respond and feel comfortable responding to your query than some other member of the department who had little or no contact with you.

While you can be proactive in seeking answers as to "why" you didn't get in, you should allow yourself to sit with the uncomfortable feelings or feel the pain that is associated with not getting into graduate school. For some, it might be a day or two, for others a couple of weeks. You also might not realize that, in the world of graduate school applications, rejection is common. Applicants tend to talk about their successes but not say a word about their failed attempts. Some of the most successful people have received the most "nos," as they are more likely to have applied to more programs than those fearful of rejection. If you're not feeling too great about the rejection, know that most of us have been conditioned to need external validation to prove our worth. We are not, however, only as valuable as an institution says. We need to learn how not to rely solely on external feedback to feel valued and validated.

If you are serious about pursuing an advanced degree, but have not been admitted this year, take the time and effort to prepare for the next graduate school application cycle. It is common to reapply. The next time you set out to apply, you will need to review and revise your materials carefully, looking for any gaps in your research experience or public engagement, depending on your desired field. If you didn't have the opportunity to meet with faculty in advance to talk to them about their research interests and working style, plan on that crucial legwork early in the application cycle. We would also recommend casting your net wider the second time around. If you only applied to four to five schools, you might increase your schools to eight to ten or even twelve to fifteen. In some instances, we've seen candidates apply to up to twenty schools, hoping they will land at least one school of interest. Don't let a denial or rejection stand in your way. Redirect the focus from the negative to the generative and reframe the "no" to what Yvette calls "no means next," and what we've heard others refer to as "no means not yet" and "rejection means redirection." Don't let defeat distract you from preparing from what comes next. Remember, too, we all have our timeline. Not everyone will go—or needs to or should go—to graduate school right after undergraduate or during the first time they apply. You might need to take a gap year or two or you might need to get a full-time job to get some experience and return stronger as a candidate when you're ready and willing.

THE WAITING GAME AND PLAN BS

As you approach the ominous April 15th deadline, you might realize that it is not just a dreaded tax day for many of us but it is also the final day for news about graduate school admissions and rejections, particularly if you are applying for doctoral programs. Master's programs have final decision dates that are further out, usually sometime in May or June. By mid-April, applicants who have been admitted but have yet to accept or deny a department's offer must make their preferences known, as the status of any waitlisted applicants are contingent on these. As spaces become available, that is, as accepted students turn down their offers, prospective or waitlisted students are admitted. If you are waitlisted and eventually denied admittance, and, sadly, have no other offer of admission or are unhappy with your choices, it is acceptable and smart to decide to reapply for admission in the following year or years. Though a disappointing trajectory, you can find ways to reframe your experience and take advantage of the time that you have to prepare and strengthen your candidacy as an applicant.

Denied Admission

If you are denied admission, we recommend that you take the time to process the outcome. For many, rejection leads to disappointment. Don't take it personally, although it is okay to give yourself time to feel all of your feelings, and use the opportunity to grow or strengthen your approach. For Adriana Jaramillo, a guest on the Grad School Femtoring Podcast, rejections from all the doctoral programs that she applied to right after her undergraduate studies was a blessing in disguise, for it allowed her to think through her commitment. To do so, she decided to pursue research during what became her gap year. "I . . . want to know what it's like be in academia, kind of get a feel for it, to make sure that it's something I really do want to pursue," Adriana explained, "and not something that I'm being pushed towards, because of all the talk that I've heard throughout my undergrad[uate] career with people trying to go directly into grad[uate] school." The "talk" or pressure to go into a graduate program, she noted, was not a sufficient reason to go to graduate school.[7]

In addition to taking proactive steps to reach your goals, remind yourself of your qualities and strengths and keep them, if possible, in a running list so that you can come back to them frequently and feel affirmed. Remember, too, if the stress or worry is too much or if you think your confidence or self-esteem has been shaken, seek out professional support. While cultural support systems—such as religion, spirituality, and faith—are useful, at times we need intervention specifically for our mental and emotional health. Fortunately, therapists are a bit more accessible and affordable—as well as acceptable as a form of healing—today than in the past. Don't let social and or cultural stigma or shame stop you from being your best. Know that it is common to feel discouraged, anxious, or even depressed, but find ways to begin the process of healing and wellness.[8]

Once you have processed the disappointing outcome, take the opportunity to learn from any potential mistakes you might have made. While Posselt argues that a lot of the decision-making is out of your hands, it does not mean you can't be proactive and find ways to strengthen your application for the next round of admissions. In doing so, you might learn that you need more language training or more research experience. You may also hear that the department decided to accept a small cohort of students this year because of budget cuts and the commitment to provide a five-year funding package to all admitted students, which is increasingly the trend in graduate admissions. Instead of admitting six or eight students, they admitted only two or four. You might find out, too, that the adviser or faculty member that you wanted to work with didn't admit or take any students this year, as they are retiring, relocating to another academic position, on sabbatical, or taking a year-long fellowship. These kinds of awards come in the winter or spring terms of the academic year so such news cannot be anticipated in fall when you are discussing your plans with potential advisors. Finally, you may find that you applied to a discipline that encourages gap years or full-time work experience and you have neither since you are a recent graduate from an undergraduate program.

Other potential reasons you didn't get into graduate school are that you didn't apply to any master's or postbaccalaureate programs (we discuss postbacc programs in more detail in chapter 1). Instead, you opted only for the PhD. It is becoming increasingly difficult to gain admission to a PhD program right out of an undergraduate program. If, indeed, you don't get into a doctoral program, it can be useful to pursue a master's as another option. Consider, too, postbacc programs (chapter 1), which are often fully funded and include assistance with applying to doctoral programs. You also may not have asked for enough help. If you're unsure about your materials or any aspect of the process, don't be afraid to seek answers. Plus, don't forget, it is never too late to try again. We believe you can take what you learned from an unsuccessful cycle and apply it in the future. Whether that's getting organized and submitting the materials on time, writing a statement of purpose that captures a holistic picture of who you are and what you want to achieve, tailoring each application to a specific program— rather than submitting a generic letter where you only change the names of the institutions and potential faculty advisors—or taking additional classes at a community college to acquire certifications or professional development, you will be a much stronger candidate. Think of this process too as building persistence and a thick skin.

Waitlisted: Now What?

If you are placed on the waitlist, we understand that it can be frustrating to be neither accepted nor denied. Instead, you remain in suspense. Being waitlisted means, however, that you are competitive and they want to keep you as a viable contender, should their first round of choices decide to go elsewhere, which almost always happens. Miroslava has often seen the first two to three or more of the top admitted students decide to go elsewhere, usually to a better resourced and more prestigious institution. Graduate programs keep a waitlist to make sure they can fill their incoming class and maintain their priorities for a diverse cohort. Once you learn about your status, figure out when you'll know if you have been admitted. As noted, if it's a PhD program, you'll know no later than April 15. For the master's program, that date will come later. If you've been waitlisted at your "dream" school but have been admitted to your second or third choice school, you are going to have to wait until the last possible day to keep your options open. If you receive an email or other contact from the schools that have admitted you, asking for your decision, know that you still have until April 15 to make final choices. Nevertheless, respond to the outreach, telling them you are still weighing your options and considering the best possible opportunity for you.

Being waitlisted also carries implications for funding, placing you potentially out of contention for internal support. In most cases, departments award funding packages to their top admits and provide less to others. A waitlist status often means you will get a small amount or will be forced to take out loans. We've worked with students who have been waitlisted and later admitted, but with no funding. Some of these students have opted not to accept the offer and wait until the following year. In some instances, the disappointment will come from having to decline an offer, for the funding may be woefully inadequate or the professor of interest may have suddenly decided to take a position elsewhere. Applicants often decline coveted offers of admission due to circumstances beyond their control. In such instances, please know that you are not alone.[9]

If you decide to wait for a potential admission, the first thing to do is to confirm with the program that you remain interested and wish to remain on the waitlist. If you don't hear back within a couple of weeks about your status, check in with them, again, expressing your interest. As the April 15 deadline approaches, send a weekly email inquiring about where you stand in the process. Sometimes students are advised to send in updates to graduate admissions; we would add that you can do that, but only when such units agree to consider them. Finally, keep in touch with the department. Don't ghost them or let them do that to you. Waitlist status can be hard to take but you can always find what works best for you.

Plan Bs

As you apply or consider applying to graduate school, it's important to also think about what you will do if you don't get accepted or receive enough funding, or if you change your mind and decide to pursue other goals. In other words, you need a backup or Plan B for achieving your goals, even if it doesn't include graduate school in the short term. A common choice is to take a gap year, which is discussed in more detail in chapter 1. Many of the students we have worked with in the recent past have decided to do just that when they didn't receive the news they expected to hear. If they lacked the research experience, some students decided to use the year or two to take extra classes at a community college or join a short-term program to fulfill additional graduate school requirements or to gain experience to become a more competitive candidate. Consider your intended field and whether practical or hands-on experience makes sense or is expected. We've also seen others apply for a full-time job in order to save money. If they had few resources or came from impoverished families and could not afford to pay for graduate school, particularly master's degrees, which tend to provide less funding than doctoral programs, some students have decided to work for a year or two. We agree that sometimes opting for employment to save for graduate school makes sense. Indeed, we don't encourage taking out hefty loans, which will likely stay with you for years to come and dampen your future prospects. Lastly, some applicants have waited another year and found work at a research lab when they could not find an optimal faculty advisor or program to match their interests. Such choices, if they become available, give you the opportunity to network with those who might be able to make introductions or open doors. Consider what makes sense professionally, financially, and personally.

This can also be an opportune moment to make a significant life change, such as reconsidering your current employment, if you've come to realize how much you dislike or dread your work or how much it drains you, and to rethink more generally where you are in life and where you want to be. It might be a good time to explore new opportunities in other areas of full-time work. Or, perhaps you take on an internship in a new field or volunteer in an area related to your graduate school interests. In doing so, you would be allowing yourself e much-needed experience for graduate school admissions. You might decide to gain a certificate or enroll in a post-baccalaureate program or other similar work that strengthens your application. Finally, rather than pursue education as an outlet, some turn to travel or passion projects to pass the time and figure out what they want to do in the future. Be creative. Now is the time.

Above all, though, we recommend staying connected with family, friends, and members of your communities throughout the process, from thinking about applying to hearing back from the institutions. As you might have learned or will learn, the process for applying to graduate school can be isolating. Remember those who are in your corner and have your back no matter what the outcome. Use them as a sounding board for your frustrations, challenges, and victories, no matter how small. If you don't feel comfortable sharing with them or disclosing personal inner thoughts and feelings of doubt, turn to online community sources for mental health assistance or support groups. You need to remain connected through these months of institutional testing and evaluating. Use all your resources at your disposal. You won't regret it.

We dedicated this chapter to removing the veil over the graduate school admissions process to help you understand how decisions are made behind closed doors. The review process, as we discussed, is complicated, competitive, and secretive and is influenced by the needs and desires of, as well as the biases of, the faculty, institution, and academia. These considerations can and will vary year-by-year; they are dependent on the demand for the program as well as the financial health of the college or university. That said, you do have some control in what happens to your application, that is, how it is evaluated and judged.

We also spent time discussing what can be stressful months of waiting to hear back on the status of your application. We advise that whether you are accepted, rejected, or waitlisted, you develop contingency plans—or Plan Bs—for moving forward, regardless of which way you are headed. If you are accepted, think about the next steps you need to take to submit your final materials, make the move to another location, and prepare for your next adventure. If you've been denied admission, investigate to the best of your ability what aspects of your candidacy need improvement or what you can do to enhance your skill set and chances down the road. Consider too what you will and can do to prepare a stronger application. Whether a gap year, taking online or in-person classes at a community college, or taking on an internship, find ways to remain connected and in pursuit of your professional and personal goals. If waitlisted, remain invested and connected to the program, especially if it is an institution that was at the top of your list. You may have to wait for a few extra weeks or months to hear the final word, but remember you will have an answer sooner than later. Similar to rejection, think about what you will and can do if you end up being admitted but with no funding offer or if you are rejected altogether.

We want to close by reiterating the need for you to take care of yourself holistically—mind, body, and spirit—during this process, which can be stressful. If you need support, seek it from professionals or an online support group. Reach out to family and friends, as well. While they may not understand your need to pursue a graduate degree at your particular stage in life, those who care and want the best for you will appreciate your drive and commitment.

KEY TAKEAWAYS

- This chapter shared insights on what happens after you have clicked "submit" on a graduate school application, including detailing some of the complex and dynamic criteria and debates involved in making admissions decisions.

- We complicated notions of merit and remind the reader of what is and is not in their control within the application.

- We talked about what to do if you have been waitlisted, when to consider creating a backup plan, and what those plans can look like.

- Lastly, we shared insights on how to deal with rejection and what to keep in mind if you decide to apply again.

9

INTERVIEWS,
RELATIONSHIPS,
AND FUNDING

AN ESSENTIAL COMPONENT OF THE graduate school application process is getting to know the specific opportunities available at each program on your list. Believe it or not, the faculty in the program are equally interested in getting to know you, your strengths and weaknesses, and how you might enhance its research specialties, curriculum, and diversity. Much of the initial "meet-and-greet" or evaluation that takes place between you and those at the institution happens through interviews, open houses or preview days, and one-on-one meetings with potential graduate advisors or officers in the department, and, possibly, with graduate admissions representatives. We advise you to do your homework before the event or trip. Think of these meetings as not only opportunities to network professionally but also to establish potential long-term relationships that will shape your future career. To help you prepare, in this chapter we have laid out some guidelines on how this process typically unfolds and what it means for you.

INTERVIEWS

The most common way for programs to get to know applicants—beyond the application—is an interview. Given the competitive nature of the graduate school admissions process and the high stakes of admitting individuals for two to six, or even more, years of study, many graduate programs have turned to interviews to evaluate applicants holistically. Interviews allow admissions committees to get to know a candidate beyond the grade point averages, scores, and carefully curated essays that make up applications, and to do so before they make the commitment to take on a student for the long term. Many programs, however, lack the resources to take the extra step of the interview and continue to rely solely on the application as the basis for their choices. Whatever the case may be for the programs on your list, you need to become familiar with the interview process, as it will follow you beyond graduate school.

Graduate school interviews are no walk in the park and can be nerve-wracking, especially if you're a first-generation, low-income, and/or nontraditional Student of Color and are unfamiliar with navigating predominantly white and elite spaces. Feelings of inadequacy often rear their ugly heads, as does another familiar voice, the impostor phenomenon, which can make its presence felt as the day and time of the event approaches. Having experienced similar bouts of fear and anxiety, we know what it's like to negotiate spaces where you feel like you're out of your league. We want you to remind yourself that, in carrying out this portion of the application process, you have a greater purpose, which is to achieve a graduate degree and your professional and personal goals that the degree will aid. Remember, too, the committee would not have invited you for a session if they didn't think you had the qualities and interests to make you a worthy contender. They would not want to waste their time if they didn't think you had what was needed to succeed in a graduate program. Instead of believing negative self-talk and limiting beliefs, reframe this as a great opportunity and think about how you might best prepare for your interview(s).

Let's break down what's involved in an interview.[1] With the growing familiarity with online chats and meetings, expect that any pre-admissions interview will be virtual and last no more than thirty to sixty minutes, giving departments the opportunity to meet more applicants than they might have done in the past or in person. The purpose of a sit-down session is for an admissions committee—usually composed of faculty, administrators, and sometimes a current graduate student—to get to know you better and become familiar with your strengths and any potential weaknesses. The committee will likely ask you about your current and future research and teaching interests and/or plans after graduate school. Be ready with answers. Anticipate questions and prepare ahead of time, ideally a few weeks before the interview. You can write out some helpful notes and post them next to you so that you can glance at them during your conversation when necessary. Don't let them overwhelm you, however; clearly mark them and attach them to convenient locations. Remember, you are always being assessed. From the moment you meet them online to when you say goodbye, you will be judged or evaluated. Accordingly, try your best not to be late, as it does not leave a good first impression. Don't forget, either, to "check your tech," that is, test out your equipment, including the computer, software, your digital background (if you're using one), and the strength or quality of the internet in the space that you plan to use for the interview. Ask a friend to call you to ensure that all is well. Also, make sure that you have appropriate lighting from the front, not from behind, unless you want the screen to appear dark. If possible, sit in front of a window with natural lighting. Be sure, too, that your background isn't distracting. Remove anything personal or unkempt that might appear on screen. Ultimately, it's up to you to reveal as much as you want, but we would caution against over-sharing in the admissions process.

You might not realize it, but the interview is also an opportunity for the committee to showcase the assets of their institution, making them appear to be an attractive and inviting place for you and others like you interested in graduate study. At the meeting, they might make it a point to share some of the highlights or strengths of the academic program, including the interdisciplinary nature of the work or of their standing among their peers. Indeed, some programs will work hard to convey their selectivity and prestige. Don't be put off if it seems excessive. Sometimes you need to break through the window dressing or shell to get to know people better, in this case, professors, administrators, and likely nervous graduate students. Academia doesn't always encourage warmth and familiarity, especially in institutions with solemn and rigid traditions. Nevertheless, you can get a sense of the culture or climate of a department as you go through the interview process.

Finally, the time you spend with the committee is a great way for you to learn more about both individual faculty and the collective. In the short time you have to get to know them, ask about the most critical elements for your ability to attend graduate school: funding, advising, femtoring and/or mentoring, and if applicable, resources for parents, LGBTQ+, undocumented, and disabled students. Inquire too about their attitudes beyond the lab or classroom, and try to do so without seeming to be overly aggressive or underwhelmed by their presence. Observe their body language and respond accordingly. You shouldn't assume that everyone in the department brings or has similar perspectives, but certainly their role as representatives says a lot about the power dynamics in the program or department. If they seem unhappy or uninterested, it's likely they were obligated to participate. Or, if they are enthusiastic, warm, and friendly, they probably enjoy the work.

Before the interview, be sure to prepare, as noted earlier. Develop questions specifically tailored to the individual unit or program. Don't write generic questions that you then recycle for each interview. Find out information about as many people as you can. Begin your research with the website, but don't trust it to tell you everything, for they are not always updated. If you notice the content is old, reach out to the graduate advisor or potential faculty advisors for insights on the program, including the faculty, administrators, and/or graduate students you will meet during the interview. Read as much as you can about the department, institution, and community. Be sure to review what went into your application packet, in case they ask you questions about any of your statements or other components. If it's not made explicit, ask about any dress code or what is appropriate to wear. In our experience, business casual attire is normally expected, even in an online interview, but keep in mind that every department is different and ultimately we would want you to feel your best on your interview day.

During the interview, be ready to respond to the questions concisely and directly. If you are comfortable doing so, make eye contact with the interviewer. If the interview is virtual, as it likely will be, look at the device's camera as much as possible, rather than looking down or to the side of the computer screen, as this will make you appear to be making eye contact. Make sure to also practice good posture, enunciate and project your voice enough to be heard clearly, and try to remain engaged with the conversation. You want to leave a good impression, as word gets around, especially in specialized fields. It's a smaller network than you might think. Additionally, listen to what they are asking or saying and try your best not to interrupt. You can jot down notes as you listen to the question, but try not to lose "eye contact" for too long. Wait for opportune times to respond, when you sense the right moment in the conversation. If you find yourself unable to sit for an interview or have the camera on for the entire interview time—for whatever reason— consider requesting an accommodation or informing them of your needs. An institution that appreciates and practices principles of diversity, equity, and inclusion will make the proper modifications.

As you might have guessed, the interview plays a significant role in the decision to offer you admission, as it provides the committee an opportunity to become more familiar with who you are and your interests and to determine whether you are a good match for the program. Though it may not end up playing the most important role, it's possible too that it can make or break your chances for admission, depending on what is said and how it is said. Remember to always express your enthusiasm and to show that you're an ideal candidate for them and that they're a good fit for you too. But don't try to be someone you're not. Lean into your identity in whatever way feels appropriate and safe to you. Don't apologize for who you are, or for your values or beliefs. You want to be in a place where you believe you can thrive, so it needs to be a program that's welcoming for returning, nontraditional, BIPOC, LGBTQ+, first-generation, and/or low-income students, as needed. Most importantly, be kind to yourself, regardless of how the interview goes.

Given the significance of the questions that they will ask you and your need to prepare responses, we include a list of potential queries below. While you don't need to answer every single one as some contain similar components, be ready to respond to variations on these. If you're feeling particularly intimidated or fearful, carry out a mock interview where you practice responding to questions from a trusted femtor or mentor as well as fellow students or friends. Have them ask you these questions and then evaluate your responses. If possible, repeat the three-minute speech, also known as the elevator pitch—where you give a succinct overview of your research, that is, the subject, method, sources, and findings—so that it rolls off the tongue and you get comfortable talking about your research experiences and interests. The more you practice, the better you will feel in your ability to engage fully. As we've learned over the years, candidates with more experience with interviews will almost always have a stronger outcome than those who don't or who didn't simulate a session.

Common Grad School Interview Questions

RESEARCH

- Why did you apply to this program? What is it about this program that attracts you?
- Tell us about your previous research experiences and how it has prepared you for graduate study.
- What specific skills or experiences have you had that make you particularly prepared to be a PhD student?
- Who would you like to work with and what would you like to work on in graduate school?
- What do you see as the major trends in your field of study? Where do you see the field headed in the next five to ten years?
- What is the last essay and/or book you read? What are you currently reading?
- If your work is interdisciplinary, how do you see yourself bridging the different fields?
- You might be asked about a specific profession if you have mentioned it in your essays or if it is relevant to the program: Have you shadowed a school psychologist/archeologist/curator? Do you know what they do?

PROFESSIONAL

- Can you tell me more about your working style and the type of mentorship you seek?

- How do you work under pressure and how do you deal with conflict?
- Can you tell us about a time you struggled and how you handled that situation?
- What are your strengths and weaknesses?
- Where do you see yourself in the next five years? Ten years?
- Why are you pursuing a PhD?

PERSONAL

- Tell us about yourself. How do you imagine contributing to our program?
- What are you looking for in a graduate program and graduate school experience?
- How do you plan to fund your graduate education?
- If there are GPA concerns, they might ask you about it: "What about your grades? I see here you earned an X this term. What happened?"
- Can you picture yourself living in this location?
- Where else are you applying? Do you have other interviews?
- What are your top choices and how would you rank them? (Trick question! Do not answer this directly. You might say "it depends," or "I'm excited about all the programs I applied to for different reasons; I'll be weighing the pros and cons after I understand my options better.")

Questions for You to Ask Interviewers

To help you get started with the questions *you* can bring to the interview, we provide a comprehensive list below. As you know by now, you will need to prepare program-specific questions that you will ask at the end of the interview, usually the time that the committee entertains and answers them. The more specific and nuanced your query, the better impression you will make with the committee. Pay attention, as well, to each individual, whether it is the graduate advisor or a first-year graduate student. Everyone matters. You never know whose work or insight will be most valued.

- What kind of funding or financial support is provided and how does it compare to living expenses?

- What kinds of teaching and research requirements are expected in the program?

- What kind of formal and informal support networks exist in the program and the campus more broadly? Does the departmental and campus culture encourage mentoring?

- Do curricula address racial, ethnic, gender, cultural, and disability issues?

- Does the program or campus have a diverse group of students, faculty, and administrators? And, does the program or campus support the needs of diverse students?

- Does the program or campus have symposia on issues pertaining to graduate students or have graduate education workshops for undergraduates?

- How much access do students have to faculty and graduate school administrative staff?

- How robust is the communication between the graduate school and students? For example, are there newsletters or social media outlets?

- Does the institution have comprehensive wellbeing services with a professional staff equipped to serve a diverse student population?

- What kinds of opportunities exist for scholarly discussions among students and faculty in interdisciplinary and multidisciplinary settings?
- How much professional development programming does the program or campus provide graduate students? Do you offer professional development funding?
- What are the kinds of jobs alumni of this program can expect?
- What kind of resources and support are available for students with children?

After your interview has been completed, don't forget to send thank-you notes. We think emailing them is fine. If you're curious as to how you handled the interview, you might ask them in that same note for any feedback they might want to provide. Don't be surprised, however, if you don't hear back. Unfortunately, it's not too common in academia to receive input on any interviews or applications, though the trend is changing. If necessary, follow up by providing any additional documentation that they request, including a supplemental writing sample.

PREVIEW DAYS

In contrast to interviews, preview days or open houses are less intensive and much friendlier, as they take place after admissions decisions have been made and you have been accepted. As such, they serve different purposes than pre-admission interviews. Open houses are usually dedicated to showcasing the strengths of the department in order to recruit admitted students—getting them to sign their Statement of Intent to Register (or SIR)—and generally to make the program, campus community, and larger region seem like an attractive place for you to study, work, and live. They often include overviews of the general program and, if relevant, specific fields, one-on-one meetings with potential advisors and current graduate students, campus tours, and usually a group meal, either lunch or dinner, including everyone who's been admitted and is in attendance. It is your opportunity to get to know your potential cohort and the institution at which you might spend the next several years completing your degree.

If you're invited to a preview day, do whatever you can to attend. Most programs will let you know if they can cover any costs associated with travel, including transportation, accommodations, and meals. In our experience, graduate divisions often set aside monies to assist departments and programs with the recruitment of first-generation, low-income, and/or nontraditional Students of Color like yourself. If it is not offered, ask if you qualify for any support for attending an open house. You may also request an itinerary, if it's not made available, as it will help you to keep track of the schedule and learn who else you will meet. An itinerary will also help you if you need special assistance getting around or other accommodations for your needs. Be sure to inquire before you go.

If you're taking classes or working on the day or days of the campus visit, you'll need to plan for the time away. Let your professors or employers know, if you feel comfortable, about missing class or work for the event. In many cases, professors are understanding and will provide you with alternate options to make up work that you missed. If needed, show them the communication you've received about the preview day. If you don't want to let an employer or others know about your future plans for fear of them knowing you plan to leave your job sometime soon, see if you can find alternatives. Most open houses are on Fridays so it might be possible for you to have the day off or make up the work another day. As a last resort, set up online meetings with the graduate advisor, potential faculty advisors, and current graduate students instead of attending the day. Remember, as Yvette says on the Grad School Femtoring Podcast, "You're the one with the reins, . . . the one in control because they're trying to schmooze [you]. They're trying to impress you. They're trying to show their best selves to . . . get you to their program. [Y]ou should feel really good if you're going in and you've already been admitted."[2]

Our final word of advice about preview days is that you need to remember that the program or department will be looking to attract you, especially if you're a first-generation, low-income, and/or nontraditional Student of Color. If you're Black, queer or non-binary, a parent, or have another identity that causes you some concern, you will want to know if the space is safe and free of mental, emotional, and/or physical threat. Historically, academia has been a ground for developing and strengthening white supremacy, scientific racism, classism, homophobia, and ableism, among other "isms." Today, many institutions are slowly coming around to reckoning with those troubled pasts and attempting to implement initiatives to diversify the faculty, curriculum, and students. You are certainly within your rights to ask faculty about how they address diversity in the classroom and curriculum and about the demographics of the program.[3] Many, although not all, faculty and administrators understand the value of diverse perspectives and the excellence that is gained through expansive experiences and points of view. We have a long way to go in meeting goals for diversity, equity, and inclusion in academia, but we have many supportive individuals and initiatives in place than we had in the recent past to help us achieve representation in higher education and beyond.

Nevertheless, it is necessary for you to see beyond the performative nature of the open house to understand the culture of the program. For that, you need to be a keen observer, listener, and participant. Don't just sit and watch what everyone is doing or saying. Get involved. Ask questions and join discussions and campus tours or any social events, usually organized by graduate students, that will help you to see yourself (or not) thriving in the culture and environment of the program. Query the graduate students, who are a key resource in providing you with an inside look at what really goes on in the program on a daily, weekly, and monthly basis. Unlike faculty or administrators, they have less to lose if you decide to go elsewhere. Usually, graduate students are open to frank conversations as they often see themselves reflected in you and your eagerness to join the academic community, even if it's only during graduate school.

If possible, you should also talk with alumni, either during preview days or in the days leading up to your decision to SIR. Contact at least one or two and ask similar questions as you would of current students about the climate, that is, about the welcoming nature (or not) of the program as it pertains to issues of race, ethnicity, class, gender, sexuality, disability, and age. Learn about alumni placement rates and outcomes as well. What are the trajectories of alumni? What are they doing with their degrees?[4] Don't ignore alumni or graduate students, especially those whose identities or experiences more closely align with your own. Seek them out. We believe they are invaluable assets in your graduate program search. To that end, here we provide a list of optional questions to ask potential graduate student peers.

Questions To Ask Graduate Students

RESEARCH AND COURSES

- What's it like to work with your advisor?
- Are first-year graduate students paired up with a faculty advisor? How are faculty advisors selected?
- What does a graduate seminar look like? What type of courses are offered regularly in this program?
- What are the expectations for writing and reading?
- How long does it typically take for students to graduate?
- What type of relationships does the department have with alumni, if any?

PERSONAL AND FUNDING

- What does it feel like to be a graduate student, specifically, a first-generation, low-income, and/or nontraditional Student of Color? Are you happy with your decision to come here? Would you do it all over again?

- Where do graduate students live? Is it affordable here? What are some options?

- Do you have access to graduate student housing? Family housing? Is it subsidized? Do you feel safe, as a first-generation/low-income/nontraditional Student of Color?

- Do students live close to campus? Do they commute? Do they have access to a shuttle or public transportation or how do they get around? How much does parking cost?

- How do you like your healthcare? Does the health insurance include vision, dental, and/or mental health services?

- Do you receive funding? Is it enough to live on? Did you have to take out student loans?

- When and how often do students TA in this department?

COMMUNITY

- What is the relationship between the department and the surrounding community?

- What is the surrounding community like? Demographics? Class? Politics?

- What do graduate students do for fun on this campus?

- What are the graduate organizations like? Do you have a student union?

- Where would I find affinity groups?

GRADUATE SCHOOL RELATIONSHIPS

Interviews and especially preview days or open houses are excellent opportunities to lay the groundwork for developing solid relationships with the people and the programs that will support you throughout your time in graduate school. As soon as you have submitted your SIR, we encourage you to establish working relationships with a faculty advisor and, when possible, seek out femtors and mentors who will work in conjunction with your advisor. Remember, as we've noted elsewhere, they need not be the same person. If they are, that's great. If not, you have the chance to expand your professional and social networks, which—like in almost all professions—are key to your success, regardless of how you envision it. Given that these relationships are fundamental to your goals, we will walk you through this process for securing a reliable and trustworthy advisor, femtor, and/or mentor.

To develop a strong and reliable relationship, we recommend that, before you agree to work together, you meet and talk with them about their advising, femtoring, and/or mentoring style or styles. This is an opportunity, as well, for you to identify your own. To do so, you might begin by asking them to discuss their approaches to guiding, teaching, and/or encouraging students in and outside the classroom. As their advisee, you will likely have to take seminars or join labs that they oversee as well as meet with them during office hours. By having an understanding of their expectations, you will be better equipped to meet their demands when you take a course or begin to draft the first chapter of your dissertation. You might also ask them about how often they like to meet with students and what it is that's accomplished at those meetings. If you know you like frequent interaction, consistent feedback, and hands-on support, be sure to communicate this with a potential advisor who might have other ideas of what it means to advise.

In your meetings with them, you will also want to ask if or how they determine goals with their students, and whether they set tasks, deadlines, and/or follow-up meetings. While communication is key when you're developing a strong relationship with an advisor, you also must clarify each other's expectations and communication styles or preferences. Do they like meeting often, remotely or in person, or do they prefer to be hands off and allow for independence on behalf of the student? Do they prefer email, phone, or text or a combination of all three? We encourage you to find out these details ahead of time as well as where they are in their career. Are they early-career *assistant professors* (without tenure, and likely more focused on their research than mentorship)? Are they mid-career *associate professors* (with tenure and likely a fairly heavy load of service, including mentorship)? Or, are they well-established *full professors* (with seniority and experience, yet perhaps out of touch with the life of a graduate student)? What is their availability and willingness to work with you? Sometimes people early in their career are available and supportive and sometimes they're not because they're working really hard to try to secure tenure. However, a faculty member's career path doesn't always determine how they approach working with students. To determine the match between you and them, communicate as openly and frankly as possible. Neither of you will regret it.

Another approach to figuring out compatibility is to find out with whom they have worked or with whom they are currently working and to determine what those individuals have to share about them and their advising, femtoring, and/or mentoring styles. Besides determining whether this person is a good match, academically and professionally, you should also figure out if they are a good fit personally. Are they kind or generous, especially to first-generation, low-income, and/or nontraditional Students of Color? Or, are they toxic and hurtful? Even if you choose an advisor who turns out not to be the person for you or that you thought they were, you can find someone else. This prospect might be tricky in a small program, where you have few options and everyone knows each other's business, but it is usually still possible. Try and do this early in your program if you can. We recommend you keep it as professional as possible. Even if the true reason for your desire to switch is a clash in personality or mentoring styles, they don't need to know that. To avoid burning bridges, you might explain that the fit or match with research interests was not ideal. In most cases, they will understand.[5]

GRADUATE SCHOOL BUDGETS, FUNDING PACKAGES, AND ADVOCATING FOR YOURSELF

To build a strong foundation for graduate school, particularly as it pertains to funding, we advise you to begin with developing a budget that reflects your anticipated expenses and sources of income while you are enrolled in school. If you've been accepted to a PhD program, you have a good chance of obtaining a four-to-five year package, as most programs will not admit applicants without some form of support. This applies to recipients of DACA, or Deferred Action for Childhood Arrivals, California AB-540 Dream Scholars, and others who are exempt from nonresident in-state tuition. Programs understand that the lack of financial means sets you up to struggle and, ultimately, fail, given the length of time you will spend in school. PhD programs, in contrast to master's programs, can also afford to provide financial support, as they rely on graduate students to assist in lecture courses and to reap the departmental benefits that come from large enrollments. If you've been admitted to a master's program, you are likely to receive little funding, however. Typically, master's programs are unable to absorb the costs, as they provide few opportunities for graduate students to serve as assistants in large courses. In our experience, master's programs run well into the tens of thousands—in some cases, up to sixty thousand dollars a year for tuition and housing for a two-to-three-year program in a region with a high cost of living. A doctoral program will likely cost you much less, especially if you are able to secure a four-to-five year offer in a lower cost area. Many master's programs can, however, assist with finding awards for you, so don't discount that possibility.[6]

Either way, we encourage you to develop a budget. Begin with a one-year budget and then multiply it by the number of years you project you will be in school. While your budget will vary from year to year, the mainstays will not change: tuition and/or fees, housing, food, transportation (personal car or public transit, and consider the cost of traveling to see friends or family if you will be moving away from them), as well as phone and other services. If you are a parent, you need to factor in the costs for childcare, or if you have special medical issues, you will have to include those costs as well. Be sure to pay attention to the cost of living in the area, as it can vary significantly from region to region, determining whether you will be able to make the move or not or how you will live.

Once you figure out your expenses, you'll be able to determine how your income or funding award, if any, meets your needs. If you have a significant gap, it's not uncommon to ask the department or graduate division on campus for assistance, even after they have made you an award offer. Ask about any additional scholarships, fellowships, or on-campus employment opportunities as well as any funding for relocation (we say more about the "ask" below). Sometimes departments and graduate divisions have small pockets of money—$500, $750, or $1000—for use toward moving. Even if they cannot offer more money, they can always tell you where to apply or to consult with your advisor, who might be able to hire you as a research assistant. While it might feel awkward or seem risky, especially for already marginalized populations such as DACA students, it is expected that you will advocate for yourself. As Yvette has reminded her podcast listeners, "no one's going to go out of their way to just give it to you, especially because you've already SIR-ed." But chances are the program will do what it can to make your educational goals possible, as it has an interest in your attending once you are admitted. The worst that can happen is that they turn you down. We have often seen the reverse come true.[7]

Be aware that graduate school funding packages come in all shapes and sizes. No two are alike. The most typical forms of support are the teaching or research assistantships, which are usually compensated with tuition, fee remission, and basic health benefits as well as a stipend for living expenses. A *teaching assistantship* requires you to work 25 to 50 percent time (ten to twenty hours a week, though you often spend more than that amount of time) as a discussion or section leader for a lecture course. A *research assistantship*, which is more common in the sciences, where professors fund their labs and pay graduate students with the support of large government grants, involves carrying out research—either your own or that of a professor or both. You normally work similar hours and receive similar benefits as you would if you were a teaching assistant. Teaching and research assistantships usually come from your home department and are part of what is called departmental-level funding. The assistantships are often part of multi-year *funding packages* that might also include *fellowships*, which are stipends that are free from any employment obligations and, as such, are coveted and competitive. Fellowships are more typically given out at the university level rather than the department level, so you will be in competition for these with students in many programs. Many departments also include research and travel grants to advance your investigations or fieldwork and to attend and present at national conferences.

In addition to the mix of grants, fellowships, teaching, and research assistantships, some programs may provide reimbursement for relocation costs—to cover the expenses related to moving and transitioning, especially across state lines or the country—as well as stipends for summer research so that you do not have to take on heavy teaching or employment as well.[8] The largest part of your graduate funding package usually comes from your academic department and is often awarded on a competitive basis. Even diversity awards, which are provided to first-generation, low-income, and/or nontraditional Students of Color, are based on rankings of applicants. Keep in mind that, if you are attending a public university using state-funded sources of support, DACA recipients, AB-540 students, and others exempt from in-state tuition are eligible to apply. Nevertheless, we strongly urge you to inquire with the graduate division or school about the policies and practices impacting undocumented students. Each campus will have unique approaches.

To give you a sense of what multi-year funding packages look like, we have provided you with a list of possible scenarios. Please note that these may not represent the type of support you get offered if admitted. Unfortunately, we have no guarantee that you'll receive money for any graduate program.

Sample Funding Packages

SAMPLE #1—PHD

We are pleased to award you the X Fellowship. This Fellowship provides $3,000/year for the first three years of study. Our offer of admission includes a full financial aid award of:

- a taxable yearly stipend of $34,000 (paid over 9 months, bi-monthly)
- full graduate tuition and fees
- a laptop computer

SAMPLE #2—PHD

I am pleased to announce that you have been recommended as one of the recipients of an X Fellowship. This fellowship includes:

- full tuition for the academic year
- full health insurance subsidy
- an annual stipend of $24,000 (paid over 9 months, monthly)
- a signing bonus of $750 to cover relocation expenses

SAMPLE #3—PHD

The X fellowship provides financial support for four years of study.

- In years 1 and 2 you will receive a $30,000 stipend for living expenses plus payment of tuition and fees
- In years 3 and 4 you will receive funding in the form of teaching or research appointments and/or departmental fellowships
- In year 5 you will be eligible to apply for a dissertation-year fellowship

SAMPLE #4—PHD

The X fellowship provides a six-year departmental package, which includes the following:

- Year 1: Stipend of $24,000 for the academic year and summer stipend of $6,000.
- Year 2: Teaching Assistantship salary of $24,000 and summer stipend of $6,000.
- Year 3: Teaching Assistantship salary of $24,000 and summer stipend of $6,000.
- Year 4: Stipend of $24,000 for the academic year and summer stipend of $6,000.
- Year 5: Stipend of $24,000 for the academic year and summer stipend of $6,000.
- Year 6: Teaching Assistantship salary of $24,000.

SAMPLE #5—PHD

I am pleased to offer you the X Fellowship for the X academic year. Your award is $25,000. The amount represents payment of full tuition and campus fees as well as a stipend for two terms. The department strongly encourages new students to seek Teaching Assistant and Research Assistant positions once you are enrolled.

SAMPLE #6—MA/MS

I am pleased to inform you that you have been awarded a scholarship in the amount of $15,000. We expect to provide the same level of funding for your second year.

SAMPLE #7—MA/MS

We are pleased to inform you that you've been awarded a scholarship of 35% towards your tuition.

SAMPLE #8—MA/MS

You have been selected for the X Scholarship, a full-tuition award that includes a quarterly stipend of $8,500 for up to two years and a $500 research grant.

SAMPLE #9—POSTBACC

As an X fellowship recipient, you will receive a department scholarship of $10,000 for your first year and $10,000 for your second year, and a teaching assistantship of $2,200 per semester. We also provide some support for travel to conferences and applications to PhD programs.

SAMPLE #10—POSTBACC

As an X fellow, you will receive an annual salary of $45,000. We are pleased to also offer you a relocation stipend in the amount of $2,500.

Remember, funding opportunities are also available through private sources located outside of your institution at the local, state, national or international level. Pay attention to the stipulations of each program, however, especially those supported with federal funds, as DACA, AB-540, and other exempted students may be ineligible to apply. The benefit of these fellowships is that they allow you to focus on your research rather than having teaching, research, or service obligations. Among the most common and well known include:

NATIONAL ACADEMIES OF SCIENCES, FORD FOUNDATION FELLOWSHIP PROGRAMS

This program provides funding to increase diversity of the professoriate. It provides predoctoral, dissertation, and postdoctoral dissertation fellowships on a competitive basis and will be available until 2028 or when the funding is exhausted.[9]

PAUL AND DAISY SOROS FELLOWSHIPS FOR NEW AMERICANS

This organization makes available fellowships for immigrants and children of immigrants for the first two years of graduate school.[10]

NATIONAL SCIENCE FOUNDATION, GRADUATE RESEARCH FELLOWSHIP PROGRAM

This unit of the federal government awards fellowships for graduate study in STEM or in STEM education.[11]

SOCIAL SCIENCE RESEARCH COUNCIL

The council awards fellowships to researchers targeting specific problems, promoting institutional change, and expanding networks.[12]

These applications can be overwhelming and unwieldy, especially if you are now returning to graduate school after a prolonged hiatus from higher education or you've had little exposure to formal research training and mentorship programs. They require submitting multiple essays, letters of recommendation, CVs, and transcripts. While they might seem similar to graduate school applications, they often require exceptional care and attention, as they are generally more competitive.[13]

To make the process feasible, we encourage you to set up a study group for accountability, including a regular check-in with a peer or peers. Find someone else or others who are also applying to fellowships and set aside time to prepare your documents together. Exchange materials and/or establish goals with them. If you have a successful application or know of someone who has had success, share the resource, as the best way to draft strong statements is to read ones that have been awarded. If you cannot leave your home for extended periods of time to meet with the group, consider doing it remotely, over Zoom or using a Google document, where you can use the chat feature to check in on each other every half hour to find out what progress you've made. Don't do it alone unless you truly work best that way. We've found that working in a community at strategic moments can vastly improve the efficiency and efficacy of completing graduate school materials.

In addition to fellowships, you will have other opportunities for support through internships or employment on campus where you serve as a graduate student assistant or as a femtor or mentor to undergraduates or others. These opportunities allow you to gain professional experience, academic credit, or both, and some are paid as well. Many units on campus, including the graduate school or graduate division as well as student affairs or student support services, have graduate student positions that provide partial or full tuition, fee remissions, and benefits equivalent to a research or teaching assistantship. These can be priceless opportunities, for they not only pay the bills but expand your professional and social networks on campus. You never know what people you might meet or what doors might open to you beyond your program or department. But again, inquire as to whether there are state- or federally-funded programs or organizations on campus, as some may limit eligibility to permanent legal residents and US citizens.

Much less desirable, but available, are loans from either private and public lending institutions, which you must pay back with interest. Pay particularly close attention to private loans from banks. They carry hefty interest rates that can set you back many years, if not decades. Federal loans, too, are available, both subsidized and unsubsidized, but again, unfortunately DACA students are not eligible. Subsidized loans, often considered the "better" option, do not require you to pay interest while you're an enrolled student, whereas unsubsidized loans generate interest immediately. We want to remind you to take a look at a loan repayment calculator before agreeing to take on any student loans so that you have a good idea of how long it will take to pay them back. We have witnessed students who, after reviewing a loan calculator, made the decision to take on less student debt and work more side jobs to cover the difference. It is ultimately up to you to make such a big financial decision. Don't forget, for these loans and any other funding you will receive, you will need to fill out the Free Application for Federal Student Aid (FAFSA). All undergraduate and graduate students—with the exception of undocumented students, including DACA recipients—must fill this out, even if you are not interested in federal loans. The FAFSA helps graduate programs determine your eligibility for need-based fellowships. In some states, like in California, you are eligible to apply for in-state financial aid. Inquire with the graduate division for specific details.[14]

As we've tried to encourage you to do throughout the process, take proactive steps, especially if you're unhappy with the funding offer at your first choice school. If that's the case, ideally you will have a second funding offer that is equally strong or, better, stronger so that you can use it as leverage to negotiate the one at your top institution. If you don't have another offer, don't think you cannot ask for a bump or an increase in your support. Yes, you can, as we noted earlier. Let's say, for instance, you've only been admitted to a PhD program and it offers full funding. That includes support for five years, with two of fellowships and three a mix of teaching and research assistantships. Not included, however, are summer funds or relocation expenses. How will you make the transition over the summer months to your new location without support for housing, food, and transportation, especially if you've recently left a job or graduated from a master's or bachelor's program? Or, if you're moving across the country from Los Angeles to New York or within the state from Brawley to Berkeley, California? If you're low-income or have considerable debt, ask the program for some relief. If they cannot assist you immediately, they may be able to direct you to a place on campus that provides such emergency funds. They may ask you to hold onto your receipts or provide a stipend outright.[15]

"But how does one do that?" you might ask. "How do we, as first-generation, low-income, and/or nontraditional Students of Color take the initiative to make such a request?" We understand that making demands from institutions is not an easy prospect or a comfortable position. We suggest taking small steps. First, draft an email, saying "thank you so much for this offer. I'm really excited at the prospect of starting in this program or attending this university." Next, tell them what you have in hand. "I also wanted to let you know that I've been accepted at University of X. They have offered a stipend of X amount along with tuition, fees, and housing. I'm really interested in your program and am wondering if you all might be able to match or, ideally, increase the stipend that you have offered me. This will allow me to make a more informed decision. I look forward to hearing back from you." Finally, attach a copy of the funding offer from the other university. That last bit of information will help your case tremendously, as

they see the lengths to which the competition—other institutions—
have placed their bets on you. They may not be able to match, dollar
for dollar, the competing package, but they might be able to provide
more aid in other ways, either through in-kind (non-cash support) or in
cash support.[16]

To help you craft a pointed message enabling you to negotiate a
funding offer, we have provided a sample email template. Again, we
cannot guarantee that you'll receive more funding with this approach.
But, from our experience, it has worked for many in the past. When in
doubt, reach out to a trusted femtor or mentor and ask them to review
a draft before you send it out.

NEGOTIATING FUNDING EMAIL TEMPLATE #1

SUBJECT LINE: Inquiry Regarding Funding Offer

Hello/Dear Dr./Professor [**last name**],

Thank you for the generous offer of admission and funding. [**name
of university and program**] is among my top choices for graduate study
and I am very interested in joining the incoming class. Before I can
commit to this program, I wanted to let you know about another more
generous offer I received and request that you consider increasing my fellowship aid. My current funding package includes [**list the offer**]. I also
received the following offer from [**name of university and program**],
which includes [**list the offer**].

Once again, I would like to emphasize how grateful I am to be offered
a spot in the incoming class. As I am committed to a career in [**profession**] after graduation and as a [**say more about your background**], my
financial aid package is a critical factor in my decision-making process. I
have attached a copy of my award letter from [**other program**]. Please let
me know if I can provide any additional information to assist you in considering my request.

Sincerely,/Best,/Respectfully,

[**your full name**]

In sum, successfully applying to and getting into graduate school is no walk in the park. Fundamentally, however, we believe it should not be shrouded in mystery or reserved to a select few. As we've reiterated throughout the chapter and the book, our purpose is to remove the veil from the process. In this discussion, we've talked about all you need to know to prepare to the best of your ability for an interview for the admissions process. We've provided sample questions that you will likely receive and ones that you might use when it's your turn to ask the questions. We also talked about the differences between the pre- and post-admission interviews and preview days or open houses. They each serve their purpose and carry a decidedly different tone and mood. Whenever possible, take advantage of preview days. Visit the institution and get to know current graduate students, alumni, and potential cohort-mates. Above all, use the time to establish solid relationships with potential advisors. While the process can be intimidating or unnerving, we have provided you with sample queries you can ask faculty about their working style and approaches to advising, femtoring, and/or mentoring. If you feel uncomfortable, do mock interviews with supportive femtors, mentors, or peers.

Equally important to establishing strong relationships with potential advisors and learning everything possible about the institution is negotiating the best funding possible. For that, establish your budget, know your monetary needs, and figure out ways to cover any potential gaps. Institutions have ways of finding support or will often assist you in trying to secure additional funds, even if you are a DACA recipient or qualify for exemption from in-state tuition. (DACA students must be particularly careful about how they navigate the post-graduate experience.) Don't let the initial award discourage you from negotiating for more security for yourself and any dependents. To that end, we have provided tips and tricks on how to advocate for yourself and negotiate more for financial means. We do not advise you to incur significant debt, especially if you are interested in pursuing the academic track. Jobs in industry, government, and health care are likely to yield more financial returns. Nevertheless, you want to be careful with how much you owe when all is said and done. We hope that these insights have provided you with valuable information as you proceed on your path towards your professional and personal goals.

KEY TAKEAWAYS

- We broke down the graduate school interview process and how to prepare for it.
- We provided you with a list of common graduate school interview questions to help you prepare for in-person or virtual interviews.
- We also shared a list of questions that you may ask interviewers and graduate students during interview days or open houses.
- We noted the differences between interviews and open houses or preview days.
- We stressed the importance of forming strong relationships with your advisor(s)and other femtors and mentors.
- We taught you how to create a budget and what funding opportunities are available to graduate students, such as fellowships, teaching assistantships, research assistantships, internships, on-campus employment, and student loans.
- We demystified the funding process by offering several sample funding packages to give you an idea of what they might look like for doctoral, master's, and postbacc programs.
- Lastly, we discussed the option to negotiate for more funding or a stronger funding package and shared sample email templates to do so.

10

YOU SAID YES, NOW WHAT?

Preparing for the Transition into Graduate School
and Beyond

|||||||||||||||||||||||||||||||||||||||||||||||||||||||||||||||||||||||||||||||||||||||||||||||||||||||||||||||||||||||||||||||||||||||||||||||||||||||||||||

CONGRATULATIONS! YOU'VE ACCEPTED a graduate school
offer. You may be feeling a wide range of emotions from
excitement to relief to disbelief—and perhaps even a bit of
apprehension. You are not alone. You have reached a mile-
stone with getting into graduate school, as too few first-generation, low-income, and/or nontraditional Students of
Color are able to reach this goal. And you have also made a
big commitment by agreeing to attend. We encourage you
to take the time to rejoice and commemorate this achievement rather than immediately worrying about what comes
next. Allow yourself a moment to pause all other commitments to make space for a celebration in which you can build
a valuable memory with those who have supported you in
this journey. This is also a good time to sit down and reflect
on how far you have come in your professional and personal
growth. If no one else has told you already, please know that
we are incredibly proud of you and we also look forward to

hearing about your achievements. Before we go, we cannot finish this book without offering some insight on how to prepare for a successful transition into graduate school and beyond into your career and life.

PREPARING FOR THE BIG MOVE

Two primary concerns for incoming graduate students are how to prepare for the big move and what to do in the summer months before starting graduate school. Whether you are moving to a different city, state, or even country, planning for your move takes time. You have many logistics to consider: determining your housing options, the cost of a moving truck or shipping materials, the expenses of securing an apartment or rental home, and figuring out how to make ends meet until you receive your first stipend payment. When it comes to your housing options, it can be helpful to reach out to your graduate student contacts in the program you're attending. Where do the graduate students live? Do they live on or off-campus? Do they live close by or commute? Can your contacts put the word out among current graduate students to help you find an apartment, house, and/or room someone is moving out of? Are there graduate student and/or family housing options that are subsidized, that is, offered at a discounted rate? Are there opportunities for you to become a resident assistant for graduate or undergraduate student housing so that you can decrease your housing costs? Are there community and university housing services, a housing community, or an online housing resource you can work with to identify your options? Do they provide options for parents, LGBTQ+, or disabled students? What does the timeline to apply for graduate student housing look like? Sometimes you are asked to apply many months in advance to secure a spot and you may encounter a long waitlist. If, however, you are applying for an apartment in the local community, you might not need to do this until a month or two before you plan to move in. Do your research on your housing options to ensure they meet your needs: preferred location, budget, living environment, and resources in proximity.

We also recommend anticipating and keeping track of moving expenses. This means creating a budget and deciding how you are going to relocate. If you have never moved too far from home to either attend college or start a job, you might not realize how quickly costs can add up to move to another city or state. If you decide to do it yourself, you will need to pay for a truck rental and fuel as well as packing supplies or, if you decide you would rather travel more quickly across a long distance, you will need to cover airfare and added luggage fees or shipping costs. If it's within your budget, you may decide to hire a moving company. You might need to account, too, for the cost of furniture if your apartment is unfurnished. All of this can easily add up to thousands of dollars, especially after you make the first rent payment, usually first and last month and a one-month security deposit, at your new place. After creating a budget for your moving costs, reach out to any family, friends, or acquaintances who you know in the area to see if they might be able to help you pack on one end, and unload or unpack on the other. And, if you're concerned over how you're going to afford the move, reach out to your department. It does not hurt to ask if they provide any funds for relocation expenses or if the graduate division or the university can help you with the cost of airfare. We have seen students do this successfully, although it depends on each department as well as the individual support of professors who may have the funds to help their students offset relocation costs. Another option is to secure a temporary or summer job that will help you save for these expenses. In some cases, students are able to move to their graduate program in the summer and start a research assistant position in their department or take summer courses, such as language courses, that may also come with funding support. If you are struggling financially, reach out to your loved ones and community to see if there are other resources you can tap into for you to achieve your dreams.

THE SUMMER BEFORE YOU START

A common question Yvette has received from countless students is what to do the summer before starting graduate school. Even without taking into account the stressful process of moving, the summer before starting graduate school can be an anxiety-inducing time. You too may be wondering what you can do to prepare for this big transition. It is not uncommon to have doubts and limiting beliefs, such as, "I'm not ready," "I don't know enough," or "they're going to realize they made a mistake in admitting me." Trust us when we say that you were admitted because you are qualified and you more than deserve to be there. However, if you'd like our input on what to do over the summer, here are a few suggestions, which we hope you'll find useful.

First, we believe you should prioritize taking a break in the summer. In other words, rest. In graduate school, you will have few opportunities to relax, particularly in the summer months, as most will be dedicated to carrying out research and writing, preparing for exams, and sometimes teaching or another job. Keep in mind you can find many ways to press pause. Downtime can include passive or active as well as physical, mental, and spiritual activity. Passive rest includes sleeping and napping, while active rest can involve low-intensity forms of exercise. Taking a break can also involve spending time with loved ones who energize us or it can include retreating temporarily from social media. Tranquility can mean taking things slowly or giving yourself time to reflect and assess where you are in your career and life goals. It can also mean picking up a new hobby to help put your mind at ease when you feel concerned about the start of your graduate program. In short, taking time for yourself means doing things that are nourishing and meaningful so that you can feel restored and ready.

Something else to prioritize before starting graduate school is getting your finances in order. We recommend that you update your existing budget or create a new one to reflect your anticipated income and expenses in graduate school. We want to make sure you can afford to attend graduate school, ideally without having to take on any debt. You have many options to create a budget or spending plan. They include a zero-based budget, pay-yourself-first budget, and the 50/30/20 budget, which recommends allocating 50 percent of income towards necessary costs, 30 percent towards discretionary costs, and 20 percent towards paying debt and saving money. You can learn more about different budgeting styles by reading books on financial literacy, especially those aimed at People of Color, such as Tiffany Aliche's *Get Good with Money*. What all budgeting methods have in common is that they account for the money that comes in (income) and the money that goes out (expenses). You want to make sure that you are spending within or below your means—in other words, that you are spending as much or less than what you are making. By creating a budget and tracking your numbers, ideally each month, you'll know if you are within, below, or above your budget and can make changes accordingly. The more comfortable you are with your numbers, the more you'll be able to make informed decisions about how to navigate graduate school from a financial standpoint.

Where things get difficult is when students neglect to think about financial planning in their graduate school careers. In most cases, they simply don't know what a budget is and don't know how to create and manage one, as many—ourselves included—were not raised in homes where we talked about money. Often, this was because we had so few means that it was shameful to talk about what we lacked and what that said about us, particularly in a consumerist, capitalist society. Without a financial plan, however, students quickly run into unfortunate surprises in the middle of the semester or quarter where they find themselves with little left in their account. We have also witnessed students who are overjoyed that they received a "full funding" package yet do not realize the first stipend payment will not be disbursed until later in the semester or quarter. This means that they may struggle to afford their expenses during the first month or few months of graduate school.

Graduate students also often realize later in their programs that their funding package is not enough to pay for living expenses because of hidden costs that are not covered by departmental or university sources. These might include fees for attending academic conferences, securing memberships for national associations, and other university requirements. Students are often unaware, as well, of the difference in living expenses between their old and new location. But if you can anticipate some of these money matters and continue learning about financial literacy and personal finance, you will be in a much better position than the nearly 48 million Americans who have student debt from their undergraduate and graduate education. And, keep in mind that most of these are individuals who have had the option of taking on federal student loans. Others do not have this privilege, such as DACA recipients, who must rely solely on personal savings or on high-interest private loans and scholarships to pay for their education. We believe financial planning is critical for low-income, first-generation, and/or nontraditional Students of Color because many of us do not have a financial safety net derived from generational wealth, whereas our middle- and upper-class peers in grad school may be able to turn to their parents for regular help or even have inheritances or generous college funds.

Once you have created a budget, if you realize that your expenses are higher than your anticipated income, it might be a good idea to take on a part-time or full-time job in the summer to save up for graduate school, despite our admonition to focus on rest. You have many options to monetize your knowledge and skills. Tutoring, housesitting, dogsitting, babysitting, and/or finding university-based sources of employment as a graduate student mentor, advisor, or research assistant are all common ways to supplement your income without committing to a more regular job. If you are creative and persistent, you may find a source of support that you enjoy and can rely on throughout the academic year to help you meet your financial goals. Do not underestimate, too, the ways that identifying external sources of income may actually help you exercise and strengthen your existing professional skills. In some graduate programs, having a job outside of your studies may be discouraged, but it is ultimately up to you to make that decision based on your personal circumstances and needs.

Besides focusing on your financial health and awareness, we encourage you to focus on activities that bring you pleasure. For many, this includes reading. We have seen incoming graduate students create summer reading lists and plow through as much as they can in their research areas so that they can be well-versed in the field by the time they start coursework. We do not advise taking this route, however, because no amount of reading in one summer will prepare you for the two to three years of coursework ahead of you. If anything, you may end up starting your program feeling burned out. Reading, however, is not a bad thing, especially if you do it for pleasure and at a relaxing pace. Miroslava finds, for instance, that reading beautifully written, richly textured narratives—usually historical fiction or fiction—helps her improve her writing by providing role models for what I seek to produce. Do you have a book that you have been wanting to read for fun, but you haven't been able to? The book need not be related to your program or discipline. Have you been tempted to listen to an audiobook but felt that you did not have the time to do it? Now would be a good time to take on some leisurely listening or reading, as you may not have this level and form of free time available once you start your graduate program.

Networking and building community is yet another ideal activity to do over the summer in preparation for starting graduate school. Reach out to individuals in the program you'll be attending, whether they are in your cohort or a few years ahead of you. Meet with them. If you live close by or if you plan to move to the area early, consider meeting in person. Reach out to the professors in the program. Some of them might be away for the summer and may not be responsive, but if they are available, you may develop a good relationship with them early on.

What advice do these individuals have to offer to incoming students? Where can you access resources for students like you at your institution? Where can you find like-minded individuals or affinity groups? Who is going to be part of your graduate school support system? Support systems in the form of peers, femtors, and mentors can help to increase your sense of self-efficacy and resilience in graduate school, increasing your chances of having a successful outcome. If networking does not come easy to you, consider reaching out to just two to three people before your program starts and see where those conversations take you. As you gain momentum, consider reaching out to more people and make time to strengthen existing relationships that are valuable to you.

WELLNESS, SELF-CARE, AND STRESS MANAGEMENT IN GRADUATE SCHOOL

It can be easy to disregard your health and wellness as you try to figure out how to acclimate to a new location, university, and program. We urge you to consider incorporating wellness, self-care, and stress management practices into your daily life now to ensure that the work you do is sustainable and does not burn you out or make you sick. Yvette knows from first-hand experience what can happen when you overwork your body and do not listen to the signs of exhaustion. She developed a series of chronic illnesses in graduate school that continue to shape her daily life today. In this section we will walk you through a series of tools and strategies to consider as part of your self-care, wellness, and stress-reduction toolkit.

Taking care of yourself is something best practiced regularly in micro and macro forms. Micro forms of self-care can include deep breathing exercises, listening to a short guided meditation, petting your dog or cat, taking a brief five-to-ten minute walk, and scheduling mini-breaks in between meetings for you to decompress. Macro forms of self-care are the bigger or more time- and energy-consuming tasks that can include scheduling and saving for your first vacation, seeing a specialist to assess and/or treat a physical or mental health concern that continues to bother you, upholding a firm boundary against a toxic family member, and leaving an unfulfilling job. Self-care is a highly individual practice and while there is no right or wrong way to do it, it is important to be mindful—or consciously aware—of what feels right or wrong for you, your body, mind, and spirit, especially as you navigate graduate school in a setting where taking care of yourself and putting yourself first is rarely encouraged.

Another way to protect your wellness is by setting healthy boundaries around your academic work. Setting boundaries is the act of communicating and upholding your personal needs and values as a means of self-preservation. In academia, it can take place in a variety of forms such as not responding to emails after a certain hour, not working on a certain day of the week, limiting the number of service requests you agree to take on, and continuously advocating for yourself when others are not respecting or are unaware of your limitations. Within academic culture there is an expectation for you to work at all times and all hours of the day without regard for your personal circumstances. In fact, while the number of hours that a professor works each week is not always clear, many would agree that professors, and especially female professors, work well over the expected forty-hour work week, and some expect their graduate students to follow suit. With this in mind, it is important to know your capacities so that you maintain a feasible workload in graduate school.

Maintaining boundaries can be challenging, as we know from first-hand experience. One way to do so is to have a clear method for assessing what opportunities you will say "yes" to and which you will say "no" to. For some students, especially those with perfectionist and people-pleasing tendencies, it can be hard to turn down any offer for fear of disappointing others or missing an amazing chance to enhance your work or yourself. But saying yes to everything will likely lead to exhaustion and burnout. Plus, you will have many more opportunities, believe us. Might we also remind you that you cannot please everyone, in graduate school or out of it? Instead of focusing on solely pleasing others, how else might you consider what you say yes and no to? You might consider whether it will include compensation. We don't mean a financial benefit alone—though certainly that is sufficient motivation—but also possible personal and professional benefits. Might the activity be an asset or of considerable value on your CV? Is it aligned with your goals and values? Will it bring you joy? And will the compensation, whether financial or not, be equitable based on your time and experience? If you say yes to any of these questions and you have the time and energy to take this on, then you have well-thought-out reasons to accept this opportunity.

Another strategy you could implement is having a group of trusted femtors, mentors, or peers who can act as your sounding board and can offer their input or advice on opportunities as they come up. For some, this is called their "no" committee, the people who help make that difficult decision to say "no." Another option is to give yourself at least twenty-four hours to decide. If you are someone who has a tendency to want to say yes right away, it can be helpful to give yourself time to fully assess the offer before giving a firm answer. You will be amazed at how your perspective on offers will change after a day of them sitting in your inbox. Suddenly, it won't look as urgent or exciting as you thought. Miroslava likes to remind herself that when she says "no" to a service request, she is saying "yes" to her research or to her family or to some other important activity or goal. Lastly, it is important to start keeping track of opportunities that are a definite "yes" and those that are a definite "no" so that when something falls in the middle, you can more quickly determine if it's closer to the yes or no on that scale and then make your decision accordingly.

Setting boundaries will also help you with maintaining healthy work-life harmony. Rather than using the phrase *work-life balance*, we use the term *harmony* to reflect the ways that your priorities and time for personal life will shift throughout your graduate program. At times, you will prioritize academic work or your personal life but it will rarely, if ever, be a fifty-fifty split, where you are able to multitask successfully. It can be helpful to communicate your needs and get your loved ones on board when you need to prioritize academic work over family events. Similarly, you may encounter times when you must put your personal needs or your family first and set firm boundaries with your advisor and other colleagues. If you are someone who has many ongoing personal obligations, it can also be helpful to include your responsibilities within your project-management and time-management system. This can include adding personal responsibilities and deadlines on your task list and intentionally setting aside time on your calendar for personal events each week that you hold sacred or are non-negotiable.

When it comes to self-care and achieving work-life harmony, we also want to reiterate the importance of community care, especially for first-generation, low-income, and/or nontraditional Students of Color, who will not see themselves reflected by the majority of the student population, staff, faculty, or administration. Community care refers to care work that uplifts entire communities and is critical in graduate school because academia is not a space where care work is prioritized. Community care in graduate school can look like joining graduate student organizations and affinity groups, getting involved in local nonprofits and small businesses, or creating your own study, writing, or other support groups. Deciding what type of community care you want to get involved in depends on your needs and preferences because, as Dr. Angela Crumdy mentions in the Grad School Femtoring Podcast, we must create spaces in graduate school "the way we want to and with the people that we want to do it with," both inside and outside higher education, depending on what helps us feel "not only rested, but restored."[1]

Another factor to consider when starting graduate school is how you are going to advocate for yourself and your needs, especially if you are disabled and require accommodations or if you are struggling academically and believe that you could benefit from getting assessed to determine what support would help you thrive. About one in five children in the United States have learning disabilities and work with an Individual Education Plan (IEP) to receive services to support their learning. The IEP typically includes goals and strategies to help the student meet their educational needs and reach their academic potential. By the time they enter college, however, the IEP is no longer applicable and the student must work with a disability or accessibility services office to learn about the accommodations available at their university and the documentation required for these. Accommodations in graduate school can look like having access to a notetaker, receiving extended time or alternative formats for tests, sign language interpreters, accessible parking, reduced course load, voice recognition and text to speech software, and more. Even if you are unsure, it can be helpful to learn about what resources are available, as Yvette has witnessed several people discover for the first time in graduate school that they have a learning disability and qualify to receive life-changing accommodations.

If you are not disabled but have family and personal needs, you can advocate for what will allow you to succeed in your program and in life. If you are a student-parent, you may promote holding more department meetings and events during business hours, rather than evenings and weekends when childcare is difficult and more expensive to secure. If you are a commuting student, you might ask for the option to come to campus a few days a week instead of every day. If you are a working-class student, you might want to ask the department if there is an option for them to pay for conference costs like airfare or lodging upfront rather than waiting weeks or months to be reimbursed. You may not always get what you request but we would rather you ask than find out too late that you missed out on a great resource.

Burnout is another big topic among graduate students and academics in general. *Burnout* refers to a state of physical and emotional exhaustion, which within a job setting is derived from prolonged or chronic work-related stress. Burnout is manifested physically, behaviorally, and emotionally. You might experience a loss of motivation, difficulty with concentration, a change in appetite or sleep, or feel exhausted, overwhelmed, and helpless, among other signs. Burnout can occur to graduate students at any stage in their academic trajectory because of the high workload and rigor of many programs. If you find yourself struggling, we offer a few suggestions for ways to cope with and ideally overcome it. The first thing you should do is recognize the signs of burnout and rule out any other possible reasons you might be struggling. If you have other concerns, such as your mental health, seek professional support. As a graduate student, you may have access to low- or no-cost counseling and psychological services, such as individual therapy or support groups. Another thing you can do is identify the primary areas in which you need to reduce your stress by re-evaluating, modifying, and reinforcing your boundaries. Look at your workload and determine what else you can say no to so that you can replace that with time for yourself—for rest, care, and replenishment. Keep in mind that it takes time, in some cases years, to recover from burnout, and that it is normal to struggle with exhaustion. It is also acceptable to reach out to others, especially those within your support system, to open up about your struggles and learn about resources to get help. In some cases, the best option might be to take a break from your program altogether. Most graduate programs have leave of absence policies that you can look into to determine if this option would be best for you. Burnout is something we hope you do not have to experience—but if you do, you are not alone and you have ways to overcome it while still making progress in your graduate program.

CAREER DEVELOPMENT AND CAREER OPTIONS WITH AN ADVANCED DEGREE

Getting into graduate school is not enough to ensure that you reach your career and life goals. You must proactively work on your career over time by identifying your goals, values, mission, and vision in life. You must also figure out what skills are necessary for the fields and industries you are most interested in and best equipped to enter. Believe it or not, you cannot assume that your graduate program will equip you for and land you your ideal job after graduation. Even if it does, however, your career does not end with your first job. It is a lifelong process of strengthening old interests and discovering new interests and then growing within one or more careers. The sooner you learn to focus on your own personal and professional development within and outside the institutions and structures you are part of, the more smoothly you'll be able to transition from one position or title to another.

How do you create a mission, vision, and determine your values and goals? This is where the concept of personal branding is important. *Personal branding* refers to the ways that you intentionally project yourself, your identity, your values, and what you stand for to the world. This can include positioning yourself as an authority or thought leader within a particular field or skillset. One way to get started with your personal branding is to think back to your life story and trajectory. What are common arcs or themes in your life? What are your most memorable positive experiences? What are areas that you've focused on or things that you believe in? From there, can you identify some core values? When you think about your career(s) of interest, what stands out to you? Why are you pursuing your current personal and professional goals? Do your past and future goals translate easily into a singular mission that you have been seeking to execute? Can you pinpoint some ideas about the vision that you have for yourself now, in the short term, and in the long term? Working on your personal branding will help you clarify the reasons that you are attracted to your current career interests and may open up new opportunities that you had not considered and are also in alignment with who you are and what you stand for.

Obtaining an advanced degree positions you to apply to a wide range of jobs since many industries require such training. Within the academic job market, a doctoral degree is typically required to secure a tenure-track job, that is, a full-time position in the professoriate with the security of employment upon earning tenure. Some PhDs decide instead to pursue a career in student affairs or in academic affairs, where their advanced degree is needed to run one or more programs or centers in a university campus. Outside of the academic job market, you can find many jobs in government, nonprofits, industry, and entrepreneurship where advanced degrees are required and/or offer highly valuable transferable skills. PhDs, in particular, are attractive in Edtech (short for educational technology) companies that focus on enhancing teaching and learning. They are also attractive within the User Experience (UX) industry—a field that focuses on enhancing all aspects of an end user's interactions with a particular digital product, website, or application. Within UX, PhDs are hired specifically for their research skills, both quantitative and qualitative. Outside of technical industries, PhDs are also highly attractive as grant writers, directors of nonprofits, and consultants who provide educational and research support for nonprofits and companies. In government, you may find PhDs working as policy analysts and researchers. You will also see PhDs working as editors, consultants, and coaches assisting with career and academic development, among many other entrepreneurial options. In short, as a PhD, you have a wide range of career options, despite the tendency for doctoral students to be trained for and funneled into one track, that is, the professoriate.

We believe it is important to empower you with this knowledge about career options precisely because, even if you do want to become a tenure-track professor, the state of the academic job market is bleak and does not seem to be getting better. Tenure means "an indefinite appointment that can be terminated only for cause or under extraordinary circumstances such as financial exigency and program discontinuation."[2] Tenure-track appointments are attractive because of the seeming job stability that they promise. However, these tenure line positions may not continue to exist after senior faculty leave or retire.

In fact, the American Association of University Professors' 2022 report on tenure policies indicates that 53.5 percent of formerly tenure-eligible positions in institutions of higher education have been replaced with contingent faculty appointments, that is, with non-tenured adjunct professors and lecturers.[3] This is a stark increase from the 17.2 percent of contingent faculty identified in 2004. The increase in contingent and low-paid faculty positions, decrease in tenure-track positions, and ongoing falling salaries and salary stagnation, is making it difficult for PhDs to consider a tenure-track faculty position as their only option.

Another hurdle that is making it more difficult for prospective students to survive and thrive within graduate programs is the limited funding and benefits afforded to students along with the culture of overwork, which often leads to exploitative work environments and student unrest. Students are no longer willing to tolerate such conditions, however, as was apparent at the end of 2022 when approximately "48,000 unionized academic workers across the University of California's 10 campuses walked off the job . . . calling for better pay and benefits."[4] Among the demands were an increase in pay to afford the high cost of living in California and added benefits related to childcare, family leave, healthcare, transportation, and more.[5] The outcome was that the University of California reached an agreement to offer pay increases of 20 to 80 percent depending on the position (teaching assistant, researcher, postdoctoral fellow) at a cost of "between $500 million and $570 million over the life of the contracts."[6] Each UC campus is responsible for calculating and planning for how they will absorb those costs, which in some cases will involve cutting graduate admissions and reducing their teaching assistantships, among other options. While the 2022 UC strike did not directly impact all graduate programs in California or across the country, other institutions may soon follow suit, especially in light of rising inflation and the growing student debt crisis. All of this is to say that these are real concerns and issues that will have an impact on who applies and who gets into doctoral programs in the future.

Another thing to keep in mind is that with the shrinking number of tenure-track positions and the rise of graduate student worker unrest, many questions come up about the ethics of admitting more graduate students into doctoral programs than can be adequately funded while they are students and can secure a good job placement afterwards. We ask: What responsibility do universities have to provide adequate funding and benefits to newly admitted students? What responsibility do they have in preparing their graduate students for successful job placements and careers? What are the risks and benefits of pursuing a doctoral degree in programs that neither offer adequate funding nor provide training for careers outside of higher education? And what can first-generation, low-income, and/or nontraditional BIPOC students do to ensure that we best position ourselves for careers within and outside academia? We do not have all of the answers but what we do know is that some graduate programs are already making decisions around their graduate school admissions process with this in mind, which may include reducing the number of admitted students and providing learning and training opportunities for alternative-academic ("alt-ac") or non-academic ("non-ac") career paths. Nevertheless, it is not safe to assume that if you do everything right—and by that we mean, if you meet your program's academic milestones, publish, teach, and provide service—you will land a coveted tenure-track position. Similarly, earning tenure is no easy feat and among those that do secure tenure, not everyone decides to keep their job. Once again, we want to emphasize the power of having options, no matter what career track you are on when earning your advanced degree.

WHAT WE BRING TO THE ACADEMIC TABLE

We want to urge you not to lose sight of what you bring to the table as a graduate student, and eventually a PhD, who has overcome many of the challenges first-generation, low-income, and/or nontraditional

Students of Color face in their lives. While this might include not having sufficient financial means to consider postgraduate education or being unaware of the hidden curriculum, we face constant hurdles—institutional and individual—along our journey. Despite the many barriers, or, rather, because of them, many of us have developed a hunger and will to fight for equity and inclusion for our families and communities in the larger society, as our ancestors have done before us. Miroslava knew why she wanted to go to graduate school and what she wanted to achieve, despite internal voices—that is, the impostor phenomenon—that kept telling her that she wasn't cut out for or would never make it in graduate school. She took those doubts and used them to fuel her desire to research, write, and recover the voices of Communities of Color, especially of women, that had been buried in the dustbins of history for too long. She came with a purpose to graduate school: to reconstruct the histories of women specifically and people generally of Mexican descent, with all their failings and successes, in the United States. While some may call it a "political purpose," she responds, "what part of history is not political?" This purpose helped her overcome her darkest moments when she wanted to give it up, when she thought it was too hard, and when she believed she would fail. She knew she could not give up and let down her subjects. She often asked herself, as overly confident graduate students sometimes do, "if I don't carry out this project, who will?"

As first generation, low-income, and/or nontraditional Students of Color, we bring many assets to the academic table of graduate school. Our experiences, insights, and perspectives are not as common as you might think, especially in the "ivory tower" where homogeneity and conformity is expected and taught from day one. While the institution might work hard to mold or pound you into its own likeness (and you'll know this work when you see and feel it) it is your prerogative to resist becoming an agent in this cause. Rather, we encourage you and applaud your willingness to fight for and retain your identity, values, and mission while you are pursuing a graduate degree. Certainly, you will face resistance from professors, peers, and others who don't agree with your views. While you should listen to them, ultimately we encourage you to stand firm with your beliefs and to do the work—the research and writing as well as the creative work—that supports your ideas and points of view. If your perspective changes through the course of your studies, don't be too surprised. That has happened to all of us and that is what we call growth. Ultimately, graduate school is about growing academically, professionally, and personally and using that to further your dreams and desires.

Again, congratulations! You have made it to the end of our collective journey where we have shared insights derived from research and first-hand experiences about what you need to know to successfully apply and get into graduate school. In this chapter, we explored some of the major concerns for incoming graduate students about how to prepare for the big move and what to do in the summer months before starting a program. As noted, you will need to consider the costs associated with moving and housing and to make plans to cover those expenses. We also discussed essential "to dos" over the summer months before starting your program. Above all, recall that it is important to rest and take a respite from all your hard work. That doesn't mean not thinking about your future. Rather, we suggest that, while you take a mental break from your academic work, you focus on your finances and the significance of creating and working with a budget year-round, despite how little you think you might make as a graduate student. Now more than ever, it is important to know where and how you are spending every dollar. If you're finding budgeting too stressful and you're unable to relax because of the stress, pick up a new hobby or renew your love for an old one. It's always important to have interests outside of graduate school. That might be joining a running group, learning a new language, or taking dance and cycling classes, as we did, but you have many other options to choose from. Believe it or not, many of these activities are subsidized by the university, enabling you to take advantage of the more affordable prices provided to students. Finally, if at all possible, find ways to reach out and network with your advisor or your peers. It's never too early to start building relationships. We don't suggest being pushy or forcibly integrating yourself into a relationship or relationships. Those take time to develop. Don't be concerned if it takes a while—a quarter or semester or two—before you feel connected and comfortable with your advisor and cohort. That's perfectly fine, but if you feel something is amiss, go with your gut instinct and consider finding a new advisor.

In addition to discussing what to do and how to prepare before arriving on campus, we also reviewed the importance of wellness, self-care, and stress management and the variety of strategies you can employ to make sure you are taking care of yourself holistically. Find what works best for you on a daily basis as well as on a monthly or quarterly schedule. Remember, too, the importance of setting boundaries for your health and academic wellness. As a first-generation, low-income, and/or nontraditional Student of Color, you may be called on—more than once—to "speak for" others like you in department events or in campus-wide graduate student organizations. Learn when to say "yes" and when to say "no." This is a valuable lesson that sometimes even we don't always know how to manage. We both admittedly still struggle with saying no, but are getting better at it.

We also want to remind you that securing a doctorate doesn't necessarily mean the path to the professoriate. On the contrary, as we have seen, PhDs are having an incredibly difficult time landing a tenure-track career. Plus, we know you have many more options and urge you to explore a variety of career options and opportunities for growth. A PhD secures you not only a foot in the door but also the potential for rapid upward mobility within your specific sector. Finally, remember that you—as a first-generation, low-income, and/or nontraditional Student of Color—bring fresh perspectives to the academic table based on your experiences, which are not commonly found among the majority of those in elite institutions. Nevertheless, you can find ways, as an individual and in community—to cultivate a space you can call your own and reclaim what is rightfully yours and ours: equity, inclusion, and belonging in higher education and beyond.

KEY TAKEAWAYS

- This chapter focused on how to prepare for starting graduate school, including how to plan for a move to a different city, state, or even country and what to focus on during the summer before you start graduate school.

- We shared several wellness, self-care, and stress management strategies to help you thrive.

- In an effort to be transparent, we also discussed the reality of limited funding in graduate programs, the culture of overwork in academia, the shrinking number of tenure-track positions, and the rise of student unrest across the United States. We also talked about how these realities may have an impact on who applies and gets into graduate school, what funding opportunities will be available, and what career options you may have.

- We wrapped up this last chapter by urging you to remember your assets and what you bring to the table as a first-generation, low-income, and/or nontraditional Student of Color.

CONCLUSION

The Impact of *Is Grad School for Me?*

WHEN THINKING ABOUT the impact that we hope this book will have for first-generation, low-income, and/or nontraditional Students of Color, we cannot help but look back at our experiences in college and in graduate school, where such a guide would have been life-changing. Having an opportunity to not only receive support during one's graduate school journey but also the guidance to take stock of one's future is critical. We understand how incredibly isolating, frustrating, and overwhelming it can be to navigate new spaces, especially when you are the first in your family and community to do so and/or if you are one of few people who look like you or have your circumstances in your program of choice. This is why we hope to have made this process a bit easier and straightforward.

We hope that this book reaches the hands of college students and graduates far and wide seeking to return to school. We acknowledge that we did not, and could not, address the hurdles and obstacles faced by all populations who come from disenfranchised and impoverished communities. However, we anticipate that this will be one of many books soon to come to help close these gaps. We also hope the book will be read by faculty who are mentoring diverse students as well as administrators who are invested in learning about and minimizing common obstacles that a large portion of their student population may be facing. We can envision training for faculty and administrators nationwide that would include this book as required reading. Lastly, this guide would also be useful to staff and community members who work closely with college and college-bound students who are interested in or may benefit from an advanced degree. This could include people working with grad prep programs, institutes, and courses at colleges and universities nationwide.

We also hope that this book will help to minimize gatekeeping of institutional knowledge, debunk any graduate school misconceptions, and ultimately, empower our readers to take control of their education, careers, and lives. One of the biggest "aha!" moments I, Yvette, have discovered in my educational and career trajectory was realizing that no amount of hard work or studying would guarantee that I would land my dream job or that being a "good" student wouldn't necessarily pay off in the form of a "good" job—one with a competitive salary, benefits, manageable workload, and hospitable environment. Instead, I needed to work "smarter," or rather, strategically, to clarify my values, mission, and vision as well as my need and capacity levels, and then build and maintain relationships and skills that could open up opportunities in alignment with those things. We hope that similarly you can come to this understanding and take the necessary steps to make progress in meeting your lifelong goals.

Our larger dream and desire is that, by facilitating access to institutions of higher education, these spaces become more diverse and equitable. We realize that this will not happen overnight. We also understand that, just because we have more first-generation, low-income, and/or nontraditional Students of Color in academia, we will not necessarily have more diverse classrooms and curriculum and inclusive policies and practices. No. We need to teach about the source of the inequality and denaturalize the disparities as well the myths of meritocracy built into institutions of higher education and the larger society. We should not be content to allow the institutionalized and oftentimes invisible forms of racism, sexism, classism, homophobia, ableism, and ageism, among other isms, to continue. We need to find and create the tools and the language to pry and call them out across a variety of institutions and workplaces. One way to do so is to learn about these hidden rules and systemic inequities and then take action towards change because, as activist, educator, and author Angela Davis once said, "I am no longer accepting the things I cannot change. I am changing the things I cannot accept."

Notes

INTRODUCTION

1. Mary Church Terrell, "The Progress of Colored Women" (Washington, DC: Smith Brothers, Printers, 1898). https://www.loc.gov/item/90898298.

2. Center for First-Generation Success, "Defining First-Generation," November 20, 2017, https://firstgen.naspa.org/blog/defining-first-generation, accessed June 18, 2022.

3. "Yesterday's Non-Traditional Student is Today's Traditional Student," Center for Postsecondary and Economic Success (2015), http://www.clasp.org/resources-and-publications/publication-1/CPES-Nontraditional-students-pdf.pdf, accessed June 18, 2022.

4. For more on Students of Color in higher education, see Morgan Taylor and Jonathan M. Turk, "Race and Ethnicity in Higher Education: A Look at Low-Income Undergraduates," American Council on Education, https://www.equityinhighered.org/resources/ideas-and-insights/race-and-ethnicity-in-higher-education-a-look-at-low-income-undergraduates/, accessed June 21, 2022.

5. RTI Data Source, "First-Generation College Graduates, Race/Ethnicity, Age, and Use of Career Planning Services," Center for First-Generation Student Success and NASPA, https://firstgen.naspa.org/files/dmfile/FactSheet-011.pdf, accessed June 21, 2022. For the 26 percent figure from 2006, see Jennifer Engle, Adolfo Bermeo, and Colleen O'Brien, "Straight from the Source: What Works for First-Generation College Students" (Washington, DC: Pell Institute for the Study of Opportunity in Higher Education, 2006).

6. Taylor and Turk, "Race and Ethnicity in Higher Education."

7. Ibid.

8. For studies on institutional neglect generally and microaggressions specifically, see, for instance, Tara J. Yosso, *Critical Race Counterstories along the Chicana/Chicano Educational Pipeline* (New York: Routledge, 2013); and, Daniel Solorzano, Miguel Ceja, and Tara Yosso, "Critical Race Theory, Racial Microaggressions, and Campus Racial Climate: The Experiences of African American College Students," *Journal of Negro Education* (2000), 60–73. For research on transfer students and the challenges they face, see, for example, Frankie Santos Laanan, S. S. Starobin, and L. E. Eggleston, "Adjustment of Community College Students at a Four-year University: Role and Relevance of Transfer Student Capital for Student Retention," *Journal of College Student Retention: Research, Theory & Practice* 12 (2010), 175–209; Frankie Santos Laanan and Dimpal Jain, "Advancing a New Critical Framework for Transfer Student Research: Implications for Institutional Research," *New Directions for Institutional Research* 170 (2016), 9–21. For useful and specific ways for students of color to succeed in higher education, see Anne H. Charity Hudley, Christine Mallinson, and Mary Bucholtz, *Talking College: Making Space for Black Language Practices in Higher Education* (New York: Teachers College Press, 2022).

9. Rackham Graduate School at the University of Michigan, *How to Mentor Graduate Students: A Guide for Faculty* (2019), p. 8. Available from https://rackham.umich.edu/faculty-and-staff/facilitating-academic-success/mentoring-advising. Cited in Graduate Division, UC Santa Barbara, "Best Practices for Faculty Mentoring of Graduate Students," June 7, 2022, https://ext-prod.graddiv.ucsb.edu/sites/default/files/2022–08/Grad%20Council%20Best%20Practices%20for%20Faculty%20Mentoring%20of%20Graduate%20Students%20%281%29.pdf, accessed September 15, 2022.

10. See, for instance, Gabriella Gutiérrez y Muhs, Yolanda Flores Niemann, Carmen G. González, and Angela P. Harris, eds., *Presumed Incompetent: The Intersections of Race and Class for Women in Academia* (Louisville: University Press of Colorado, 2012); Gabriella Gutiérrez y Muhs, Yolanda Flores Niemann, Carmen G. González, eds., *Presumed Incompetent II: Race, Class, Power, and Resistance of Women in Academia* (Louisville: University Press of Colorado, 2020); Atia Sattar, "Academic Motherhood and the Unrecognized Labors of Non-Tenure Track Faculty Women of Color," *Academe* 109 (2022), https://www .aaup.org/article/academic-motherhood-and-unrecognized-labors-non-tenure-track-faculty-women-color; Kelly Marie Ward, "Crafting the Conditions for Professional Membership: Women of Color Navigating Inclusion into Academia," *Sociology Quarterly* 63 (2022), 497–515. For more on emotional labor, see, for instance, Gemma Hartley, *Fed Up: Emotional Labor, Women, and the Way Forward* (New York, NY: Harper One, 2018).

11. "Pursuing a Master of Library Science and Bilingual School Librarianship" with Jeffrey Merino, in Yvette Martínez-Vu, *Grad School Femtoring Podcast*, episode 141, June 10, 2022.

12. National Science Foundation, Division of Science Resources Statistics, *U.S. Doctorates in the 20th Century*, NSF 06–319, Lori Thurgood, Mary J. Golladay, and Susan T. Hill (Arlington, VA 2006), chapter 2; Lawton M. Hartman, *Graduate Education: Parameters for Public Policy: Report Prepared for the National Science Board* 69, no. 2. (Washington, DC: US Government Printing Office, 1969), 4–5.

13. For more on the early history of higher education in the white mainstream, see, for instance, John R. Thelin, *A History of American Higher Education* (Baltimore, MD: John Hopkins University Press, 2011); John S. Brubacher and Willis Rudy, *Higher Education in Transition: A History of American Colleges and Universities* (New York: Routledge, 2017). Equally comprehensive studies on African Americans, Native Americans, Mexican Americans, Puerto Ricans, and white women are still wanting. Nevertheless, the literature is in development. See, for instance, Pero Gaglo Dagbovie, "Black Women Historians from the Late 19th Century to the Dawning of the Civil Rights Movement," *The Journal of African American History* 89 (Summer 2004): 241–261; Margaret Smith Crocco and Catty L. Waite, "Education and Marginality: Race and Gender in

Higher Education, 1940–1955," *History of Education Quarterly* 47 (2007): 69–91; Bobby Wright and William G. Tierney, "American Indians in Higher Education: A History of Cultural Conflict," *Change: The Magazine of Higher Learning* 23 (1991): 11–18; Christopher Tudico, "Before We Were Chicanas/os: The Mexican American Experience in California Higher Education, 1848–1945, (PhD diss., University of Pennsylvania, 2010); Barbara Miller Solomon, *In the Company of Educated Women: A History of Women and Higher Education in America* (New Haven: Yale University Press, 1985).

14. Derrick P. Alridge, "On the Education of Black Folk: W. E. B Du Bois and the Paradox of Segregation," *Journal of African American History* 100 (2015), 478. See also Heather Andrea Williams, *Self-Taught: African American Education in Slavery and Freedom* (Chapel Hill: University of North Carolina Press, 2005).

15. The figures come largely from "Key Events in Black Higher Education: JBHE Chronology of Major Landmarks in the Progress of African Americans in Higher Education," *Journal of Blacks in Higher Education*, https://www.jbhe .com/chronology/, accessed August 14, 2022.

16. For more on Bouchet, see Andy Piascik, "Edward Alexander Bouchet: The First African American to Earn a PhD from an American University," February 12, 2022, https://connecticuthistory.org/edward-alexander-bouchet-the-first-african-american-to-earn-a-phd-from-an-american-university, accessed August 12, 2022. For more on Du Bois and the granting of his PhD, see David Pilgrim, "Was W. E. B. Du Bois the First African American to Receive a Ph.D.?" Jim Crow Museum, Ferris State University, https://www.ferris.edu/HTMLS /news/jimcrow/question/2009/may.htm, accessed Aug 12, 2022. See also Henry Louis Gates Jr. and Evelyn Brooks Higginbotham, eds., *African American National Biography* (New York: Oxford African American Studies Center, 2006).

17. Alridge, "On the Education of Black Folk," 477.

18. For more on Du Bois, see W. E. B. Du Bois, *Souls of Black Folk*, introduction by Manning Marable (New York: Routledge, 2015 [1903]); W. E. B. Du Bois, *Black Reconstruction in America*, introduction by H. Mack Jones (New York: Routledge, 2017 [1935]). Du Bois was one of the most influential intellectuals, scholars, public figures, and writers of the twentieth century. In 1909, he was a founding member of the National Association for the Advancement of Colored People (NAACP), one of the foremost and earliest advocates for civil rights.

19. Victoria-María MacDonald, "American Latino Theme Study: Education Demanding their Rights: The Latino Struggle for Educational Access and Equity," https://www.nps.gov/articles/latinothemeeducation.htm, accessed August 14, 2022; Victoria-María MacDonald and Benjamin Polk Hoffman, "'Compromising La Causa?': The Ford Foundation and Chicano Intellectual Nationalism in the Creation of Chicano History, 1963–1977," *History of Education Quarterly* 52, no. 2 (2012), 251–81. For more on George I. Sánchez, see, for instance, Carlos Kevin Blanton, *George I. Sánchez: The Long Fight for Mexican American Integration* (New Haven: Yale University Press, 2015). For more on Martha Bernal, see Julia Weis, "Dr. Martha Bernal, The First Latina with a PhD in Psychology," https://salud-america.org/dr-martha-bernal-the-first-latina-with-a-phd-in-psychology, accessed August 14, 2022; "Women Who Achieve: Martha Bernal," Pennsylvania Psychiatric Institute, https://ppimhs.org/newspost/women-who-achieve-martha-bernal, accessed August 16, 2022.

20. For more see, for example, Clifford E. Trafzer and Joel R. Hyer, eds., *Exterminate Them: Written Accounts of the Murder, Rape, and Enslavement of Native Americans During the California Gold Rush* (East Lansing: Michigan State Uuniversity Press, 1999). For more on the boarding school experience, see, for instance, Clifford E. Trafzer, Jean A. Keller, and Lorene Sisquoc, eds., *Boarding School Blues: Revisiting American Indian Educational Experiences* (Lincoln: University of Nebraska Press, 2006); Brenda J. Child, *Boarding School Seasons: American Indian Families, 1900–1940* (Lincoln: University of Nebraska Press, 1998). For the establishment of an American Indian college in California, see, for instance, Lorena V. Márquez, *La Gente: Struggles for Empowerment and Community Self-Determination in Sacramento* (Tucson: University of Arizona Press, 2020), chapter 4.

21. Will Bunch, *After the Ivory Tower Falls: How College Broke the American Dream and Blew Up Our Politics—And How to Fix It* (New York: William Morrow, 2022).

22. National Science Foundation Division of Science Resources Statistics, *U.S. Doctorates in the 20th Century*, 5.

23. Ibid., chapter 3, figures 3.13 and 3.14.

24. Maricel Quintana-Baker, "A Profile of Mexican American, Puerto Rican, and Other Hispanic STEM Doctorates: 1983 to 1997," *Journal of Women and Minorities in Science and Engineering* 8 (2002): 118. For more information on "Other Hispanics," see pp. 99–100.

25. Elvia Ramírez, "'No One Taught Me the Steps': Latinos' Experiences Applying to Graduate School," *Journal of Latinos & Education* 10 (July 2011): 204.

CHAPTER 1. DEMYSTIFYING GRADUATE SCHOOL
AND THE HIDDEN CURRICULUM

1. Jessica McCrory Calarco, *A Field Guide to Grad School: Uncovering the Hidden Curriculum* (Princeton, NJ: Princeton University Press, 2020), 1.

2. For early studies unpacking the curriculum, see Robert Dreeben, *On What is Learned in Schools* (Reading, MA: Addison-Wesley Publishing Co., 1968); Philip N. Jackson, *Life in Classrooms* (New York: Holt, Rinehart and Winston, Inc., 1968); Norman Overly, ed., *The Unstudied Curriculum* (Washington, DC: Association of Curriculum and Supervision, 1970); Michael W. Apple, "The Hidden Curriculum and the Nature of Conflict," *Interchange* 2, no. 4 (1971), 27–40; Henry A. Giroux and Anthony N. Penna, "Social Education in the Classroom: The Dynamics of the Hidden Curriculum," *Theory & Research in Social Education* 7, no. 1 (1979): 21–42.

3. Julie R. Posselt, *Inside Graduate Admissions: Merit, Diversity, and Faculty Gatekeeping* (Cambridge: Harvard University Press, 2016), 3.

4. Ibid., 4–6.

5. Ibid., 9.

6. Ibid., 10.

7. Ibid., 12, 13.

8. D. W. Sue, "Whiteness and Ethnocentric Monoculturalism: Making the 'Invisible' Visible," *American Psychologist* 59, no. 8 (2004): 762.

9. David Hemphill and Erin Blakely, "Narratives of Progress and the Colonial Origins of Schooling," *Counterpoints* 456 (2015): 1–28.

10. "Ethical Chisme and Harsh Realities of Grad School," with Sirenia Sanchez, in Yvette Martínez-Vu, *Grad School Femtoring Podcast*, episode 62, May 21, 2021.

11. Susan K. Gardner, "Student and Faculty Attributions of Attrition in High and Low-Completing Doctoral Programs in the United States, *Higher Education 58* (2009): 97.

12. Ibid., 99.

13. Leonard Cassuto, "Ph.D. attrition: How much is too much?" *Chronicle of Higher Education,* July 1, 2013, http://chronicle.com/article/PhD-Attrition-How-

Much- Is/140045, accessed June 20, 2022. For more, see Cassuto and Robert Weisbuch, *The New Ph.D.: How to Build a Better Graduate Education* (Baltimore, MD: Johns Hopkins University Press, 2021); and, for the pioneer in the field, see Barbara E. Lovitts, *Leaving the Ivory Tower: The Causes and Consequences of Departure From Doctoral Study* (Lanham, MD: Rowman & Littlefield, 2001).

14. For more, see "Surviving Grad School Qualifying Exams," in Yvette Martínez-Vu, *Grad School Femtoring Podcast*, episode 41, October 30, 2020.

15. Vivien Collingwood, Joris Buis, Vincent Visser, and Ger Post, *Academic Skills for Interdisciplinary Studies* (Amsterdam: Amsterdam University Press, 2017).

16. Steven G. Brint, Lori Turk-Bicakci, Kristopher Proctor, and Scott Patrick Murphy, "Expanding the Social Frame of Knowledge: Interdisciplinary, Degree-Granting Fields in American Colleges and Universities, 1975–2000," *The Review of Higher Education* 32, no. 2 (2009): 155–83.

17. Calarco, *A Field Guide to Graduate School.*

18. Leonard Cassuto, "To Apply or Not Apply," *Chronicle of Higher Education,* June 7, 2013.

19. For more on gap years, see William Fitzsimmons, "Time Out or Burn Out for the Next Generation," *New York Times,* December 6, 2000; Karl Haigler and Rae Nelson, *The Gap-year Advantage: Helping Your Child Benefit From Time Off Before or During College* (New York: Macmillan, 2005).

20. Gap Year Association, "What is a Gap Year?," https://www.gapyear association.org/what-is-a-gap-year-2, accessed, May 20, 2022.

21. Nina Hoe Gallagher, "Research Statement," Gap Year Association, https://www.gapyearassociation.org/gap-year-research, May 20, 2022.

22. For more, see "Taking a Gap Year: Things to Consider," in Yvette Martínez-Vu, *Grad School Femtoring Podcast*, episode 52, March 5, 2021.

23. "How to Get Out of Your Own Way," with Wendy Amara, in Janesse Torres, *Yo Quiero Dinero: Personal Finance for Latinas*, podcast, episode 164.

CHAPTER 2. IS GRADUATE SCHOOL RIGHT FOR ME?

1. "How to Advocate for Yourself in Grad School" with Amanda Peña, in Yvette Martínez-Vu, *Grad School Femtoring Podcast*, episode 129, March 25, 2022.

2. When first-generation students have older siblings who are also first-generation and have graduated with a four-year degree, the younger siblings are still considered first-generation; the designation is based on family generation.

3. "Confidence Building and Defining Career Success on Your Terms" with Dr. Jasmine Escalera, in Yvette Martínez-Vu, *Grad School Femtoring Podcast*, episode 147, July 22, 2022.

4. Ibid.

5. For guidebooks, see, for instance, Donald Asher, *Graduate Admissions Essays: Write Your Way into the Graduate School of Your Choice*, 4th ed. (Berkeley: Ten Speed Press, 2012); Kaplan, *Get into Graduate School: A Strategic Approach* (New York: Simon & Schuster, 2003); Harold Greene and Matthew W. Greene, *Greenes' Guides to Educational Planning, Making It Into a Top Graduate School, 10 Steps to Successful Graduate School Admission* (New York: Harper Collins, 2001); American Psychological Association, *Getting In: A Step-By-Step Plan For Gaining Admission to Graduate School in Psychology*, 4th ed. (Washington, DC: APA Publishing, 2014); Jesus Reyes, *The Social Work Graduate School Applicant's Handbook*, 2nd ed. (Harrisburg, PA: White Hat Communications, 2005).

6. Rick Seltzer, "Failing to Keep Up: Recent Increases in Number of Minority Administrators Don't Keep Up with Demographic Shifts, but New Study Finds Broad Pay Equity," *Inside Higher Education*, March 2, 2017, https://www.insidehighered.com/news/2017/03/02/racial-gap-among-senior-administrators-widens, accessed June 23, 2022.

7. Quote cited in Daniel Solorzano, Miguel Ceja, and Tara Yosso, "Critical Race Theory, Racial Microaggressions, and Campus Racial Climate: The Experiences of African American College Students," *Journal of Negro Education* (2000): 60. For the original essay, see Chester Pierce, J. Carew, D. Pierce-Gonzalez, and D. Wills, "An Experiment in Racism: TV Commercials," in *Television and Education,* ed. Charles Pierce (Beverly Hills, CA: Sage, 1978), 62–88. The literature on microaggressions is vast and growing. For more see Janice McCabe, "Racial and Gender Microaggressions on a Predominantly-White Campus: Experiences of Black, Latina/o and White Undergraduates," *Race, Gender & Class* (2009): 133–151; Tabitha L. Grier-Reed, "The African American Student Network: Creating Sanctuaries and Counterspaces for Coping with Racial Microaggressions in Higher Education Settings," *The Journal of Humanistic Counseling, Education and Development* 49, no. 2 (2010): 181–88; Lindsay Pérez Huber

and Daniel G. Solorzano, "Racial Microaggressions as a Tool for Critical Race Research," *Race Ethnicity and Education* 18, no. 3 (2015): 297–320; Celeste Nichole Lee and Mark Hopson, "Disrupting Postracial Discourse: Black Millennials' Response to Postracial Ideology and the Continued Impact of Racial Microaggressions on College Campuses," *Southern Communication Journal* 84, no. 2 (2019): 127–39.

8. Quote cited in Solorzano, Ceja, and Yosso, "Critical Race Theory," 60. For the original essay, see Peggy C. Davis, "Law as Microaggression," *Yale Law Journal* 98 (1989): 1559–79.

9. Solorzano, Ceja, and Yosso, "Critical Race Theory," 67–68.

10. Quote cited in Solorzano, Ceja, and Yosso, "Critical Race Theory," 62. For the original study, see Claude M. Steele and Joshua Aronson, "Stereotype Threat and the Intellectual Test Performance of African Americans," *Journal of Personality and Social Psychology* 69 (1995): 797–811. For Steele's more recent work, see Steele, *Whistling Vivaldi: How Stereotypes Affect Us and What We Can Do* (New York: W. W. Norton & Company, 2011).

11. Solorzano, Ceja, and Yosso, "Critical Race Theory," 71.

12. Tara J. Yosso, William A. Smith, Miguel Ceja, and Daniel G. Solórzano, "Critical Race Theory, Racial Microaggressions, and Campus Racial Climate for Latina/o Undergraduates," *Harvard Educational Review* 79, no. 4 (2009): 673.

13. Ibid., 669.

14. Ibid, 672; for more on the racially assaultive "words that wound," see Mari J. Matsuda, Charles R. Lawrence, III, Richard Delgado, and Kimberlé Williams Crenshaw, "Words That Wound: Critical Race Theory, Assaultive Speech, and the First Amendment," eds. Mari J. Matsuda, Charles R. Lawrence, III, Richard Delgado, and Kimberlé W. Crenshaw (Boulder, CO: Westview Press, 1993).

15. Yosso, Smith, Ceja, and Solórzano, "Critical Race Theory, Racial Microaggressions, and Campus Racial Climate for Latina/o Undergraduates," 664.

16. Quote cited in ibid., 675. For the full cite, see William A. Smith, Tara J. Yosso, and Daniel G. Solórzano, "Challenging Racial Battle Fatigue on Historically White Campuses: A Critical Race Examination of Race-Related Stress," in *Faculty of Color: Teaching in Predominantly White Colleges and Universities*, ed. C. A. Stanley (Bolton, MA: Anker, 2006), 299–32.

17. K. L. Nadal, D. P. Rivera, and M. J. H. Corpus, "Sexual Orientation and Trans-Gender Microaggressions: Implications for Mental Health and

Counseling," in *Microaggressions and Marginality: Manifestation, Dynamics, and Impact,* ed. D. W. Sue (Hoboken, NJ: John Wiley & Sons, 2010), 217–40.

18. A. Jordan Wright and Ryan T. Wegner, "Homonegative Microaggressions and Their Impact on LGB Individuals: A Measure Validity Study," *Journal of LGBT Issues in Counseling* 6, no. 1 (2012): 37.

19. Ibid., 50.

20. Michael R. Woodford, Jill M. Chonody, Alex Kulick, David J. Brennan, and Kristen Renn, "The LGBQ Microaggressions on Campus Scale: A Scale Development and Validation Study," *Journal of Homosexuality,* 62:12 (2015): 1661. See also Sierra K. Dimberg, D. Anthony Clark, Lisa B. Spanierman, and Rachel A. Van Daalen, "'School Shouldn't Be Something You Have to Survive': Queer Women's Experiences with Microaggressions at a Canadian University," *Journal of Homosexuality* 68, no. 5 (2021): 709–32.

21. University of California, Office of the President, "Campus Climate Project Final Report," March 2014, p. 72, https://campusclimate.ucop.edu/_common/files/pdf-climate/ucsystem-full-report.pdf, accessed June 25, 2022. For details of the survey, see "An Ethos of Respect and Inclusion," UCOP, March 19, 2014, https://campusclimate.ucop.edu/results, accessed June 25, 2022. Climate refers to "the current attitudes, behaviors and standards of faculty, staff, administrators and students concerning the level of respect for individual needs, abilities and potential (University of California, Office of the President, "Campus Climate Survey: What is Campus Climate? Why Does It Matter?," https://campusclimate.ucop.edu/what-is-campus-climate, accessed June 25, 2022).

22. University of California, Santa Barbara, Campus Climate Project Final Report, March 2014, p. 53–54, *https://campusclimate.ucop.edu/_common/files/pdf-climate/ucsb-full-report.pdf,* accessed June 25, 2022.

23. University of California, Office of the President, "Campus Climate Study, Executive Summary: Campus Climate Study for the University of California System," p. 14, https://campusclimate.ucop.edu/_common/files/pdf-climate/ucsystem-summary.pdf, accessed June 25, 2022..

24. United States Department of Education, "The Beginning Postsecondary Students Longitudinal Study (BPS), 2012–2017," https://nces.ed.gov/surveys/bps/about.asp, accessed May 30, 2022.

25. Claire Wladis, "Opinion: Many Student-Parents Drop Out Because They Don't Have Enough Time for Their Schoolwork," *The Hechinger Report,*

Covering Innovation and Inequality in Education, July 24, 2018, https://hechinger-report.org/opinion-many-student-parents-drop-out-because-they-dont-have-enough-time-for-their-schoolwork-research-shows/, accessed May 30, 2022. See also Nicole Lynn Lewis, "How Colleges Tell Student-Parents They Don't Belong," *The Atlantic Online,* May 26, 2021.

26. Cecilia Caballero, Yvette Martínez-Vu, Judith Pérez-Torres, Michelle Téllez, and Christina Vega, eds., *Chicana Motherwork Anthology* (Tucson: University of Arizona Press, 2019), 6–7.

27. Amanda Márquez, "The Graduate Student Experience: The Parents' Perspective" (PhD diss., Alliant International University, 2021); Hyeon Jean Yoo and David T. Marshall, "Understanding Graduate Student Parents: Influence of Parental Status, Gender, and Major on Graduate Students' Motivation, Stress, and Satisfaction," *Journal of College Student Retention: Research, Theory & Practice* (January 2022): 1–24.

28. Lewis, "How Colleges Tell Student-Parents They Don't Belong."

29. Solorzano, Ceja, and Yosso, "Critical Race Theory," 62.

30. Ibid., 62–63.

31. Georgetown Law Library, "Civil Rights in the United States, A Brief History," https://guides.ll.georgetown.edu/c.php?g = 592919&p = 4170925, accessed May 13, 2022.

32. Ilona Bray, "What's a Crime of Moral Turpitude According to U.S. Immigration Law?," https://www.nolo.com/legal-encyclopedia/what-s-crime-moral-turpitude-according-us-immigration-law.html, accessed May 15, 2022.

33. American Immigration Council, "Fact Sheet, Aggravated Felonies: An Overview," March 16, 2021, https://www.americanimmigrationcouncil.org/research/aggravated-felonies-overview, accessed May 15, 2022.

34. National Council of State Legislatures, "Undocumented Student Tuition: Overview," June 9, 2021, https://www.ncsl.org/research/immigration/tuition-benefits-for-immigrants.aspx, accessed May 14, 2022.

35. University of California, Office of the President, "UC Campus Climate Study, Executive Summary," p. 15.

36. Rosie B., "Personal Statement," March 15, 2022. Permission to quote given in personal communication.

37. Undergraduate students at UC Berkeley first organized the Underground Scholars program in 2013 and it was officially recognized as the Underground

Scholars Initiative in 2014. Today, nearly every University of California campus has a USI chapter and they continue to build throughout the state.

38. "Contextualizing Higher Ed Models and Academia's Hidden Curriculum," with Jamaal Muwwakkil, in Yvette Martínez-Vu, *Grad School Femtoring Podcast*, episode 133, April 15, 2022.

CHAPTER 3. MYTHS AND MISCONCEPTIONS OF GRADUATE SCHOOL DEBUNKED

1. Katie Langin, "A Wave of Graduate Programs Drop the GRE Requirement," *Science*, May 2019, https://www.science.org/content/article/wave-graduate-programs-drop-gre-application-requirement, accessed June 30, 2022.

2. For more on holistic review and implicit bias, see Julie R. Posselt, *Inside Graduate Admissions: Merit, Diversity, and Faculty Gatekeeping* (Cambridge: Harvard University Press, 2016); J. D. Kent and M. T. McCarthy, "Holistic Review in Graduate Admissions: A Report from the Council of Graduate Schools" (Washington, DC: Council of Graduate Schools, 2016), https://cgsnet.org/wp-content/uploads/2022/01/CGS_HolisticReview_final_web.pdf.

3. "How to Advocate for Yourself in Grad School," with Amanda Peña, in Yvette Martínez-Vu, *Grad School Femtoring Podcast*, episode 129, March 25, 2022.

4. "Wellness and Content Creation in Graduate School," with Dr. Angela Crumdy, in Yvette Martínez-Vu, *Grad School Femtoring Podcast*, episode 135, April 29, 2022.

5. Aleksandra Kuzior, Karolina Kettler, and Lukasz Rab, "Great Resignation—Ethical, Cultural, Relational, and Personal Dimensions of Generation Y and Z Employees' Engagement," *Sustainability* 14 (2022): 6764.

6. Leonard Cassuto and Robert Weisbuch, *The New PhD: How to Build a Better Graduate Education* (Baltimore, MD: Johns Hopkins University Press, 2021), 10.

7. Dick Startz, "First-Generation College Students Face Unique Challenges," Brookings, Brown Center Chalkboard, April 25, 2022, https://www.brookings.edu/blog/brown-center-chalkboard/2022/04/25/first-generation-college-students-face-unique-challenges, accessed June 30, 2022.

8. Radomir Ray Mitic, "Insights into First-Generation Doctoral Students," Council of Graduate Schools Brief, March 2022, 1, https://cgsnet.org/wp-content

/uploads/2022/03/CGS_CP_First-Gen-Doc-Students_ForWeb.pdf, accessed June 30, 2022.

9. "Secrets of Successful Nontraditional Paths Into Graduate School," in Yvette Martínez-Vu, *Grad School Femtoring Podcast*, episode 138, May 20, 2022.

10. Ibid.

11. Posselt, *Inside Graduate Admissions*.

12. Rev, "ADA Compliance for Colleges & Universities: Laws Protecting People with Disabilities," February 28, 2020, https://www.rev.com/blog /speech-to-text-accessibility/ada-compliance-for-colleges-universities, accessed July 5, 2022.

13. Nanette Goodman, Michael Morris, and Kelvin Boston, "Financial Inequality: Disability, Race and Poverty in America," National Disability Institute, 2019, p. 5, https://www.nationaldisabilityinstitute.org/wp-content/uploads /2019/02/disability-race-poverty-in-america.pdf, accessed July 6, 2022.

14. "The Americans with Disabilities Act (ADA) defines disability as 'a physical or mental impairment that substantially limits one or more major life activities' or 'being regarded as having such an impairment'" (ibid., 7).

15. Colleen Flaherty, "Mental Health Crisis for Grad Students," *Inside Higher Ed*, March 6, 2018, https://www.insidehighered.com/news/2018/03/06/new-study-says-graduate-students-mental-health-crisis, accessed July 5, 2022. For more on African Americans, see Goodman, Morris, and Boston, "Financial Inequality."

16. Flaherty, "Mental Health Crisis."

17. Ibid.

18. "What Everyone Needs to Know About Disability and Academia," with Liu Miao, in Yvette Martínez-Vu, *Grad School Femtoring Podcast*, episode 143, June 24, 2022.

19. "Impostor [Phenomenon] as a High Achieving First-Gen Grad Student," with Samantha González, in Yvette Martínez-Vu, *Grad School Femtoring Podcast*, episode 139, May 27, 2022.

20. Miroslava Chávez-García, "Negotiating Power and Privilege," LatinX Talk, January 2019, https://latinxtalk.org/2019/01/15/strategies-for-negotiating-power-and-privilege-in-academia1.

21. "Impostor [Phenomenon] as a High Achieving First-Gen Grad Student."

22. Rebecca Covarrubias, A. Romero, and M. Trivelli, "Family Achievement Guilt and Mental Well-Being of College Students," *Journal of Child and Family Studies* 24, no. 7 (2015): 2031–37; Melissa Cloyd, "Family Achievement Guilt as Experienced by First-Generation College Students: A Phenomenology" (PhD diss., Liberty University, 2019).

CHAPTER 4. GETTING ORGANIZED AND CREATING THE GRAD SCHOOL LIST

1. "Five Key Reasons To Contact Faculty Before Applying to Grad School," in Yvette Martínez-Vu, *Grad School Femtoring Podcast*, episode 152, August 26, 2022. See "Contacting & Meeting with Prospective Faculty," in Yvette Martínez-Vu, *Grad School Femtoring Podcast,* episode 35, August 28, 2020, and "What Faculty Think and Say about Grad Students," with Dr. Ester Trujillo, Yvette Martínez-Vu, *Grad School Femtoring Podcast*, episode 78, August 20, 2021.

CHAPTER 6. THE PERSONAL AND DIVERSITY STATEMENTS

1. Jasper Elan Hunt, "How I Explained a Gap in My CV When Applying to Graduate School," *Nature,* May 29, 2019, https://www.nature.com/articles /d41586–019–01696–4, accessed June 14, 2022.

CHAPTER 8. THE APPLICATION REVIEW PROCESS AND PLAN BS

1. Julie R. Posselt, *Inside Graduate Admissions: Merit, Diversity, and Faculty Gatekeeping* (Cambridge, MA: Harvard University Press, 2016), 2.

2. Ibid., 6.

3. Ibid., 8–10.

4. Ibid., 11.

5. Ibid., 17.

6. On rejections, see "No Means Next," in Yvette Martínez-Vu, *Grad School Femtoring Podcast*, episode 51, February 19, 2021.

7. "Gap Years, Rejection, and Reapplying to Grad Programs," with Adriana Jaramillo, in Yvette Martínez-Vu, *Grad School Femtoring Podcast*, episode 115, January 28, 2022.

8. For more on how to handle disappointments, see "Compassionate Ways," in Yvette Martínez-Vu, *Grad School Femtoring Podcast*, episode 136, May 6, 2022.

9. "Declining an Offer," in Yvette Martínez-Vu, *Grad School Femtoring Podcast*, episode 53, March 12, 2021.

CHAPTER 9. WHAT GRAD PROGRAMS WANT TO KNOW ABOUT YOU AND WHAT YOU NEED TO KNOW ABOUT THEM

1. For more on interviews, see "Preparing for a Grad School Interview," episode 13, January 5, 2020, and "Zoom Interview," episode 47, January 15, 2021, both in Yvette Martínez-Vu, *Grad School Femtoring Podcast*.

2. "Grad School Open House," in Yvette Martínez-Vu, *Grad School Femtoring Podcast*, episode 14, January 12, 2020.

3. "You Got into Grad School, Now What?," in Yvette Martínez-Vu, *Grad School Femtoring Podcast*, episode 49, January 29, 2021.

4. For more on this point, see ibid.

5. "Establishing a Good Relationship with your Advisor," in Yvette Martínez-Vu, *Grad School Femtoring Podcast*, episode 48, January 22, 2021.

6. "You Got into Grad School, Now What?"

7. For more, see "Accepting an Offer With Little to No Funding," in Yvette Martínez-Vu, *Grad School Femtoring Podcast*, episode 58, April 23, 2021.

8. "Negotiating a PhD Funding Package," in Yvette Martínez-Vu, *Grad School Femtoring Podcast*, episode 21, February 28, 2020.

9. See Ford Foundation Fellowship Programs, https://sites.nationalacademies.org/PGA/FordFellowships/index.htm, accessed August 30, 2022. As of September 2022, Ford announced they would sunset the program in 2028.

10. Paul & Daisy Soros Fellowships for New Americans, https://www.pdsoros.org/?gclid=CjwKCAjw6raYBhB7EiwABge5KuGndzh9qh8mb1n50OHT4UFKDLJ_a4IkTHQzuBzzfFZfnyOb_PTcchoC_WoQAvD_BwE, accessed August 30, 2022.

11. National Science Foundation, Graduate Research Fellowship Program, https://www.nsfgrfp.org, accessed August 30, 2022.

12. Social Science Research Council, "Mobilizing Social Science for the Public Good," https://www.ssrc.org/about-us/, accessed August 30, 2022.

13. "Ford and NSF Fellowships, What Are They and Tips," in Yvette Martínez-Vu, *Grad School Femtoring Podcast*, episode 39, October 2, 2020.

14. For more see "Accepting an Offer With Little to No Funding," episode 58, April 23, 2021 and "What You Need to Know About Student Loans," episode 67, June 25, 2021, both in Yvette Martínez-Vu, *Grad School Femtoring Podcast*.

15. For more see "Negotiating a PhD Funding Package" and "Accepting an Offer With Little to No Funding"

16. For more, see ibid.

CHAPTER 10. YOU SAID YES, NOW WHAT?

1. "Wellness and Content Creation in Graduate School ," with Dr. Angela Crumdy, in Yvette Martínez-Vu, *Grad School Femtoring Podcast,* episode 135, April 29, 2022.

2. American Association of University Professors, Issues, "Tenure: What is academic tenure?" n.d., https://www.aaup.org/issues/tenure, accessed October 2, 2022.

3. Insight Into Diversity, "AAUP Releases First Tenure Study Since 2004, Revealing Major Changes in Faculty Career Tracks, June 22, 2022," https://www.insightintodiversity.com/aaup-releases-first-study-on-tenure-since-2004-revealing-major-changes-in-faculty-career-tracks, accessed October 2, 2022.

4. "Read our full coverage of the UC academic workers' strike," *The Los Angeles Times*, November 30, 2022, https://www.latimes.com/california/story/2022–11–30/read-our-full-coverage-of-the-uc-strike-of-48–000-academic-workers, accessed March 7, 2023.

5. Ibid.

6. "To afford historic labor contract, UC considers cutting TAs, graduate student admissions," *The Los Angeles Times*, January 27, 2023, https://www.latimes.com/california/story/2023–01–27/uc-scrambling-to-pay-big-wage-gains-for-academic-workers-grad-student-cuts-loom, accessed March 7, 2023.

Acknowledgments

Meeting each other when we did and how we did was more than uncanny. In some ways, it was inevitable and perhaps preordained. We first met at UCSB at the McNair Scholars Program where Yvette served as the Associate Director and Miroslava was a candidate for the Faculty Director position, a role which she eventually assumed. Within weeks of getting to know each other, we realized we had many things in common. We both were UCLA alumnae, we both had a passion for mentorship—Miroslava in her role as a faculty member and Yvette with her Grad School Femtoring Podcast—and we both had lost a parent or two at the age of twelve, which meant that we both had the experience of having to grow up quickly and take on the role of a parent or parents. As it became clear to each of us, we had matured sooner than our peers or our chronological age revealed. Whether we knew it or not at the time, we found in each other kindred spirits, we might say. One had a few decades of analog experience under her belt, while the other had the acumen, drive, and know-how of the new generation. You couldn't ask for a more perfect fit.

After a year of getting to know each other's working style, Yvette broke the news that she would be leaving the McNair Scholars Program to pursue her passion of working with clients to provide them with the insights she had gained as a femtor. Hearing the announcement crushed many staff and students who had come to rely on Yvette's steady guiding hand as well as care and concern for the whole individual. Yet, we all soon realized that Yvette's decision was best for all of us, as it meant she would have the opportunity to impart her wisdom to many more people beyond the walls and halls of McNair at UCSB. Miroslava saw Yvette's decision as an admirable and fearless endeavor that few folks in a similar position dared carry out. We wished her well on her new journey.

Within weeks of Yvette's move abroad, Miroslava asked her if she had ever considered writing a book to complement her successful podcast. "I thought you'd never ask!" she responded in her enthusiastic voice. We then talked about the possibility of working on a guide together: Yvette with her content and contacts in the world of podcast mentorship and Miroslava with her networks in academia and publishing. Fortunately, Miroslava's colleague, Elizabeth "Beth" DePalma Digeser, a professor of history at UCSB, did us the wonderful favor of contacting her editor at UC Press, Eric Schmidt, who publishes books in ancient history, a far cry from what we wanted to put out. We didn't anticipate or think that he or the press might take on this project.

Lo and behold and much to our surprise, Beth, Miroslava's colleague, told us that Eric was interested and that I should contact him. We then met with Eric and LeKeisha Hughes, Eric's amazing assistant at the time and now an acquiring editor, and pitched them our idea, which they encouraged endlessly. We were both amazed and grateful for their enthusiasm and unflagging support. Truth be told, Miroslava—who had worked with several presses in the past—remained a bit skeptical and incredulous at the warm reception and genuine interest for the work and for us. Every time we met with Eric and LeKeisha, we both had to pinch ourselves to make sure we weren't dreaming and that this guide would come to light. This is all a long way to say that we thank the heavens and the stars for connecting our paths, as well as for taking us down a journey to work with some of the most supportive individuals we have met.

I, Miroslava, would like to acknowledge my co-author, Yvette, for all of her wisdom, patience, and organizational skills to keep the project moving ahead.

I have learned so much and am grateful for all that we have done together. Our journey is only just beginning. I would also like to thank my colleagues, especially Beth DePalma Digeser for putting us in touch with Eric and LeKeisha. We would like to thank all those who contributed to the book by allowing us to share their insights and tips on graduate school and life more generally. I am especially indebted to all the femtors and mentors who have shaped and influenced my academic career as well as my professional and personal life. Among my greatest champions and sources of strength are Vicki L. Ruiz, Denise Segura, Catherine Cenize Choy, Theresa Delgadillo, Alexandra M. Stern, Rosie Bermudez, Lorena Márquez, and Lorena Oropeza. Mentors who have provided invaluable guidance over the years and who have not already been mentioned include Ernesto Chávez, Norris Hundley Jr., Kevin R. Johnson, and George J. Sánchez. Among the greatest role models I have had over the years are those who are no longer with us, but they deserve a special thank you. My dear tía Beatriz Chávez, her spouse, my tío Paco Chávez, who raised me and my brother and their own children, Alicia Robertson and Gloria Chávez. My tía Lupe Montes, who died way too young, my mother's older sister, Asunción Alvarado, and all those in my parents' generation who have left this earth.

I would like to acknowledge, as well, my family, especially my spouse and partner, Ebers García, and my two children, Eli García and Evan García, as well as our loving and boisterous companion, Chiquita. I love you all! ¡Los quiero mucho!

I, Yvette, am incredibly grateful to the following individuals who have supported me through this book-writing process. I'd like to start by thanking my co-author and femtor, Dr. Miroslava Chávez-García. I have had many mentors over the years but she is one of the few who has shown me what femtorship looks like in theory and practice through kindness, unconditional support, and radical honesty. I also want to again thank our amazing co-editors LeKeisha Hughes and Eric Schmidt, whose enthusiasm and backing in this project has made this all possible. I also want to thank my ride or die comadres who I met in college through the Mellon Mays Undergraduate Fellowship, Dr. Cecilia Caballero and Dr. Ester Trujillo. Our ongoing chats and pep talks have provided me with the emotional support to keep going during difficult physical and mental health days. I also want to thank my fierce spiritual sister, Dr. Elana Jefferson, who has reminded me when to slow down and honor my body. I'm incredibly grateful for the folks who have cheered me on and provided support in the form of co-working sessions, check-in meetings, and sharing space with me: Maceo Nafisah Cabrera-Estevez, Patty Favela, Dr. Hortencia Jiménez, Samhar Khalfani, Dr. Evingerlean D. B. Hudson, Dr. Nancy Morales, Dr. Judith Pérez-Torres, Christina Rodríguez, Dr. Emmanuela Stanislaus, Dr. Michelle Tellez, Diana Valdivia, Cynthia Pong, and Dr. Christine Vega. I would also like to express my gratitude to the guests of the Grad School Femtoring Podcast, including those quoted in this book, as well as to all of the individuals who generously shared their sample successful graduate school essays with us. Your willingness to share your stories, knowledge, and writing with us have helped to shape and strengthen this book.

Finally, I would like to express my sincerest thank you to *mi familia*, especially to *mi mamá* Rosaura, my sister Itzel, my *tío* Roberto, my *tía* Irma, my husband Joshua, and my two children, Emiliano and Ely Rosaura. *Muchísimas gracias,* I love you all!

Glossary

ABD, OR ALL BUT DISSERTATION A student who has completed all doctoral requirements except for their dissertation.

ADMISSIONS COMMITTEES The groups of people assigned to review your application, including faculty, administrators, and, sometimes, other graduate students.

ADJUNCT PROFESSOR A contingent professor who often teaches on a limited-contract or part-time and is ineligible for tenure. Many adjunct professors hold temporary appointments with low pay and without benefits.

ADVISING A process of guiding a student along an academic track, that is, on course requirements, exams and exam preparation, and writing and defending the thesis and/or dissertation.

ASSISTANT PROFESSOR Also known as a "tenure-track" professor, this is an early-career or entry-level professor without tenure and likely focused primarily on their research and tenure process.

ASSOCIATE PROFESSOR A mid-career or mid-level professor with tenure who may be pursuing the option of promotion to full professor by producing research and scholarship.

ATTRITION The departure of students from educational settings either because they are dropping out or being pushed out.

AUDITION A sample performance that one may give to be granted admission into a music, theater, or other performance-based program.

BIPOC Black, Indigenous, and People of Color.

BURNOUT A state of physical and emotional exhaustion derived from prolonged or chronic stress.

COLORBLIND ADMISSIONS A graduate school admissions process that does not pay attention to ethnic and racial differences, among other "isms," a process which often increases disparities.

COMMITTEE Members of the faculty (typically three to five) who supervise a graduate student's work and may serve as mentors, provide constructive feedback, and evaluate the work before a final exam or defense.

COMPREHENSIVE EXAMS Also known as qualifying exams, these exams are typically given to doctoral students after the completion of coursework and before they begin their dissertation.

CURRICULUM VITAE (CV) A document meant to summarize your academic achievements, including your experience, accomplishments, and skills.

DEGREE INFLATION The need to have higher degrees for positions that in the past required bachelor's degrees or no degrees.

DEMO A live or prerecorded demonstration of your abilities related to that discipline (for example, a teaching demo demonstrates your teaching abilities).

DISSERTATION A long piece of writing based on original research that is often required to obtain a doctoral degree.

DISSERTATION DEFENSE The meeting with the committee where a doctoral candidate is asked to "defend" or entertain any lingering questions or concerns about the study before it is officially submitted and considered completed.

DIVERSITY STATEMENT A graduate school admissions essay that demonstrates how your personal background and/or your academic, research, career interests have come together to contribute to diversifying higher education and academia more generally.

DOCTORAL DEGREE The highest degree that you can earn in a field. Doctor of philosophy programs in particular are for individuals who are interested in pursuing a career in research or in higher education. Professional doctoral programs like the Doctor of Education (EdD), Doctor of Psychology (PsyD), Juris Doctor (JD), and Doctor of Medicine (MD) are intended for individuals who are pursuing a specific career track in education, psychology, law, or medicine, respectively.

FAMILY ACHIEVEMENT GUILT The guilt and discomfort students may feel for having more educational opportunities and college success than their family members.

FELLOWSHIP A research-related funding source that provides you with a stipend sufficient to cover anywhere from three to twelve months of expenses, allowing you the opportunity to advance in your program without having to hustle to find part-time or full-time employment.

FEMTORING Mentorship that prioritizes individual and community empowerment as well as social justice and calls attention to the ways in which this type of service work is gendered.

FIRST-GENERATION STUDENT A person whose parents did not complete a bachelor's degree. This includes individuals who may have resided with one parent who did not complete a four-year program.

FULL PROFESSOR A senior-level or experienced professor who may opt to take on a leadership role in the department (perhaps as a chair) or campus-wide (perhaps as a dean or provost). Some senior-level professors earn honorary titles like "Distinguished Professor," which is reserved for faculty who have achieved the highest levels of scholarship over the course of their careers.

FUNDING PACKAGE A series of funding sources that may be awarded to an incoming graduate student that often includes a combination of teaching and research assistantships, fellowships, and scholarships.

GAP YEAR When a student decides to take a break from education for twelve months, or sometimes longer, usually between undergraduate and graduate school, to help build their experience and resume. (Although not used this way in this book, a gap year can also refer to a break between high school and college years.)

GATEKEEPING The process of limiting access or keeping out members from certain populations.

GRADE POINT AVERAGE (GPA) The average score of your accumulated grades over time.

GRADUATE DEGREE Any advanced academic degree that goes beyond the undergraduate degree, generally a master's or doctorate.

GRADUATE RECORD EXAM (GRE) A graduate school admissions exam akin to the SAT; a series of tests, general and subject-based, that measure your skills in verbal reasoning, quantitative reasoning, critical thinking, analytical skills, and subject-specific topics.

GRANT A funding source that provides money for specific research- or project-related activities, including maintaining labs in STEM fields, fostering interdisciplinary collaboration across the humanities and social sciences, and/or carrying out a number of archival, recovery, or digital projects.

HIDDEN CURRICULUM The set of cultural beliefs and practices of the institution that you are expected to know but are not explicitly taught.

HIGHER EDUCATION Formal study and training beyond high school, including the bachelor's, master's, and doctoral degrees.

HOLISTIC REVIEW An admissions review process in which the admissions committee takes into account all aspects of the applicant's lived experiences and how that contributes to their preparedness and overall fit for the program.

HOMONEGATIVE MICROAGGRESSIONS Daily forms of verbal, behavioral, and /or environmental abuse or slights aimed at sexual minorities.

IMPLICIT BIAS Preconceived notions of an individual's ability and/or inability based on group stereotypes. This also refers to informal forms of discrimination that occur without conscious knowledge.

IMPOSTOR PHENOMENON A term that has recently supplanted the misleading term "impostor syndrome," which individualizes beliefs or thoughts of personal inabilities or shortcomings, rather than attributing them to systemic, institutional barriers. Imposter phenomenon is not a diagnosable condition but rather a common psychological experience of having the belief that one is a fraud intellectually or professionally.

KANBAN A method of productivity and workflow that involves a visual system for managing your work as it goes through a process.

LECTURER A non-tenure-track professor or instructor hired by a university to teach part-time or full-time. Some lecturers have what is called "Security of

Employment" and are deemed to be exceptional teachers, provide service to the university, and may hold leadership responsibilities. There are also "Senior Lecturers" who may have responsibilities similar to Full Professors, like leading labs, supervising student researchers, and teaching full-time.

LETTER OF RECOMMENDATION An endorsement by the writer, typically a professor or related professional, indicating that you have the necessary strengths, attributes, and potential to be successful in your chosen field of study.

LOW-INCOME We define low-income as students whose income falls at or below the poverty line. This also includes any populations who come from disenfranchised or under-resourced communities. In this book we use California guidelines for "low-income" but the income levels vary widely across the United States.

MASTER'S DEGREE A credential you can earn after completing your bachelor's degree that includes research-based as well as applied or professional terminal programs.

MENTORING A process of guiding, teaching, and learning that happens between the mentor—the guide or teacher—and the mentee—the student or learner—in a variety of contexts and with a wide range of goals.

MONOTASKING Unlike multitasking, this refers to the practice of focusing on one task at a time.

NONTRADITIONAL STUDENTS Those whose age is twenty-five or over, including adult students who often have family and work responsibilities that can interfere with successful completion of educational goals.

PERSONAL BRANDING The ways that you intentionally project yourself, your values, your identity, and what you stand for to the world.

PERSONAL STATEMENT A graduate school admissions essay that centers on how your personal background and experiences have shaped or influenced your graduate school interests and career goals.

PORTFOLIO A carefully curated collection of work that can include your art, advertising, animation, or architectural plans, among others.

POST-BACCALAUREATE (POSTBACC) PROGRAMS Educational programs completed after graduating with a bachelor's degree and almost always before a master's or doctoral degree.

PROSPECTUS An academic proposal for the dissertation. Typically, it includes the project's scope, central questions, intervention in the literature, methods and sources, and chapter summaries.

QUALIFYING EXAMS See "comprehensive exams."

RACIAL BATTLE FATIGUE A term coined by William Smith that refers to the forms of race-related environmental stress that can hinder achievement and exacerbate mental, emotional, and physical stress.

RACIAL MICROAGGRESSIONS Unconscious and subtle forms of racism or racist acts, comments, or forms of communication.

RE-ENTRY STUDENTS Students who are returning to college after a prolonged absence from school.

RESEARCH ASSISTANTSHIP A form of employment that involves carrying out research—either your own or that of a professor or both. Similar to a teaching assistantship, a research assistantship may involve working 25 to 50 percent of your time (10 to 20 hours a week) to receive a stipend and benefits.

RESEARCH INSTITUTION A university with high research activity.

SABBATICAL A paid leave of absence given to a professor to dedicate more time towards their research and writing than is possible when they are teaching full time.

STANDARD OPERATING PROCEDURE A set of instructions that lays out the step-by-step process for carrying out a procedure, task, or project.

STATEMENT OF PURPOSE A graduate school admissions essay that conveys your academic, research, and career interests and goals and how they align with the program you are applying to.

STUDENTS OF COLOR A term we use to refer to any student who is Black, Brown, or non-white and self-identifies as a Person of Color.

TEACHING ASSISTANTSHIP A form of employment where you assist an instructor or professor, who is the primary leader of a course, in communicating the main themes, concepts, and insights to the students who are enrolled in the class. It typically requires you to work 25 to 50 percent time (10 to 20 hours a week) to receive a stipend and benefits. This position may involve serving as a discussion or section leader for a lecture course, grading assignments, and holding office hours.

TEMPLATE A predefined document with a layout and text that you can modify and reuse each time you need to work on a similar task.

TIME-BLOCKING Defining and assigning certain periods of time on your calendar to a predetermined type of task.

TIME TO DEGREE The total time from enrollment to graduation.

TRANSCRIPTS A record of your courses and grades for the years you spent at an institution of higher education, including community college.

WRITING SAMPLE A manuscript that provides evidence of your written work, research experience, and academic potential.

Bibliography

Alridge, Derrick P. "On the Education of Black Folk: W. E. B Du Bois and the Paradox of Segregation." *Journal of African American History* 100 (2015): 473–93.

American Association of University Professors. "Tenure: What is Academic Tenure?" n.d. https://www.aaup.org/issues/tenure, accessed October 2, 2022.

American Immigration Council. "Aggravated Felonies: An Overview." March 16, 2021. https://www.americanimmigrationcouncil.org/research/aggravated-felonies-overview, accessed May 15, 2022.

American Psychological Association. *Getting In: A Step-By-Step Plan For Gaining Admission to Graduate School in Psychology.* 4th ed. Washington, DC: APA Publishing, 2014.

Apple, Michael W. "The Hidden Curriculum and the Nature of Conflict." *Interchange* 2 (1971): 27–40.

Asher, Donald. *Graduate Admissions Essays: Write Your Way into the Graduate School of Your Choice.* 4th ed. Berkeley: Ten Speed Press, 2012.

Blanton, Carlos Kevin. *George I. Sánchez: The Long Fight for Mexican American Integration*. New Haven: Yale University Press, 2015.

Bourdieu, Pierre. *The State Nobility: Elite Schools in the Field of Power*. Stanford, CA: Stanford University Press, 1998.

Bray, Ilona. "What's a Crime of Moral Turpitude According to U.S. Immigration Law?" *Nolo.com*. N.d. https://www.nolo.com/legal-encyclopedia/what-s-crime-moral-turpitude-according-us-immigration-law.html, accessed May 15, 2022.

Brint, Steven G., Lori Turk-Bicakci, Kristopher Proctor, and Scott Patrick Murphy. "Expanding the Social Frame of Knowledge: Interdisciplinary, Degree-Granting Fields in American Colleges and Universities, 1975–2000." *The Review of Higher Education* 32 (2009): 155–83.

Brubacher, John S., and Willis Rudy. *Higher Education in Transition: A History of American Colleges and Universities*. New York: Routledge, 2017.

Bunch, Will. *After the Ivory Tower Falls: How College Broke the American Dream and Blew Up Our Politics—And How to Fix It*. New York: William Morrow, 2022.

Caballero, Cecilia, Yvette Martínez-Vu, Judith Pérez-Torres, Michelle Téllez, and Christina Vega, eds. *The Chicana Motherwork Anthology*. Tucson: University of Arizona Press, 2019.

Cassuto, Leonard. "Ph.D. Attrition. How Much is Too Much?" *Chronicle of Higher Education*, July 1, 2013. http://chronicle.com/article/PhD-Attrition-How-Much- Is/140045/, accessed June 20, 2022.

———. "To Apply or Not Apply." *Chronicle of Higher Education*, June 7, 2013.

Cassuto, Leonard, and Robert Weisbuch. *The New PhD: How to Build a Better Graduate Education*. Baltimore, MD: Johns Hopkins University Press, 2021.

Center for First-Generation Success. "Defining First-Generation." November 20, 2017. https://firstgen.naspa.org/blog/defining-first-generation, accessed June 18, 2022.

Charity Hudley, Anne H., Christine Mallinson, and Mary Bucholtz. *Talking College: Making Space for Black Language Practices in Higher Education*. New York: Teachers College Press, 2022.

Chávez-García, Miroslava. "Negotiating Power and Privilege." LatinX Talk, January 2019. https://latinxtalk.org/2019/01/15/strategies-for-negotiating-power-and-privilege-in-academia1.

Child, Brenda J. *Boarding School Seasons: American Indian Families, 1900–1940.* Lincoln: University of Nebraska Press, 1998.

Collingwood, Vivien, Joris Buis, Vincent Visser, and Ger Post. *Academic Skills for Interdisciplinary Studies.* Amsterdam: Amsterdam University Press, 2017.

Covarrubias, Rebecca, A. Romero, and M. Trivelli. "Family Achievement Guilt and Mental Well-Being of College Students." *Journal of Child and Family Studies* 24, no. 7 (2015): 2031–37.

Cloyd, Melissa. "Family Achievement Guilt as Experienced by First-Generation College Students: A Phenomenology." PhD diss., Liberty University, 2019.

Dagbovie, Pero Gaglo. "Black Women Historians from the Late 19th Century to the Dawning of the Civil Rights Movement." *The Journal of African American History* 89 (Summer 2004): 241–61.

Davis, Peggy C. "Law as Microaggression." *Yale Law Journal* 98 (1989): 1559–79.

Dimberg, Sierra K., D. Anthony Clark, Lisa B. Spanierman, and Rachel A. Van Daalen. "'School Shouldn't Be Something You Have to Survive': Queer Women's Experiences with Microaggressions at a Canadian University." *Journal of Homosexuality,* 68 (2021): 709–32.

Dreeben, Robert. *On What is Learned in Schools.* Reading, MA: Addison-Wesley Publishing Co., 1968.

Du Bois, W E.B. *Black Reconstruction in America.* Introduction by Mack H. Jones. New York: Routledge, 2017 [1935].

———. *Souls of Black Folk.* Introduction by Manning Marable. New York: Routledge, 2015 [1903].

Engle, Jennifer, Adolfo Bermeo, and Colleen O'Brien. "Straight from the Source: What Works for First-Generation College Students." Washington, DC: Pell Institute for the Study of Opportunity in Higher Education, 2006.

Espinosa, Lorelle L., Morgan Taylor, and Jonathan M. Turk. "Race and Ethnicity in Higher Education: A Status Report." Washington, DC: American Council on Education, 2019.

Fitzsimmons, William. "Time Out or Burn Out for the Next Generation." *New York Times,* December 6, 2000.

Flaherty, Colleen. "Mental Health Crisis for Grad Students." *Inside Higher Ed,* March 6, 2018. https://www.insidehighered.com/news/2018/03/06/new-study-says-graduate-students-mental-health-crisis, accessed July 5, 2022.

Gap Year Association. "What is a Gap Year?" N.d. https://www.gapyear association.org/what-is-a-gap-year-2, accessed May 20, 2022.

Gardner, Susan K. "Student and Faculty Attributions of Attrition in High and Low-Completing Doctoral Programs in the United States." *Higher Education* 58 (2009): 97–112.

Gates, Henry Louis, Jr., and Evelyn Brooks Higginbotham, eds. *African American National Biography.* New York: Oxford African American Studies Center, 2006.

Georgetown Law Library. "Civil Rights in the United States, A Brief History." N.d. https://guides.ll.georgetown.edu/c.php?g=592919&p=4170925, accessed May 13, 2022.

Giroux, Henry A., and Anthony N. Penna. "Social Education in the Classroom: The Dynamics of the Hidden Curriculum." *Theory & Research in Social Education* 7 (1979): 21–42.

Goodman, Nanette, Michael Morris, and Kelvin Boston. "Financial Inequality: Disability, Race and Poverty in America." National Disability Institute, 2019, p. 5, https://www.nationaldisabilityinstitute.org/wp-content/uploads/2019 /02/disability-race-poverty-in-america.pdf, accessed July 6, 2022.

Graduate Division, UC Santa Barbara. "Best Practices for Faculty Mentoring of Graduate Students." June 7, 2022. https://ext-prod.graddiv.ucsb.edu/sites /default/files/2022–08/Grad%20Council%20Best%20Practices%20for%20 Faculty%20Mentoring%20of%20Graduate%20Students%20%281%29.pdf, accessed September 15, 2022.

Greene, Harold, and Matthew W. Greene. *Greenes' Guides to Educational Planning, Making It Into a Top Graduate School, 10 Steps to Successful Graduate School Admission.* New York: Harper Collins, 2001.

Grier-Reed, Tabitha L. "The African American Student Network: Creating Sanctuaries and Counterspaces for Coping with Racial Microaggressions in Higher Education Settings." *Journal of Humanistic Counseling, Education and Development* 49 (2010): 181–88.

Gutiérrez y Muhs, Gabriella, Yolanda Flores Niemann, Carmen G. González, and Angela P. Harris, eds. *Presumed Incompetent: The Intersections of Race and Class for Women in Academia.* Louisville: University Press of Colorado, 2012.

Gutiérrez y Muhs, Gabriella, Yolanda Flores Niemann, and Carmen G. González, eds. *Presumed Incompetent II: Race, Class, Power, and Resistance of Women in Academia.* Louisville: University Press of Colorado, 2020.

Haigler, Karl, and Rae Nelson. *The Gap-Year Advantage: Helping your Child Benefit From Time Off Before or During College.* New York: Macmillan, 2005.

Hartley, Gemma. *Fed Up: Emotional Labor, Women, and the Way Forward.* New York: Harper One, 2018.

Hartman, Lawton M. *Graduate Education: Parameters for Public Policy* 69, no 2. Washington, DC: US Government Printing Office, 1969.

Hemphill, David, and Erin Blakely. "Narratives of Progress and the Colonial Origins of Schooling." *Counterpoints* 456 (2015): 1–28.

Hoe Gallagher, Nina. "Research Statement." Gap Year Association. N.d. https://www.gapyearassociation.org/gap-year-research, accessed May 20, 2022.

Hunt, Jasper Elan. "How I Explained a Gap in My CV When Applying to Graduate School." *Nature,* May 29, 2019. https://www.nature.com/articles/d41586–019–01696–4, accessed June 14, 2022.

Insight Into Diversity. "AAUP Releases First Tenure Study Since 2004, Revealing Major Changes in Faculty Career Tracks." June 22, 2022. https://www.insightintodiversity.com/aaup-releases-first-study-on-tenure-since-2004-revealing-major-changes-in-faculty-career-tracks, accessed October 2, 2022.

Jackson, Philip N. *Life in Classrooms.* New York: Holt, Rinehart and Winston, Inc., 1968.

Kaplan. *Get into Graduate School: A Strategic Approach.* New York: Simon & Schuster, 2003.

Kent, J. D., and M. T. McCarthy. "Holistic Review in Graduate Admissions: A Report from the Council of Graduate Schools." Washington, DC: Council of Graduate Schools, 2016. https://cgsnet.org/wp-content/uploads/2022/01/CGS_HolisticReview_final_web.pdf.

"Key Events in Black Higher Education: JBHE Chronology of Major Landmarks in the Progress of African Americans in Higher Education." *Journal of Blacks in Higher Education.* N.d. https://www.jbhe.com/chronology, accessed August 14, 2022.

Kuzior, Aleksandra, Karolina Kettler, and Lukasz Rab. "Great Resignation—Ethical, Cultural, Relational, and Personal Dimensions of Generation Y and Z Employees' Engagement." *Sustainability* 14 (2022): 6764.

Langin, Katie. "A Wave of Graduate Programs Drop the GRE Requirement." *Science,* May 2019. https://www.science.org/content/article/wave-graduate-programs-drop-gre-application-requirement, accessed June 30, 2022.

Lee, Celeste Nichole, and Mark Hopson. "Disrupting Postracial Discourse: Black Millennials' Response to Postracial Ideology and the Continued Impact of Racial Microaggressions on College Campuses." *Southern Communication Journal* 84 (2019): 127–39.

Lewis, Nicole Lynn. "How Colleges Tell Student-Parents They Don't Belong." *The Atlantic Online,* May 26, 2021.

Lovitts, Barbara E. *Leaving the Ivory Tower: The Causes and Consequences of Departure From Doctoral Study.* Washington, DC: Rowman & Littlefield, 2001.

MacDonald, Victoria-María. "American Latino Theme Study: Education Demanding their Rights: The Latino Struggle for Educational Access and Equity." https://www.nps.gov/articles/latinothemeeducation.htm, accessed August 14, 2022.

MacDonald, Victoria-María, and Benjamin Polk Hoffman. "'Compromising La Causa?': The Ford Foundation and Chicano Intellectual Nationalism in the Creation of Chicano History, 1963–1977." *History of Education Quarterly* 52 (2012): 251–81.

Márquez, Amanda. "The Graduate Student Experience: The Parents' Perspective." PhD diss, Alliant International University, 2021.

Márquez, Lorena V. *La Gente: Struggles for Empowerment and Community Self-Determination in Sacramento.* Tucson: University of Arizona Press, 2020.

Martínez-Vu, Yvette. *Grad School Femtoring Podcast.* 2020–22. https://gradschool femtoring.com/podcast.

Matsuda, Mari J., Charles R. Lawrence III, Richard Delgado, and Kimberlé W. Crenshaw. *Words That Wound: Critical Race Theory, Assaultive Speech, and The First Amendment.* Boulder, CO: Westville Press, 1993.

McCabe, Janice. "Racial and Gender Microaggressions on a Predominantly-White Campus: Experiences of Black, Latina/o and White Undergraduates." *Race, Gender & Class* (2009): 133–51.

McCrory Calarco, Jessica. *A Field Guide to Grad School: Uncovering the Hidden Curriculum.* Princeton, NJ: Princeton University Press, 2020.

Miller Solomon, Barbara. *In the Company of Educated Women: A History of Women and Higher Education in America.* New Haven: Yale University Press, 1985.

Mitic, Radomir Ray. "Insights into First-Generation Doctoral Students." Council of Graduate Schools Brief, March 2022, https://cgsnet.org/wp-content

/uploads/2022/03/CGS_CP_First-Gen-Doc-Students_ForWeb.pdf, accessed June 30, 2022.

Nadal, K. L., D. P. Rivera, and M. J. H. Corpus. "Sexual Orientation and Trans-Gender Microaggressions: Implications for Mental Health and Counseling." In *Microaggressions and Marginality: Manifestation, Dynamics, and Impact,* edited by D. W. Sue, 217–40. Hoboken, NJ: John Wiley & Sons, 2010.

National Academies. "Ford Foundation Fellowship Programs." N.d. https://sites.nationalacademies.org/PGA/FordFellowships/index.htm, accessed August 30, 2022.

National Council of State Legislatures. "Undocumented Student Tuition: Overview." June 9, 2021. https://www.ncsl.org/research/immigration/tuition-benefits-for-immigrants.aspx, accessed May 14, 2022.

National Science Foundation Division of Science Resources Statistics. *U.S. Doctorates in the 20th Century,* NSF 06–319, Lori Thurgood, Mary J. Golladay, and Susan T. Hill. Arlington, VA: National Science Foundation, 2006.

National Science Foundation, Graduate Research Fellowship Program. https://www.nsfgrfp.org, accessed August 30, 2022.

Overly, Norman, ed. *The Unstudied Curriculum.* Washington, DC: Association of Curriculum and Supervision, 1970.

Paul & Daisy Soros Fellowships for New Americans. "Honoring America's Immigrant Experience: A Graduate School Fellowship for New Americans." N.d. https://www.pdsoros.org/?gclid=CjwKCAjw6raYBhB7EiwABge5KuGndzh9q h8mb1n5oOHT4UFKDLJ_a4IkTHQzuBzzfFZfnyOb_PTcchoC_WoQAvD_ BwE, accessed August 30, 2022.

Piascik, Andy. "Edward Alexander Bouchet: The First African American to Earn a PhD from an American University." February 12, 2022. https://connecticuthistory.org/edward-alexander-bouchet-the-first-african-american-to-earn-a-phd-from-an-american-university, accessed August 12, 2022.

Pérez Huber, Lindsay, and Daniel G. Solorzano. "Racial Microaggressions as a Tool for Critical Race Research." *Race Ethnicity and Education* 18 (2015): 297–320.

Pierce, Chester, J. Carew, D. Pierce-González, and D. Wills. "An Experiment in Racism: TV Commercials." In *Television and Education,* edited by Charles Pierce, 62–88. Beverly Hills, CA: Sage, 1978.

Pilgrim, David. "Was W. E .B. Du Bois the First African American to Receive a Ph.D.?" Jim Crow Museum, Ferris State University, https://www.ferris

.edu/HTMLS/news/jimcrow/question/2009/may.htm, accessed August 12, 2022.

Posselt, Julie R. *Inside Graduate Admissions: Merit, Diversity, and Faculty Gatekeeping.* Cambridge: Harvard University Press, 2016.

Quintana-Baker, Maricel. "A Profile of Mexican American, Puerto Rican, and Other Hispanic STEM Doctorates: 1983 to 1997." *Journal of Women and Minorities in Science and Engineering* 8 (2002): 99–121.

Rackham Graduate School at the University of Michigan. *How to Mentor Graduate Students: A Guide for Faculty.* 2019. https://rackham.umich.edu/faculty-and-staff/facilitating-academic-success/mentoring-advising.

Ramírez, Elvia. "'No One Taught Me the Steps': Latinos' Experiences Applying to Graduate School." *Journal of Latinos & Education* 10 (July 2011): 204–22.

Rev. "ADA Compliance for Colleges & Universities: Laws Protecting People with Disabilities." February 28, 2020. https://www.rev.com/blog/speech-to-text-accessibility/ada-compliance-for-colleges-universities, accessed July 5, 2022.

Reyes, Jesús. *The Social Work Graduate School Applicant's Handbook.* 2nd ed. Harrisburg, PA: White Hat Communications, 2005.

RTI Data Source. "First-Generation College Graduates, Race/Ethnicity, Age, and Use of Career Planning Services." Center for First-Generation Student Success and NASPA. https://firstgen.naspa.org/files/dmfile/FactSheet-011.pdf, accessed June 21, 2022.

Santos Laanan, Frankie, and Dimpal Jain. "Advancing a New Critical Framework for Transfer Student Research: Implications for Institutional Research." *New Directions for Institutional Research* (2016): 9–21.

Santos Laanan, Frankie, S. S. Starobin, and L. E. Eggleston. "Adjustment of Community College Students at a Four-Year University: Role and Relevance of Transfer Student Capital for Student Retention." *Journal of College Student Retention: Research, Theory & Practice* 12 (2010): 175–209.

Sattar, Atia. "Academic Motherhood and the Unrecognized Labors of Non-Tenure Track Faculty Women of Color." *Academe* 109 (2022). https://www.aaup.org/article/academic-motherhood-and-unrecognized-labors-non-tenure-track-faculty-women-color.

Seltzer, Rick. "Failing to Keep Up: Recent Increases in Number of Minority Administrators Don't Keep Up with Demographic Shifts, But New Study Finds Broad Pay Equity." *Inside Higher Education,* March 2, 2017. https://www

.insidehighered.com/news/2017/03/02/racial-gap-among-senior-administrators-widens, accessed June 23, 2022.

Smith Crocco, Margaret, and Catty L. Waite. "Education and Marginality: Race and Gender in Higher Education, 1940–1955." *History of Education Quarterly* 47 (2007): 69–91.

Smith, William A., Tara J. Yosso, and Daniel G. Solórzano. "Challenging Racial Battle Fatigue on Historically White Campuses: A Critical Race Examination of Race-Related Stress." In *Faculty of Color: Teaching in Predominantly White Colleges and Universities,* edited by C. A. Stanley, 299–232. Boston, MA: Anker, 2006.

Social Science Research Council. "About Us." https://www.ssrc.org/about-us, accessed August 30, 2022.

Solorzano, Daniel, Miguel Ceja, and Tara Yosso. "Critical Race Theory, Racial Microaggressions, and Campus Racial Climate: The Experiences of African American College Students." *Journal of Negro Education* (2000): 60–73.

Startz, Dick. "First-Generation College Students Face Unique Challenges." Brookings, Brown Center Chalkboard, April 25, 2022. https://www.brookings.edu/blog/brown-center-chalkboard/2022/04/25/first-generation-college-students-face-unique-challenges, accessed June 30, 2022.

Steele, Claude M. *Whistling Vivaldi: How Stereotypes Affect Us and What We Can Do.* New York: W. W Norton & Company, 2011.

Steele, Claude M., and Joshua Aronson. "Stereotype Threat and the Intellectual Test Performance of African Americans." *Journal of Personality and Social Psychology* 69 (1995): 797–811.

Sue, D. W. "Whiteness and Ethnocentric Monoculturalism: Making the 'Invisible' Visible." *American Psychologist* 59, no. 8 (2004): 761–69.

Taylor, Morgan, and Jonathan M. Turk. "Race and Ethnicity in Higher Education: A Look at Low-Income Undergraduates." American Council on Education. https://www.equityinhighered.org/resources/ideas-and-insights/race-and-ethnicity-in-higher-education-a-look-at-low-income-undergraduates/, accessed June 21, 2022.

Terrell, Mary Church. "The Progress of Colored Women." Washington, DC: Smith Brothers, Printers, 1898. https://www.loc.gov/item/90898298.

Thelin, John R. *A History of American Higher Education.* John Hopkins University Press, 2011.

Torres, Janesse. *Yo Quiero Dinero: Personal Finance for Latinas*. Podcast. Episode 164, "How to Get Out of Your Own Way, with Wendy Amara," August 6, 2022. https://yoquierodineropodcast.com/podcasts/episode-164.

Trafzer, Clifford E., and Joel R. Hyer, eds. *Exterminate Them: Written Accounts of the Murder, Rape, and Enslavement of Native Americans During the California Gold Rush*. East Lansing: Michigan State University Press, 1999.

Trafzer, Clifford E., Jean A. Keller, and Lorene Sisquoc, eds. *Boarding School Blues: Revisiting American Indian Educational Experiences*. Lincoln: University of Nebraska Press, 2006.

Tudico, Christopher. "Before We Were Chicanas/os: The Mexican American Experience in California Higher Education, 1848–1945." PhD diss., University of Pennsylvania, 2010.

United States Department of Education. "The Beginning Postsecondary Students Longitudinal Study (BPS), 2012–2017." https://nces.ed.gov/surveys /bps/about.asp, accessed May 30, 2022.

University of California, Office of the President. "Campus Climate Study, Executive Summary: Campus Climate Study for the University of California System." https://campusclimate.ucop.edu/_common/files/pdf-climate/ucsystem-summary.pdf, accessed June 25, 2022.

———. "Campus Climate Project Final Report." March 2014. https:// campusclimate.ucop.edu/_common/files/pdf-climate/ucsystem-full-report.pdf, accessed June 25, 2022.

———. "UC Campus Climate Study, Executive Summary: Campus Climate Study for the University of California System." https://campusclimate.ucop.edu /_common/files/pdf-climate/ucsystem-summary.pdf, accessed June 25, 2022.

———. "Campus Climate Survey." https://campusclimate.ucop.edu/what-is-campus-climate, accessed June 25, 2022.

———. "An Ethos of Respect and Inclusion." March 19, 2014. https://campus-climate.ucop.edu/results/, accessed June 25, 2022.

University of California, Santa Barbara. "Campus Climate Project Final Report." March 2014. https://campusclimate.ucop.edu/_common/files/pdf-climate/ucsb-full-report.pdf, accessed June 25, 2022.

Ward, Kelly Marie. "Crafting the Conditions for Professional Membership: Women of Color Navigating Inclusion into Academia." *Sociology Quarterly* 63 (2022): 497–515.

Weis, Julia. "Dr. Martha Bernal, The First Latina with a PhD in Psychology." https://salud-america.org/dr-martha-bernal-the-first-latina-with-a-phd-in-psychology, accessed August 14, 2022.

Williams, Heather Andrea. *Self-Taught: African American Education in Slavery and Freedom*. Chapel Hill: University of North Carolina Press, 2005.

Wladis, Claire. "Opinion: Many Student-Parents Drop Out Because They Don't Have Enough Time for Their Schoolwork." *The Hechinger Report, Covering Innovation and Inequality in Education*, July 24, 2018. https://hechinger-report.org/opinion-many-student-parents-drop-out-because-they-dont-have-enough-time-for-their-schoolwork-research-shows, accessed May 30, 2022.

"Women Who Achieve: Martha Bernal." Pennsylvania Psychiatric Institute. https://ppimhs.org/newspost/women-who-achieve-martha-bernal, accessed August 16, 2022.

Woodford, Michael R., Jill M. Chonody, Alex Kulick, David J. Brennan, and Kristen Renn. "The LGBQ Microaggressions on Campus Scale: A Scale Development and Validation Study." *Journal of Homosexuality*, 62 (2015): 1660–87.

Wright, A. Jordan, and Ryan T. Wegner. "Homonegative Microaggressions and Their Impact on LGB Individuals: A Measure Validity Study." *Journal of LGBT Issues in Counseling* 6 (2012): 34–54.

Wright, Bobby, and William G. Tierney. "American Indians in Higher Education: A History of Cultural Conflict." *Change: The Magazine of Higher Learning* 23 (1991): 11–18.

"Yesterday's Non-Traditional Student is Today's Traditional Student." Center for Postsecondary and Economic Success, 2015. http://www.clasp.org/resources-and-publications/publication-1/CPES-Nontraditional-students-pdf.pdf, accessed June 18, 2022.

Yoo, Hyeon Jean, and David T. Marshall. "Understanding Graduate Student Parents: Influence of Parental Status, Gender, and Major on Graduate Students' Motivation, Stress, and Satisfaction." *Journal of College Student Retention: Research, Theory & Practice* (January 2022): 1–24.

Yosso, Tara J. *Critical Race Counterstories Along the Chicana/Chicano Educational Pipeline*. New York: Routledge, 2013.

Yosso, Tara J., William A. Smith, Miguel Ceja, and Daniel G. Solórzano. "Critical Race Theory, Racial Microaggressions, and Campus Racial Climate for Latina/o Undergraduates." *Harvard Educational Review* 79 (2009): 659–91.

Index

B., Rosie, 78–79, 80

bachelor's degree programs, 38–39

backup plans. *See* Plan Bs

Bernal, Martha, 21–22

"Best Graduate Schools" *(US News and World Report)*, 126–27

Big Ten Academic Alliance Summer Research Program, 60

BIPOC (Black, Indigenous, and People of Color), as term, 11

Black Codes, 19

Black students, 11; academic outcomes of, 66; educational access and, 24, 25; history of, 19–21; racist policies and behaviors against, 65–66; rates of students with disabilities among, 102; safety of, 74

Black veterans, 23

Blakely, Erin, 32

"boarding schools," 22

boredom, 57

Bouchet, Edward Alexander, 20

Bray, Ilona, 76

Brint, Steven G., 45

Brown, Michael, 87

budgets and financial planning, 10, 270–71, 281, 286–88. *See also* costs; debt; funding options

Bureau of Labor Statistics, 88

burnout, 48, 87, 104, 289, 292, 294–95. *See also* mental health; wellness

Calarco, Jennifer McCrory, 29–30, 47

career development and options, 58–64, 295–99. *See also* job security

Cassuto, Leonard, 42, 89

Center for Postsecondary and Economic Success, 10

Charlottesville, Virginia attack (2017), 74

Chávez-García, Miroslava, 1–2, 4–7, 104–5

chronic pain, 102

citizenship status, 76, 77–78. *See also* DACA (Deferred Action for Childhood Arrivals) students

classism, 98–99, 102. *See also* low-income students; poverty

colorblind approach, 32. *See also* racism

community care, 293

contacting graduate students, as selection strategy, 133–38

contacting professors, as selection strategy, 128–33

costs, 62, 85–86, 98, 216, 219–22. *See also* budgets and financial planning; debt; funding options

crimes, 76–77

Crumdy, Angela, 87, 293

Cuban American students, 25

cultural capital, 32

cultural shock, 3

curriculum vitae (CV), 212–13, 222–25

DACA (Deferred Action for Childhood Arrivals) students, 270, 271, 273, 276, 278, 281, 288. *See also* citizenship status

Davis, Angela, 307

Davis, Peggy C., 66

dealbreakers, 140–41

debt, 42, 58, 85, 236, 278, 279, 281, 287–88, 298. *See also* budgets and financial planning; costs

decision-making process, 51, 54–58. *See also* selection strategies

degree inflation, 31

demonstration of abilities, 229

harmony, 292–93

Hemphill, David, 32

hidden costs of applying to graduate school. *See* costs

hidden curriculum of academia, 2, 29–30, 300

Hispanic Scholarship Fund, 232

Hispanic students, 25

holistic review process, 143

homonegative microaggressions, 67–68. *See also* LGBTQ+ students

housing options, 71, 141, 236, 264, 279, 284–85

humanities graduate programs, 18, 35; samples of diversity statements for, 204–6; samples of personal statements for, 189–91; samples of statement of purpose for, 158–62

identity: of authors, 3, 5–6; intersectionality of, 65–81; success strategy based on, 50–53, 116, 183

IEPs (Individualized Education Plans), 102, 294. *See also* accommodations (academic)

immigration laws, 76. *See also* citizenship status; DACA (Deferred Action for Childhood Arrivals) students

implicit bias, 8, 31–32, 93, 143

imposter phenomenon, 3–4, 92–93, 101, 103–5, 153. *See also* self-doubt

incarceration, 79

Institute for Colored Youth, 20

interdisciplinary approaches, 44–48

intersectional feminism, 15–17

intersectional identities and graduate school, 65–81. *See also* identity

interviews, 254–63

Jaramillo, Adriana, 247

jobs. *See* research assistantships (RAships); side jobs; teaching assistantships (TAships)

job security, 41, 47, 56, 150, 295–99. *See also* career development and options

kanban method, 114

Langin, Katie, 84

Latinx students: educational access and, 23–24; history of, 21–22; racial microaggressions against, 66–67

Latinx veterans, 23–24

Leadership Alliance Program, 60

learning disabilities, 102, 294. *See also* accommodations (academic); students with disabilities

leisure activities, 289

letters of recommendation, 99–101, 208–19

Lewis, Lynn, 72

LGBTQ+ students, 67–68, 102

life stage, impact of, 58–64

loan deferrment, 58

location-based selection strategy, 127

low-income students: costs and funding options for, 62–63, 98; defined, 10, 13; support programs for, 59. *See also* classism; poverty

male privilege, 70

Martin, Trayvon, 87

Martínez-Vu, Yvette, 1–4

master's degree programs, 33, 39–40, 83

McNair, Ronald E., Scholars Program (UCSB), 59, 96, 146, 183, 221

Mellon Foundation, 3

tenure-track *vs.* non-tenure track professoriate, 89–90, 299. *See also* professoriate

terminal master's degree program, 39

Terrell, Mary Church, 1

therapy, 247

time-blocking method, 114–15

timeline of application process, 62, 120–23, 229–36

time management strategies, 91–92, 113, 114–16. *See also* productivity

time to degree, as phrase, 41

transcripts, 216, 220

transgender students, 67–68, 102. *See also* LGBTQ+ students

transition into graduate school, 86–87, 283–303

trauma, 52, 170, 191, 206

UCLA Mellon Mays Undergraduate Fellowship, 3

UC LEADS (University of California Leadership Excellence), 59

Underground Scholars Program and Initiative, 79

unionization, 298

University of California, 298

University of California, Santa Barbara (UCSB), 68

University of Virginia, 74

User Experience (UX) industry, 297

US News and World Report (publication), 126–27

validation, 4, 55, 200, 245

violence, 74, 87

waiting game, 241, 246

waitlisting, 246, 249–50

waivers, 221. *See also* costs

wellness, 102, 290–95. *See also* burnout; mental health

white students, overview, 23–24, 25

white supremacy, 74, 87

Wladis, Claire, 70

work-life balance, 10, 91, 103, 199, 292–93

writer's block, 153, 188

writing samples, 225–26

Yosso, Tara, 66–67

Founded in 1893,
UNIVERSITY OF CALIFORNIA PRESS
publishes bold, progressive books and journals
on topics in the arts, humanities, social sciences,
and natural sciences—with a focus on social
justice issues—that inspire thought and action
among readers worldwide.

The UC PRESS FOUNDATION
raises funds to uphold the press's vital role
as an independent, nonprofit publisher, and
receives philanthropic support from a wide
range of individuals and institutions—and from
committed readers like you. To learn more, visit
ucpress.edu/supportus.